MILITARY·Living's ™

Military R.V. Camping & Rec Areas Around the World

by

William "Roy" Crawford, Ph.D.
and
Lela Ann Crawford

EDITOR - Rose C. McLain
COVER DESIGN - June Douglas
LAYOUT ARTISTS - June Douglas, Pamela Greer
ASSISTANT LAYOUT ARTIST - Bryce D. Thompson
EDITORIAL ASSISTANTS - Pamela Greer
Bryce D. Thompson
MARKETING MANAGER - William R. Crawford, Jr.
OFFICE STAFF - Anna Belle Causey, Helen
Henderson, Irene Kearney

Military Living Publications
P. O. Box 2347
Falls Church, Virginia 22042

NOTICE

The information in this book has been compiled and edited either from the activity/facility listed, its superior headquarters or from other sources which may or may not be so noted. All listed facilities and any or all information about them could change. Please note, however, that many of these RV, camping and rec areas have been in continuous operation at the same location for over 40 years. This book should be used as a guide to military RV, camping and rec areas with the above understanding. Please forward any corrections or additions to **Military Living Publications, P.O. Box 2347, Falls Church, Virginia 22042.**

This guide is published by **Military Marketing Services, Inc.**, a private firm in no way connected with the U.S. Federal or other governments. The book is copyrighted by William Roy and Lela Ann Crawford. Opinions expressed by the publisher and writers herein are their own and are not to be considered an official expression by any government agency or official.

The information and statements contained in this book have been compiled from sources believed by the publisher to be reliable and to represent the best current opinion on the subject. No warranty, guarantee or representation is made by **Military Marketing Services, Inc.**, as to the absolute correctness or sufficiency of any representation contained in this or other publications and we can assume no responsibility.

Library of Congress Cataloging-in-Publication Data

Crawford, William Roy, 1932-
    Military living's military RV, camping & rec areas around the
  world / by William Roy Crawford and Lela Ann Crawford.
       p.   cm.
    Rev. ed. of: Military living's military camping & rec areas around
  the world. c1983.
    Includes index.
    ISBN 0-914862-16-2 : $6.95
    1. Recreation areas--United States--Directories. 2. Recreation
  areas--Directories. 3. Camping--United States--Directories.
  4. Camping--Directories. 5. United States--Armed Forces-
  -Facilities--Directories. I. Crawford, Ann Caddell. II. Military
  living. III. Title. IV. Title: Military RV, camping & rec areas
  around the world. V. Series: Crawford, William Roy, 1932-
  Military living's military camping & rec areas around the world.
  UC403.C73 1988
  647'.947309--dc19   88-11738
                                                                  CIP

INTRODUCTION

You can have a lot of fun with this book. Many military families, both active duty and retired, use their recreational vehicles and camp for fun, but others camp to save money while visiting many famous tourist attractions. Most of these international attractions are referenced in the individual listings of this book. We have provided the information in this book that many military camping families have requested and which we believe will be of the most value to you. In this third edition we have retained our block/semi-chart easy-to-use format. Also, we have included full coverage of all of the Armed Forces Recreation Centers worldwide. **MILITARY RV, CAMPING & REC AREAS AROUND THE WORLD** is the first commercial book to zero in on RV, camping and recreation areas of all services worldwide to include Army, Navy, Marine Corps, Air Force and Coast Guard. We believe that we have covered most of the active locations. **YOU** may know of other locations that we did not find. Please, send us the information on any that we missed so we can research the location to share with you and your fellow military families in the next printing/edition.

The Publishers of Military Living wish to thank all military recreation and public affairs personnel who so diligently serve the military and their families. **You are real "morale boosters."**

HOW TO USE THIS DIRECTORY

Name of Installation/Facility (AL01R2)	**Comm:**
Street or Unit Designation (if required)	**ATVN:**
City/Base/APO/FPO, State, ZIP Code	**FTS:**

Location Identifier: Example (AL01R2). The first two characters (letters) are Country/State abbreviations used in Military Living's books (Contents and Listings). The next two characters are random numbers (00-99) assigned to a specific location. The fifth character (letter) is an R indicating region and the sixth character (0-9) is the regional location. The location identifiers for listings in this book are keyed to a regional map in Appendix A. The regional maps are designed to provide you with the relative geographic location of each installation/facility worldwide.

Comm: This is the commercial telephone service for the installation/facility's main or information/operator assistance number. Within the US Area Code System, the first three-digit group is the area code. For foreign country locations, the first two-digit group is the Country Code (consult your local directory or operator for specific dialing instructions). The next three-digit group is the area telephone exchange/switch number. In foreign countries the exchange number can have fewer or more digits than in the US system. The last four-digit group is the information or operator assistance number. Again, in foreign countries, this number may be fewer or more than four digits.

ATVN: The Department of Defense has a worldwide Automatic Voice Network (ATVN). The number given is for information/operator assistance.

ETS: This is the European Telephone System. The number given is for information/operator assistance.

FTS: This is the Federal Telephone System. The number given is for information/operator assistance.

LOCATION: The specific driving instructions to the installation/facility from local major cities, interstate highways and routes are in this section. RM: indicates the Rand McNally 1988 Road Atlas page number and coordinates for the installation/facility. For European listings the Hallwag Europe Atlas (HE:) is used. NMI: is the nearest military installation if the rec area is not located on post/base. NMC: is the nearest major city. The distance in miles and the direction from the installation/facility to the NMI and NMC are given.

DESCRIPTION OF AREA: This section provides a description of the RV, camping or recreation area in the listing. Special geographic and topographic features are noted. Other recreational opportunities and military support facilities are noted. Special facilities and helpful hints are included.

SEASON OF OPERATION: The time frame during which the facility is available for general use is specified in this section.

ELIGIBILITY: The category/status of uniformed/military and civilian employees who may use the facility is stated in this section.

RESERVATIONS: The procedure for establishing reservations, the mailing address, commercial, ATVN and FTS contact numbers and special instructions are contained in this section. Please call these numbers for additional information as required. Some areas have complicated priority systems. If the facilities are very limited, priority for space is often given to personnel/families of the sponsoring installation. When writing, it is advisable to include a self-addressed, stamped envelope.

CAMP FACILITIES: This section details any recreational lodging, RV spaces, camping spaces and tent spaces. The number of units is specified along with the hookup facilities available and the fee for each facility used. You should anticipate possible changes in rates/fees and facilities provided.

SUPPORT FACILITIES: Installation facilities available to visitors are listed in this section. In most cases general base support facilities have not been noted.

ACTIVITIES: This section lists the general recreational activities available to visitors.

RESTRICTIONS: Details of any restrictions, limitations and rules for the use of the facility are in this section.

Please review Appendix C, General Abbreviations. Also, note the Regional Location Maps, Appendix A. Other helpful appendices are also included in this book.

EDITOR'S NOTE

Because of budget reductions within the Federal Government, both seasons of operation and hours of operation within seasons may be reduced or otherwise changed after the press date of this book.

CONTENTS

CONTINENTAL UNITED STATES (CONUS)

LOCATION IDENTIFIER	INSTALLATION	PAGE

ALABAMA

AL07R2	Dauphin Island Recreational Complex	1
AL05R2	Lake Martin Recreation Area	2
AL11R2	Maxwell Recreation Center and Fam-Camp	2
AL09R2	McClellan Recreation Area and Campground	3
AL12R2	Redstone Arsenal Campground	3
AL10R2	Rucker Outdoor Recreation Area	4
AL13R2	Thomas Mill Creek Park	5

ARIZONA

AZ10R4	Apache Flats Campground	5
AZ14R4	Davis-Monthan Fam-Camp	6
AZ11R4	Fort Tuthill Recreation Area	7
AZ15R4	Gila Bend Fam-Camp	7
AZ12R4	Martinez Lake Recreation Area	8
AZ07R4	Williams AFB Recreation Annex (Waterdog)	9

ARKANSAS

AR05R2	Little Rock Fam-Camp	9

CALIFORNIA

CA60R4	Beale Fam-Camp	10
CA05R4	Big Bear Lake Recreation Facility	10
CA72R4	Castle Fam-Camp	11
CA03R4	Del Mar Recreation Beach	12
CA61R4	East Garrison Recreation Area and Travel Camp	12
CA62R4	Edwards Fam-Camp	13
CA76R4	El Centro NAF Campground	14
CA70R4	George Fam-Camp	14
CA02R4	Lake Isabella Recreation Area	15
CA04R4	Lake Isabella Recreation Camp	15
CA65R4	Lake O'Neill Aquatic Park	16
CA73R4	Lake Tahoe Army Recreation Facilities	17
CA24R4	Lake Tahoe CG Recreation Facility	17
CA07R4	Miramar RV Park	18
CA64R4	Mission Gorge Campground	18
CA69R4	Norton RV Park	19
CA66R4	Petaluma Coast Guard Training Center	20
CA11R4	Point Mugu Recreation Area	20
CA31R4	San Onofre Recreation Beach	21
CA63R4	Sharpe Army Travel Camp	22
CA68R4	Travis Fam-Camp	22
CA67R4	Vandenberg Fam-Camp	23

COLORADO

CO08R3	Dillon Recreation Area	23
CO01R3	Farish Memorial Fam-Camp	24
CO09R3	Lowry Fam-Camp	25

CONNECTICUT - None

DELAWARE

DE02R1   Fort Miles Recreation Area...................................... 25

DISTRICT OF COLUMBIA - None

FLORIDA

FL29R1   Avon Park Recreation Area...................................... 26
FL23R1   Coon's Creek Recreation Area................................... 27
FL01R1   Destin Army Infantry Center Recreation Area.................... 28
FL25R1   Eglin Fam-Camp... 28
FL24R1   Lake Fretwell Recreation Area.................................. 29
FL12R1   Lake Pippin, Maxwell/Gunter Recreation Area.................... 32
FL28R1   Marathon Recreation Cottages................................... 32
FL22R1   Mystic Lake Fam-Camp... 33
FL09R1   Oak Grove Trailer Park... 33
FL21R1   Orlando Travel Trailer Park.................................... 34
FL07R1   Panama City NCSC Outdoor Recreation Center..................... 35
FL10R1   Rucker Florida Recreation Area................................. 36
FL26R1   Tyndall Fam-Camp... 36

GEORGIA

GA04R1   Gordon Recreation Area... 37
GA06R1   Grassy Pond Recreation Area.................................... 38
GA19R1   Holbrook Pond Army Travel Camp................................. 38
GA05R1   Lake Allatoona Army Recreation Area............................ 39
GA01R1   Lake Allatoona NAS Recreation Center........................... 40
GA18R1   Lakeside Fam-Camp.. 41
GA07R1   Robins Fam-Camp.. 41
GA20R1   Uchee Creek Recreational Area.................................. 42

IDAHO

ID03R4   Mountain Home Fam-Camp... 42
ID02R4   Strike Dam Recreation Area..................................... 43

ILLINOIS

IL10R2   Chanute Fam-Camp... 44
IL09R2   Scott Fam-Camp... 44

INDIANA

IN04R2   Delaware Campground.. 45

IOWA - None

KANSAS

KS05R3   Kiernan/Smith Marina, Travel Camp and Beach.................... 46
KS01R3   Leavenworth RV Park.. 46

KENTUCKY

KY03R2   Camp Carlson Army Travel Camp.................................. 47
KY04R2   Eagles' Rest Travel Camp....................................... 48
KY05R2   Fletchers Fork Travel Camp..................................... 48

LOUISIANA

LA09R2	Barksdale Fam-Camp	49
LA02R2	Cotile Recreation Area	49
LA08R2	New Orleans NAS Campground	50
LA03R2	New Orleans NSA RV Park	51
LA04R2	Toledo Bend Recreation Site	51

MAINE

ME03R1	Dow Pines Recreation Area	52
ME05R1	Malabeam Lake and Fam-Camp Area	53
ME01R1	Rocky Lake	53
ME02R1	Sprague's Neck	54
ME04R1	Winter Harbor Recreation Area	55

MARYLAND

MD15R1	Andrews Fam-Camp	55
MD16R1	Annapolis Fam-Camp	56
MD03R1	Goose Creek/West Basin Recreation Area	56
MD17R1	Ritchie Outdoor Recreation Center	57
MD05R1	Solomons Navy Recreation Center	58

MASSACHUSETTS

MA10R1	Cape Cod Vacation Apartments	59
MA04R1	Cuttyhunk Island Recreation Facility	60
MA02R1	Fourth Cliff Recreation Area	60
MA08R1	Hanscom Fam-Camp	61
MA01R1	Robbins Pond Travel Camp	62

MICHIGAN

MI04R2	Point Betsie Recreation Cottage	63
MI05R2	Wurtsmith Air Force Beach and Fam-Camp	63

MINNESOTA – None

MISSISSIPPI

MS05R2	Keesler Marina	64
MS06R2	Sardis Lake Recreation Area	65

MISSOURI

MO01R2	Lake of the Ozarks Recreation Area	65

MONTANA

MT01R3	Malmstrom Fam-Camp	66
MT02R3	St. Mary's Recreation Camp	67

NEBRASKA

NE01R3	Offutt Fam-Camp	68

NEVADA

NV04R4	Nellis Fam-Camp	68

NEW HAMPSHIRE

NH03R1   Peverly Pond Recreation Area................................. 69

NEW JERSEY

NJ06R1   Barnegat Recreation Cottage................................. 70
NJ04R1   Brindle Lake Travel Camp.................................... 70
NJ02R1   Lake Denmark Recreation Area................................ 71
NJ07R1   McGuire Fam-Camp.. 71
NJ12R1   Wildwood Campground... 72

NEW MEXICO

NM06R3   Holloman Fam-Camp... 73
NM07R3   Kirtland Fam-Camp... 73
NM01R3   Lake Conchas Recreation Area................................ 74
NM08R3   Volunteer Park Travel Camp Site............................. 74

NEW YORK

NY15R1   Griffiss Fam-Camp... 75
NY14R1   Remington Pond Recreation Area.............................. 76
NY04R1   Round Pond Recreation Area.................................. 76
NY13R1   Seneca Army Depot Lakeshore Travel Camp..................... 77
NY05R1   Thayer Hotel.. 78

NORTH CAROLINA

NC09R1   Cape Hatteras Coast Guard Recreation Area................... 78
NC04R1   Cherry Point MWR Fam-Camp................................... 79
NC13R1   Fisher Fam-Camp... 80
NC07R1   New River Recreation Beach Areas............................ 80
NC14R1   Onslow Beach Campsites and Recreation Area.................. 81
NC16R1   Rogers Bay Family Campway................................... 82
NC08R1   Seymour Johnson Fam-Camp.................................... 82
NC12R1   Smith Lake Army Travel Camp................................. 83

NORTH DAKOTA

ND01R3   Grand Forks Fam-Camp.. 83

OHIO

OH03R2   Wright-Patterson Fam-Camp................................... 84

OKLAHOMA

OK06R3   Altus Fam-Camp.. 85
OK03R3   Lake Elmer Thomas Recreation Area........................... 85
OK07R3   Murphy's Meadow... 86
OK08R3   Tinker Fam-Camp... 87

OREGON - None

PENNSYLVANIA

PA10R1   Letterkenny Army Travel Camp................................ 87

RHODE ISLAND - None

SOUTH CAROLINA

SC12R1	Charleston Fam-Camp	88
SC15R1	Folly Beach Recreation Facility	89
SCO5R1	Lake Wateree Recreation Area and Fam-Camp	89
SC13R1	Myrtle Beach AF Fam-Camp	90
SC14R1	Myrtle Beach Army Fam-Camp	90
SCO2R1	Short Stay	91
SCO3R1	Weston Lake Recreation Area and Travel Camp	92

SOUTH DAKOTA

SDO2R3	Ellsworth AFB Fam-Camp	92

TENNESSEE

TNO3R2	Arnold Fam-Camp	93
TNO4R2	Navy Lake Recreation Area	94

TEXAS

TX07R3	Belton Lake Recreation Area	94
TX31R3	Bliss Family Campgrounds	95
TX29R3	Canyon Lake Army Recreation Area	96
TX30R3	Carswell Fam-Camp	96
TX01R3	Circle B Recreation Area	97
TX15R3	Elliott Lake Recreation Area	98
TX11R3	Flying K Recreation Ranch	98
TX32R3	Goodfellow Recreation Camp	99
TX33R3	Kelly Fam-Camp	99
TX34R3	Lake Amistad Recreation Area	100
TX38R3	Lake Medina Recreation Camp	101
TX16R3	Lake Texoma Recreational Annex	101
TX13R3	Laughlin Fam-Camp	102
TX35R3	Randolph Off-Base Recreation Area	102
TX36R3	Shields Park NAS Recreation Area	103
TX04R3	Shoreline Recreation Area	104
TX08R3	West Fort Hood Travel Camp	104

UTAH

UT01R4	Carter Creek Recreation Area	105
UT07R4	Hill Fam-Camp	106
UT03R4	Hillhaus Lodge	106
UT06R4	Oquirrh Hills Travel Camp	107

VERMONT - None

VIRGINIA

VA39R1	A. P. Hill Recreation Facilities	108
VA22R1	Bethel Park Recreation Area	108
VA23R1	Cameron Station Trailer Park	109
VA31R1	Cheatham Annex Recreation Cabins and RV Park	109
VA32R1	"The Colonies" Travel Park	110
VA34R1	Freedom Star Recreation Area	111
VA35R1	Lunga Reservoir	111
VA33R1	Pickett Travel Camp	112
VAO4R1	Stewart Campground	113
VAO5R1	Story Travel Camp	113
VA37R1	Yorktown CG Campground	114
VA36R1	Yorktown Naval Weapons Station Campsite	115

WASHINGTON

WA01R4	Clear Lake Resort	115
WA12R4	Cliffside RV Park	116
WA03R4	Holiday Park Fam-Camp	116
WA07R4	Jim Creek Campground	117
WA13R4	Lewis Travel Camp	118
WA14R4	Westport Recreation Park	118

WEST VIRGINIA - None

WISCONSIN

WI04R2	Rawley Point Light Recreation Cottage	119
WI03R2	Sherwood Point Cottage	120
WI01R2	Squaw Lake Recreation Area	120

WYOMING

WY02R3	Warren Fam-Camp	121

OUTSIDE CONTINENTAL UNITED STATES (OCONUS)

ALASKA

AK01R5	Birch Lake Recreation Area	122
AK16R5	Black Spruce Army Travel Camp	122
AK02R5	Eielson Fam-Camp	123
AK12R5	Elmendorf Fam-Camp	123
AK14R5	Glass Park	124
AK13R5	Ravenwood Ski Lodge	125
AK05R5	Seward AF Recreation Area	125
AK06R5	Seward Army Recreation Camp	126

GUAM

GU04R8	Guam USA and Marianas Islands Consolidated Recreation	127

HAWAII

HI01R6	Barbers Point Recreation Area	128
HI02R6	Bellows Recreation Area	128
HI08R6	Hale Koa Hotel AFRC	129
HI07R6	Hickam Harbor Recreation Area	130
HI06R6	Kaneohe Bay Beach Cottages and Campsites	131
HI04R6	KMC Volcanoes Recreation Area	131
HI05R6	Waianae Army Recreation Center	132

FOREIGN COUNTRIES

CANADA

CN01R1	North East Arm Camp	133

GERMANY

GE56R7   Bad Kreuznach Army Travel Camp.................................. 133
GE55R7   Baumholder Rolling Hills Travel Camp. 134
GE07R7   Berchtesgaden Armed Forces Recreation Center.............. 135
GE47R7   Camp Dahn Travel Camp... 136
GE08R7   Chiemsee Armed Forces Recreation Center.................... 137
GE57R7   Chiemsee AFRC Campground...................................... 138
GE10R7   Garmisch Armed Forces Recreation Center.................... 138
GE58R7   Garmisch AFRC Campground...................................... 139
GE09R7   Rhein Main Travel Camp.. 140

GREECE

GR03R9   Iraklion Campground... 141

ITALY

IT03R7   Admiral Carney Park... 141
IT09R7   Aviano Fam-Camp... 142
IT02R7   Camp Darby Campgrounds and Sea Pines Lodge................ 142
IT15R7   Lake Marola Outdoor Recreation Area....................... 143
IT08R7   Vicenza Travel Camp... 144

JAPAN

JA01R8   New Sanno U. S. Forces Center................................ 144
JA09R8   Okuma Recreation Center....................................... 145
JA10R8   Tama Hills Recreation Area.................................... 146
JA13R8   White Beach Recreation Services.............................. 147

KOREA

RK01R8   Naija Hotel and Armed Forces Recreation Center............ 148

PHILIPPINES

RP02R8   Camp John Hay Armed Forces Recreation Center.............. 148
RP01R8   Grande Island Recreation Area................................ 149

SPAIN

SP05R7   Rota Travel Camp.. 150

TURKEY

TU03R9   Erdemli Beach Area.. 151

UNITED KINGDOM

UK14R7   Machrihanish Travel Camp...................................... 151

APPENDICES

APPENDIX A - Regional Location Maps
      Region 1 - East Coast (North)............................... 153
      Region 1 - East Coast (South)............................... 154
      Region 2 - Central (North).................................. 155
      Region 2 - Central (South).................................. 156
      Region 3 - Midwest (North).................................. 157
      Region 3 - Midwest (South).................................. 158
      Region 4 - West Coast....................................... 159
      Region 5 - Alaska... 160
      Region 6 - Hawaii... 161
      Region 7 - West Europe...................................... 162
      Region 7/9-East Europe (Greece/Turkey)...................... 163
      Region 8 - Far East/Pacific................................. 164

APPENDIX B - Camping on Other Federal Property..................... 165

APPENDIX C - General Abbreviations................................. 168

Camping Facilities Directory...................................... 170

Coupons... 186

-NOTES-

CONTINENTAL UNITED STATES (CONUS)

ALABAMA

Dauphin Island Recreational Complex
(ALO7R2)

USCG Aviation Training Center
Mobile, AL 36608-9682

Comm: 205-694-6110
ATVN: 436-3635
FTS: 537-6110

LOCATION: Off base. On the Gulf of Mexico approx 40 mi S of Mobile. I-10 to AL-163 (Dauphin Island Pkwy exit); S approx 35 mi to Dauphin Island. L at dead end to E end of island. Follow signs to complex. RM: p-5, V/3. NMI: USCG Aviation Training Center, Mobile, 40 mi N. NMC: Mobile, 40 mi N.

DESCRIPTION OF AREA: Dauphin Island offers a variety of outdoor activities and sightseeing. Explore old Ft Gaines, ancient Indian shell mounds or Audubon bird sanctuary. Some military fac available at USCG Aviation Training Center.

SEASON OF OPERATION: Year round.

ELIGIBILITY: Active/Retired/DOT and DOD Civilians.

RESERVATIONS: Required, by application only, with adv payment. Summer (1 May-30 Sep): up to 60 days in adv for AD CG; up to 30 days, AD other services; up to 30 days, all others. Fall/Winter (1 Oct-30 Apr): 15-30 days in advance. Address: Special Services, Coast Guard AVTRACEN, Mobile, AL 36608-9682. Comm: 205-694-6130; ATVN: 436-3635; FTS: 537-6130.

CAMP FACILITIES:	NO UNITS	HOOKUPS	FEE
Cottages, 3 bdrm, furn except linens, bedding	13		$40-65 weekend/ 50-85 weekly
Camper Spaces	6 Hardstand	W/S/E	5 daily/25 wkly/ 15-20 weekend
Tent Spaces	20		3 daily

SUPPORT FACILITIES:			
	Beach (private)	Fish Poles/Bait	Food Vending
	Grills	Grocery (2 mi)	Laundry
	Marina	Picnic Area	Playground
	Restrooms	Sailboat Rental	Sewage Dump Sta
	Showers/Bath House		Sun Deck

ACTIVITIES:			
	Bicycling	Boating	Fishing
	Rec Equip Avail	Sailing	Swimming

RESTRICTIONS: No pets allowed. Summer: 7-day limit for cottages; 2-day minimum (weekend); 14-day limit for camper and tent sites. Fall/Winter: 14-day limit; no minimum. Patrons may wish to bring small electric kitchen appliances, lawn chairs, radio, TV, bed linens, towels, etc.

Lake Martin Recreation Area (ALO5R2)
Maxwell Air Force Base, AL 36112-5000

Comm: 205-293-1110
ATVN: 875-1110

LOCATION: Off base. Located near Dadeville, SE of Birmingham, NE of Montgomery. From Montgomery take I-85 N to AL-49. N to Stillwater Rd (2 mi N of Blue Creek bridge); turn W and proceed 2.5 mi to rec area. RM: p-5, K/11. NMI: Maxwell AFB, 60 mi SW. NMC: Montgomery, 60 mi SW.

DESCRIPTION OF AREA: Located on Lake Martin Reservoir near dam. Excellent fishing; variety of water and woods-oriented activities. Voted outstanding recreation area of the Air Force. Full range of military fac at Maxwell AFB.

SEASON OF OPERATION: Year round.

ELIGIBILITY: Active/Retired/DOD Civilians at Maxwell/Gunter AFB.

RESERVATIONS: Required. Must be made in person at Recreation Center, Bldg 834, Maxwell AFB, AL 36112-5000. Receipt of payment from Maxwell AFB required. Comm: 205-293-5496.

CAMP FACILITIES:	NO UNITS	HOOKUPS	FEE
Mobile Homes, furnished, except linens	12	W/S/E	$22-24 daily
Camper Spaces	42 Hardstand	W/S/E	6.00 daily
Tent Spaces	30	None	5.00 daily

SUPPORT FACILITIES:			
	Beach	Boat Rental	Gas
	Grocery	Ice	Laundry
	Marina	Picnic Area/fee	Playground
	Restrooms	Sewage Dump Sta	Showers

ACTIVITIES:	Fishing (lic)	Volleyball

RESTRICTIONS: Pets allowed on leash.

Maxwell Recreation Center and Fam-Camp (AL11R2)
Maxwell Air Force Base, AL 36112-5000

Comm: 205-293-1110
ATVN: 875-1110

LOCATION: On base. Take I-85 S to I-65; exit N to Day St which leads to main gate. Check in at Recreation Center, 834 Maxwell Blvd, before going to Fam-Camp. RM: p-5, Y/4. NMC: Montgomery, 1.5 mi SE.

DESCRIPTION OF AREA: Situated in a wooded area on a small lake. Martin Lake and many other fresh water lakes and reservoirs located within 50 mi. Site of Wright Brothers Flying School and historical airplanes which have been retired. Historical city of Montgomery has much to offer in the way of sightseeing. Full range of military facilities available on base.

SEASON OF OPERATION: Year round.

ELIGIBILITY: Active/Retired.

RESERVATIONS: No adv resv. Address: Maxwell Recreation Center, Bldg 834, Maxwell AFB, AL 36112-5000. Comm: 205-293-7370/6904.

Maxwell Rec Ctr & Fam-Camp, Cont'd

CAMPING FACILITIES:	NO UNITS	HOOKUPS	FEE
Camper Spaces	24 Hardstand	W/S/E	$6 dly/35 wk/125 mo
Camper Spaces	Overflow	None	3.00 daily
Tent Spaces	Open	None	3.00 daily

SUPPORT FACILITIES:			
	Boat Launch	Chapel	Comm Bldg
	Gas	Golf	Grills
	Laundry	Picnic Area	Rec Center
	Restrooms	Sewage Dump Sta	Showers
	Snack Bar	Sports Fields	Stables
	Trails		
	Equipmental Rental for All Outdoor Activities		

ACTIVITIES:	Fishing (lic)	Golfing	Jogging

RESTRICTIONS: Pets allowed on leash.

McClellan Recreation Area and Campground (ALO9R2)
Fort McClellan, AL 36205-5000

Comm: 205-238-4611
ATVN: 865-1110

LOCATION: On post. Located 3 mi N of Anniston, off AL-21. Enter Baltzell Gate to 10th St; L to 2nd St, L 2 blocks to Bldg 699. RM: p-4, G/12. NMC: Birmingham 60 mi W.

DESCRIPTION OF AREA: Located in Alabama hills W of Atlanta, GA, and E of Birmingham. Campgrounds located 3 mi from main post area on 8-acre lake. Full range of military facilities available on post.

SEASON OF OPERATION: Year round.

ELIGIBILITY: Active/Retired/DOD Civilians.

RESERVATIONS: Required. Address:Commander, USACML&MPCEN&M, ATTN: ATZN-PA-R, Ft McClellan, AL 36205-5000. Comm: 205-238-5663/5649; ATVN: 865-5663.

CAMPING FACILITIES:	NO UNITS	HOOKUPS	FEE
Camper Spaces	8 Hardstand	W/E	$6.00 daily
Camper Spaces	3 Primitive	None	4.00 daily
Tent Spaces	3 Primitive	None	4.00 daily

SUPPORT FACILITIES:			
	Archery	Go-Kart Track	Golf
	Laundry	Picnic Area	Rec Center
	Restrooms	Sewage Dump Sta	Showers
	Skeet Range	Snack Bar	Sports Fields

ACTIVITIES:	Fishing (lic)	Recreation Equipment Available

RESTRICTIONS: None.

Redstone Arsenal Campground (AL12R2)
Redstone Arsenal, AL 35898-5355

Comm: 205-876-2151
ATVN: 746-0011

LOCATION: On post. From I-65 take ALT US-72/AL-20 E; turn S on Jordan Lane to Gate 10. From US-231 (Memorial Parkway) in Huntsville, take Drake Ave W; S on Patton thru Gate 10. RM: p-4, C/9,15. NMC: Huntsville, 6 mi NE.

ALABAMA
Redstone Arsenal Campground, Cont'd

DESCRIPTION OF AREA: Situated along Tennessee River in northern Alabama. Alabama Space and Rocket Center nearby. Southern BBQ is wonderful. Full range of military facilities available on post.

SEASON OF OPERATION: Year round; no water in winter months.

ELIGIBILITY: Active/Retired/DOD Civilians.

RESERVATIONS: No adv resv. Address: Outdoor Recreation, Bldg 5129, Redstone Arsenal AL 35898-5355. Comm: 205-876-4868/6854.

CAMPING FACILITIES:	NO UNITS	HOOKUPS	FEE
Camper & Tent Spaces	23 Hardstand	W/S/E (110)	$3.00-4.50 daily
Camper Spaces	Overflow	None	None

SUPPORT FACILITIES:			
	Archery	Boat Launch	Boat Rental
	Camp Equip Rntl	Golf	Grills
	Pavilions	Picnic Area	Playground
	Rec Center	Restrooms	Sewage Dump Sta
	Showers	Skeet/Trap Range	Softball Field
	Trails		

ACTIVITIES:			
	Boating	Fishing (lic)	Hunting (lic)
	Jogging	Rec Equip Avail	

RESTRICTIONS: Pets allowed on leash. No open fires.

Rucker Outdoor Recreation Area
(AL10R2)
Fort Rucker, AL 36362-5000

Comm: 205-255-6181
ATVN: 558-1110

LOCATION: On post. From US-231, take AL-249 S to Daleville. After passing through Ft Rucker gates (approx 5 mi), R at first blinking light (Christian Rd) for approx 3 mi and follow signs. RM: p-5, Q/12. NMC: Dothan, 25 mi SE.

DESCRIPTION OF AREA: Located between Montgomery and Florida Gulf Coast on the shores of 660-acre Lake Tholocco. Full range of military facilities on post.

SEASON OF OPERATION: Year round. Camping area closed January and February.

ELIGIBILITY: Active/Retired/DOD Civilians.

RESERVATIONS: No adv resv. Address: Community Activities, Outdoor Recreation, Bldg 24201, Lake Tholocco, Ft Rucker, AL 36362-5000. Comm: 205-255-4305; ATVN: 558-4305, FTS: 533-4305.

CAMPING FACILITIES:	NO UNITS	HOOKUPS	FEE
Camper Spaces	18 Hardstand	W/E	$5.00 daily
Tent Spaces	20 Unimproved	None	3.00 daily

SUPPORT FACILITIES:			
	Archery	Beach	Boat Launch
	Boat Rental	Camp Equip Rntl	Golf
	Grills	Ice	Laundry
	Marina	Picnic Area	Pistol Range
	Rec Equip Rntl	Restrooms	Sewage Dump Sta
	Showers	Skeet Range	Snack Bar
	Stables	Trails	

Rucker Outdoor Rec Area, Cont'd

ACTIVITIES: Fishing (lic)   Hunting

RESTRICTIONS: No pets allowed.

Thomas Mill Creek Park (AL13R2)
Fort Rucker, AL 36362-5000

Comm: 205-255-6181
ATVN: 558-1110

LOCATION: Off post. Located N of Dothan on AL-97 between junctions with AL-10 and AL-95, just across the bridge from Wilson's Grocery Store. RM: p-5, P/14. NMI: Ft Rucker, 60 mi SW. NMC: Dothan, 80 mi S.

DESCRIPTION OF AREA: A 12-acre park situated on southern end of Lake Eufaula, which offers some of the best fishing in the US. The park has paved roads and a state-owned boat ramp outside the main entrance. Full range of military fac available at Ft Rucker.

SEASON OF OPERATION: Year round.

ELIGIBILITY: Active/Retired/DOD Civilians.

RESERVATIONS: Accepted for trailers only. Address: Rec Center, ITT Office, PO Drawer 189, Ft Rucker, AL 36362-5000. Comm: 205-255-5816/2997.

CAMP FACILITIES:	NO	UNITS	HOOKUPS	FEE
Mobile Home, 17.5', slp 6 self-contained, A/C, heat	3			$18.00 daily
Camper Rental, 13' & 16'	4		W/E	10-12 daily
Camper Spaces	15	Hardstand	W/E	8.00 daily
Tent Spaces	11	Improved	None	5.00 daily

SUPPORT FACILITIES:	Laundry	Pavilion/fee	Restrooms
	Sewage Dump Sta	Showers	

ACTIVITIES:	Boating	Fishing	Water Skiing

RESTRICTIONS: No pets allowed.

ARIZONA

Apache Flats Campground (AZ10R4)
Fort Huachuca, AZ 85613-6000

Comm: 602-538-7111
ATVN: 821-2151
FTS: 769-2151

LOCATION: On post. Take I-10 to AZ-90; S 25 mi to Sierra Vista and main gate of post. RM: p-8, P/10. NMC: Tucson, 75 mi NW.

DESCRIPTION OF AREA: Ft Huachuca, located at an altitude of 5,000 feet, is at the base of the Huachuca Mountains. Old mining towns of Bisbee and Tombstone are within short driving distance. Full range of military facilities on post.

SEASON OF OPERATION: Year round; restrooms closed 1 November to 1 April

ELIGIBILITY: Active/Retired/DOD and NAF Civilians.

RESERVATIONS: No adv resv. Address: US Army Garrison, Outdoor Recreation Branch, Ft Huachuca, AZ 85613-6000. Comm: 602-533-3317; ATVN: 821-3317.

CAMPING FACILITIES:	NO UNITS	HOOKUPS	FEE
Camper Spaces	4	W/S/E	$7.00 daily
Camper Spaces	6	E	5.00 daily
Tent Spaces	Limited	None	3.00 daily

SUPPORT FACILITIES:			
	Camp Equip Rntl	Chapel	Gas
	Golf	Laundry	Picnic Area
	Playgrounds	Rec Center	Sewage Dump Sta
	Skeet/Trap Range	Sports Fields	Stables
	Tennis Courts	Walking Trails	

ACTIVITIES:	Fishing	Hunting (lic)	Rec Equip Avail

RESTRICTIONS: No zoo animals. Pets must be kept indoors or on leash and controlled. They also MUST be registered at Animal Disease Prevention and Control Facility, Bldg 30022. Animals must have valid rabies certificates.

Davis-Monthan Fam-Camp (AZ14R4)

Davis-Monthan Air Force Base, AZ 85707-5000

Comm: 602-750-4717
ATVN: 361-1110

LOCATION: On base. From E, exit I-10 at Kolb Rd. N to Golf Links Rd; L on Craycroft Rd; R to main gate. From W, exit I-10 at Alvernon Way. Turn L and follow road to base. (Alvernon Way becomes Golf Links Rd at Ajo intersection.) Check in at Recreation Center, Bldg 4201. RM: p-8, N/9. NMC: Tucson, 4 mi NW.

DESCRIPTION OF AREA: Located in a wide desert valley which has beautiful weather year round. Nearby attractions include Arizona-Sonora Desert Museum, Pima Air Museum, Saguaro National Monument, Old Tucson and Reid Park and Zoo. Full range of military facilities available on base.

SEASON OF OPERATION: Year round.

ELIGIBILITY: Active/Retired/DOD Civilians/TDY Personnel.

RESERVATIONS: No adv resv. Address: Fam-Camp, PO Box 15034, Davis-Monthan AFB, AZ 85707-5000. Comm: 602-750-3717; ATVN: 361-3717.

CAMPING FACILITIES:	NO UNITS	HOOKUPS	FEE
Camper Spaces	25 Hardstand	W/S/E (110)	$8.00 daily
Camper Spaces	35	None	3.00 daily

SUPPORT FACILITIES:			
	Archery	Chapel	Gas
	Golf	Laundry	Racquetball
	Rec Center	Restrooms	Sewage Dump Sta
	Showers	Skeet Range	Snack Bar
	Sports Fields	Stables	Tennis Courts

ACTIVITIES:	Recreation Equipment Available

RESTRICTIONS: Pets allowed.

Fort Tuthill Recreation Area (AZ11R4)
Luke Air Force Base, AZ 85309-5000

Comm: 602-856-7411
ATVN: 853-1110

LOCATION: Off base. Located 4 mi S of Flagstaff. Take I-17 to exit 337 (Airport/Sedona). First road to L after entering park area at Ft Tuthill (adjoins Coconino County fairgrounds). RM: p-8, G/6. NMI: Luke AFB, Glendale, 138 mi SW. NMC: Flagstaff, 4 mi N.

DESCRIPTION OF AREA: Ft Tuthill is located at the base of the San Francisco Peaks. Tall pines, mild summer temperatures, and skiing in the winter make this an ideal vacation spot. Full range of military fac available at Luke AFB.

SEASON OF OPERATION: Mobile homes, huts and chalets: Year round.
Camping area: May-October.

ELIGIBILITY: Active/Retired/Reserve/DOD Civilians.

RESERVATIONS: Recommended up to 30 days in adv. Address: Luke Rec Area, Oak Creek Star Rte, Box 5, Flagstaff, AZ 86001; Comm: 602-774-8893; ATVN: 835-3401.

CAMP FACILITIES:	NO UNITS	HOOKUPS	FEE
Mobile Homes, furn, except bath towels	12	W/S/E	$16.00 daily
Chalets, furn	3	W/S/E	30.00 daily
Huts, furn, no bath/kit	8	E	10.00 daily
Camper Spaces	26 Hardstand	W/E	8.00 daily
Camper Spaces	10	W	6.00 daily
Camper & Tent Spaces	7 Wilderness	None	4.50 daily

SUPPORT FACILITIES:			
	Country Store	Golf (8 mi)	Grills
	Handball	Jacuzzi	Lakes (15 mi)
	Laundry	Lodge	Outdoor Rntl Office
	Picnic Area	Playground	Restrooms
	Sewage Dump Sta	Showers	Sports Fields
	Stables (6 mi)	Tennis Courts	Trails
	TV/VCR		

ACTIVITIES:			
	Boating	Day Trips	Fishing
	Hiking	Hunting	Movie Night
	Rec Equip Avail	Snow Skiing (DH & XC nearby)	

RESTRICTIONS: No pets inside facilities. Pets allowed on leash in camping area.

Gila Bend Fam-Camp (AZ15R4)
Gila Bend Air Force Auxiliary Field, AZ 85337-5000

Comm: 602-683-6201
ATVN: 853-6201

LOCATION: On base. 71 mi S of Luke Air Force Base at the Auxiliary Field. From I-10 W of Phoenix take Exit 112 (Yuma/Gila Bend); S on AZ-85 through Gila Bend; R at Gila Bend AFAF/Ajo sign approx 4.5 mi to AFAF. RM p-8, L/5. NMC: Phoenix, 48 mi NE.

DESCRIPTION OF AREA: Located between Yuma and Phoenix in an area that enjoys pleasant weather year round. Mountain areas and Mexico within easy driving distance. Full range of military facilities available on base.

SEASON OF OPERATION: Year round.

ELIGIBILITY: Active/Retired/DOD Civilians.

RESERVATIONS: Accepted for Active Duty and DOD Civilians on official orders. Address: MWR, PO Box 1022, Gila Bend AFAF, AZ 85337-5000. Comm: 602-683-6275/6102; ATVN: 853-5275/5102.

CAMPING FACILITIES:	NO UNITS	HOOKUPS	FEE
Camper Spaces	13 Gravel	W/S/TV/E	$6.00 dly/75 biwkly
Camper Spaces	6 Gravel	W/E	4.00 daily
Dry Camp Area		None	3.00 daily

SUPPORT FACILITIES:			
Boat Rental	Camp Equip Rntl	Chapel
Golf	Laundry	Picnic Area
Racquetball	Restrooms	Sewage Dump Sta
Showers	Skeet/Trap Range	Swimming Pool
Tennis Courts		

ACTIVITIES:			
Fishing	Jogging	Rec Equip Avail

RESTRICTIONS: Pets allowed on leash. Animals must have rabies shots. 14-day limit. Host and hostess are present for check-in and information (Oct-May) in site 8 area.

Martinez Lake Recreation Area (AZ12R4)

Yuma Marine Corps Air Station, AZ 85369-5000

Comm: 602-726-2011
ATVN: 951-2011

LOCATION: Off base. Located on Colorado River 38 mi N of Yuma. N on US-95; L on Imperial Wildlife Refuge access road; travel approx 10 mi. R at sign for USMC Rec Area; follow road approx 2 mi. RM: p-8, L/1. NMI: US Army Yuma Proving Ground, 15 mi N. NMC: Yuma, 38 mi S.

DESCRIPTION OF AREA: Located on land administered by the US Fish and Wildlife Service. Area provides rustic semi-private fishing camp. Campground is barren desert peninsula extending into river. Full range of military facilities available at Yuma US Army Proving Ground.

SEASON OF OPERATION: Year round.

ELIGIBILITY: Active/Retired.

RESERVATIONS: Accepted. Address: Special Services, Bldg 633, MCAS, Yuma, AZ 85369-5000; Comm: 602-726-2278; ATVN: 951-2007/2279. Recreation Area: Martinez Lake Rec Area, PO Box 72202, Martinez Lake, AZ 85365; Comm: 602-783-3422.

CAMP FACILITIES:	NO UNITS	HOOKUPS	FEE
Cabins, A/C, furn,	8		$11-12 daily/
except dishes & linens			1.00 ea add pers
Camper Spaces	17 Hardstand	W/E (110/220)	4.50-5.50 daily
Camper & Tent Spaces	4 Primitive	None	4.00-4.50 daily

SUPPORT FACILITIES:			
Boat Rental	Grills	Grocery
Marina	Picnic Area	Playground
Restrooms	Sewage Dump Sta	Showers
Snack Bar	Swimming Pool	

ACTIVITIES:			
Fishing	Horseshoes	Swimming

RESTRICTIONS: Pets allowed on leash. 7-day limit for cabins and some campsites. No weapons allowed.

Williams AFB Recreation Annex (Waterdog) (AZO7R4)
Williams Air Force Base, AZ 85240-5225

Comm: 602-988-1011
ATVN: 474-1011

LOCATION: Off base. Located on Apache Lake NE of Apache Junction on AZ-88 (Apache Trail). Obtain detailed directions from Rec Services. RM: p-8, K/8. NMI: Williams AFB, 53 mi SW. NMC: Phoenix, 75 mi SW.

DESCRIPTION OF AREA: The Recreation Annex (popularly known as "Waterdog") is located on Apache Lake at an elevation of 1,950 feet in the Tonto National Forest and has many recreational activities to offer. Waterdog gets its name from the little waterfaring animals of the salamander family that inhabit the lake and are used as bait in all warm water lakes in AZ. Driving time from Williams AFB is approx 2 hours. Full range of military fac at Williams AFB.

SEASON OF OPERATION: Year round. (Closed 2 weeks in Dec for holidays.)

ELIGIBILITY: Active/Retired/DOD and NAF Civilians at Williams AFB.

RESERVATIONS: Required. Address: MWR Logistics, Bldg 508, 82 ABG/SSS, Williams AFB, AZ 85240-5225. Comm: 602-988-5592; ATVN: 474-5592.

CAMP FACILITIES:	NO UNITS	HOOKUPS	FEE
Cabins, sleep 6	18		$20.00 daily
Camper Spaces	8	W/E	7.00 daily

Monthly rates are available October through April.
Cabins furnished, except towels; have A/C and electric furnaces.
Tent sites (free) are available at Davis Wash, next to Waterdog.

SUPPORT FACILITIES:	Barbecue Pits	Boat Rental	Boat Launch
	Fishing Tackle	Grocery Store	Lounge (in sumr)
	Picnic Area	Rec Hall	Restrooms
	Showers		

ACTIVITIES:	Boating	Fishing (lic)	Hiking
	Hunting	Skiing	

RESTRICTIONS: No swimming. Dependent children are not authorized to rent cabins on their own.

ARKANSAS

Little Rock Fam-Camp (ARO5R2)
Little Rock Air Force Base, AR 72099-5000

Comm: 501-988-3131
ATVN: 731-1110

LOCATION: On base. Located 10 mi NE of Little Rock off US-67/167 at Jacksonville. AFB exit to main gate. Check in at Base Billeting (Razorback Inn), Bldg 1024. RM: p-9, G/7. NMC: Little Rock, 10 mi SW.

DESCRIPTION OF AREA: Located in central region of state in open terrain near lakes and wooded area. Full range of military facilities available on base.

SEASON OF OPERATION: Year round.

ELIGIBILITY: Active/Retired/DOD Civilians.

RESERVATIONS: No adv resv. Address: Recreation Services, 314 CSG/SSR, Little Rock AFB, AR 72099-5000. Comm: 501-988-6164; ATVN: 731-6164.

ARKANSAS
Little Rock Fam-Camp, Cont'd

CAMPING FACILITIES:	NO UNITS	HOOKUPS	FEE
Camper Spaces	10 Hardstand	W/E (110)	$5.00 daily
Tent Spaces	Wilderness	None	3.00 daily

SUPPORT FACILITIES:			
	Boat Rental (summer weekends)		Camp Equip Rntl
	Chapel	Gas	Golf
	Grills	Picnic Area	Playground
	Racquetball	Rec Center	Sewage Dump Sta
	Sports Fields	Tennis Courts	Trailer Rental

ACTIVITIES:			
	Fishing (lic)	Hunting (lic)	Jogging
	Rec Equip Avail		

RESTRICTIONS: Pets allowed on leash.

CALIFORNIA

Beale Fam-Camp (CA60R4)
Beale Air Force Base, CA 95903-5000

Comm: 916-634-3000
ATVN: 368-1110

LOCATION: On base. Take US-70 S from Marysville for approx 12 mi to main gate of AFB. Well marked. Check in at Billeting, Bldg 2156. RM: p-10, NK/10. NMC: Sacramento, 40 mi SW.

DESCRIPTION OF AREA: Located in northern California in the midst of a variety of interesting recreational opportunities. Full range of military fac on base.

SEASON OF OPERATION: Year round.

ELIGIBILITY: Active/Retired/DOD Civilians.

RESERVATIONS: No adv resv. Address: Recreation Services, 9 CSG/SSRO, Beale AFB, CA 95903-5000. Comm: 916-634-4222; ATVN: 368-4222.

CAMPING FACILITIES:	NO UNITS	HOOKUPS	FEE
Camper Spaces (self-contained veh only)	27 Hardstand	W/S/E (110/30A)	$6.00 daily

SUPPORT FACILITIES:			
	Boat Rental	Camp Equip Rntl	Chapel
	Gas	Golf	Laundry
	Off-Road Veh	Rec Center	RV Rental
	Sewage Dump Sta	Snack Bar	Snow Skiing
	Trails		

ACTIVITIES:		
	Hunting (lic)	Recreation Equipment Available

RESTRICTIONS: Pets allowed on leash.

Big Bear Lake Recreation Facility (CA05R4)
El Toro Marine Corps Air Station, CA 92709-5000

Comm: 714-651-2100
ATVN: 997-2100

LOCATION: Off base. From I-10 at Redlands, take CA-30 N to CA-330 to CA-18 at Running Springs; R to Big Bear Lake. RM: p-15, E/25. NMI: Norton AFB, 50 mi SW. NMC: San Bernardino, 50 mi SW.

Big Bear Lake Rec Facility, Cont'd

DESCRIPTION OF AREA: Located in the San Bernardino National Forest next to Snow Summit Ski Resort. Area offers excellent fishing, boating, hiking and skiing. Full range of military facilities available at Norton AFB.

SEASON OF OPERATION: Year round.

ELIGIBILITY: Active/Retired.

RESERVATIONS: Required. Address: The Lodge, Bldg 823, MCAS El Toro, Santa Anna, CA 92709-5007. Comm: 714-651-2095/2084; ATVN: 997-2095/2084. Rec Facility (info only) Comm: 714-866-3965.

CAMP FACILITIES:	NO UNITS	HOOKUPS	FEE
Cottages	8		$40.00 daily
Motor Homes/Campers	5		5.00 daily
Tent Spaces	Unlimited	None	4.00 daily

SUPPORT FACILITIES:			
	Bicycle Rental	Boat Launch	Boat Rental
	Grills	Laundry	Picnic Area
	Playground	Rec Equip Rntl	Rec Room
	Restrooms	Sewage Dump Sta	Showers

ACTIVITIES:			
	Boating	Fishing	Hiking
	Snow Skiing	Volleyball	Water Skiing

RESTRICTIONS: No pets allowed. No vehicles over 18' in length. No campfires.

Castle Fam-Camp (CA72R4)

Castle Air Force Base, CA 95342-5000

Comm: 209-726-2011
ATVN: 347-1110

LOCATION: On base. From CA-99, exit at Buhach Rd/Castle AFB (Atwater from N or Merced from S). RM: p-10, NQ/12. NMC: Merced, 7 mi S.

DESCRIPTION OF AREA: Centrally located in San Joaquin Valley, Castle AFB is a max of two hours from some of the world's most picturesque sites and cities: Yosemite National Park, San Francisco, Sequoia and Kings Canyon Natl parks. The base is less than an hour away from the foothills of the Sierra Nevada. Full range of military facilities on base.

SEASON OF OPERATION: Year round.

ELIGIBILITY: Active/Retired/NG on AD/DOD Civilians.

RESERVATIONS: Accepted. Address: MWR Supply, 93 CSG/SSS, Castle AFB, CA 95342-5000. (Resv) Comm: 209-723-6031; (Info) Comm: 209-726-2715; ATVN: 347-2531.

CAMPING FACILITIES:	NO UNITS	HOOKUPS	FEE
Camper Spaces	6 Hardstand	W/S/E	Call For
Camper Spaces	36 Hardstand	None	Rates

SUPPORT FACILITIES:			
	Boat Rental	Camper Rental	Camp Equip Rntl
	Chapel	Gas	Laundry
	Picnic Area	Playground	Sewage Dump Sta
	Snowmobile Rntl	Sports Equip Rntl	

ACTIVITIES:			
	Boating	Fishing	Snow Skiing
	Windsurfing		

CALIFORNIA
Castle Fam-Camp, Cont'd

RESTRICTIONS: Pets allowed.

NOTE: Castle AFB no longer operates a marina at Lake McClure because the water
level is too low. They are looking into the possibility of obtaining another
area. Call MWR Supply, Comm: 209-726-2715, if you desire additional info.

Del Mar Recreation Beach (CA03R4)

Camp Pendleton Marine Corps Base
Camp Pendleton, CA 92055-5001

Comm: 619-725-4111
ATVN: 365-4111

LOCATION: On base. Exit I-5 at Oceanside. RM: p-13, SN/16. NMC: San Diego,
50 mi S.

DESCRIPTION OF AREA: Located in southern California approx 90 mi S of Los
Angeles. Campgrounds situated on 26 miles of Pacific Ocean shoreline. Full
range of military facilities available on base.

SEASON OF OPERATION: Year round (some restrictions).

ELIGIBILITY: Active/Retired.

RESERVATIONS: Req at least one month in adv. Address: Special Services, Marine
Corps Base, Camp Pendleton, CA 92055-5001. Comm: 619-725-6288; ATVN: 365-6288.

CAMP FACILITIES:	NO UNITS	HOOKUPS	FEE
Cottages	12		$23.00 daily
Camper & Tent Spaces	32	W/E	8.00 daily
Camper & Tent Spaces	44	W	6.00 daily

SUPPORT FACILITIES:			
	Archery	Bicycle Route*	Boat Rental &
	Cabanas	Chapel	Supply
	Fire Rings&Pits	Gas	Golf
	Marina	Picnic Area	Racquetball
	Rec Center	Restrooms	Sewage Dump Sta
	Snow Ski(nearby)	Tennis Courts	

*Along coastline. Groups of 10 or more must get writ-
ten permission to use route. Write JPAO, MCB, Camp
Pendleton, CA 92055-5001 at least 45 days in adv.

ACTIVITIES:	Jogging	Rec Equip Avail	Swimming

RESTRICTIONS: No pets. No bottles on beach.

East Garrison Recreation Area and Travel Camp (CA61R4)

Fort Ord, CA 93941-5600

Comm: 408-242-4200
ATVN: 929-4200

LOCATION: On post. From San Francisco, S for 100 mi on US-101; R on CA-156 for
10 mi to main gate of post. RM: p-12, SC/4. NMC: Monterey, 7 mi S.

DESCRIPTION OF AREA: Located in wooded area adjacent to Los Padres National
Forest. Easy access to many rec areas, such as scenic and historic Monterey
Peninsula, Carmel-by-the-Sea, beautiful coastline from Fort Ord south to Big
Sur. Full range of outdoor rec activities in nearby areas includes backpacking,
sailing, deep-sea fishing, surf fishing, stream fishing and snow skiing. Full
range of military facilities available on post.

East Garrison Rec Area & Travel Camp, Cont'd

SEASON OF OPERATION: Year round.

ELIGIBILITY: Active/Retired/DOD and NAF Civilians.

RESERVATIONS: No adv resv. Address: Outdoor Recreation, AFZW-PA-CRO, Bldg 3104, East Garrison Travel Camp, Ft Ord, CA 93941-5600. Comm: 408-899-3374; ATVN: 929-3466.

CAMPING FACILITIES:	NO UNITS	HOOKUPS	FEE
Camper Spaces	38	W/E	$5.00 daily
Tent Spaces	27	None	3.00 daily

SUPPORT FACILITIES:			
	Beach	Bicycle/Motor	Boat Rental
	Camp Equip Rntl	Cross Track	Chapel
	Firearms Ranges	Gas	Golf
	Grills	Ice	Laundry
	Picnic Area	Playground	Racquetball
	Rec Center	Restrooms	Scout Camping Area
	Sewage Dump Sta	Showers	Snack Bar
	Sports Fields	Stables	Tennis Courts
	Trails	Vending Machines	

ACTIVITIES:			
	Bicycling	Fishing (lic)	Hiking
	Hunting (lic)	Jogging	Rec Equip Avail
	River Rafting	Snow Ski Trips	

RESTRICTIONS: Pets allowed.

Edwards Fam-Camp (CA62R4)
Edwards Air Force Base, CA 93523-5000

Comm: 805-277-1110
ATVN: 527-1110

LOCATION: On base. Off CA-14, 18 mi E of Rosamond and 30 mi NE of Lancaster. Off CA-58, 10 mi SW of Boron and 40 mi NW of Barstow (Jct I-15 & I-40). Check in at Billeting Office. RM: p-13, SI/15. NMC: Los Angeles, 90 mi SW.

DESCRIPTION OF AREA: Located in Mojave-Lancaster-Barstow section of California's hilly desert region NE of Los Angeles metropolitan area. Convenient base for visiting Lake Arrowhead and other points of interest in the San Bernardino-Pasadena-Los Angeles complex. Full range of military facilities avail on base.

SEASON OF OPERATION: Year round.

ELIGIBILITY: Active/Retired/DOD Civilians.

RESERVATIONS: No adv resv. Address: Fam-Camp, 6510 ABG/SVH, Edwards AFB, CA 93523-5000. Comm: 805-277-3394; ATVN: 527-3394.

CAMPING FACILITIES:	NO UNITS	HOOKUPS	FEE
Camper Spaces	6 Hardstand	W/S/E	$6.00 daily
Camper Spaces	Overflow	None	3.00 daily

SUPPORT FACILITIES:			
	Chapel	Gas	Golf
	Racquetball	Sports Fields	Trails

ACTIVITIES:	
	Recreation Equipment Available

RESTRICTIONS: Pets allowed. No open fires. No feeding of wild animals.

El Centro NAF Campground (CA76R4)

El Centro Naval Air Facility, CA 92243-5001

Comm: 619-339-2555
ATVN: 958-8555

LOCATION: On base. From I-8 at Seeley, take Drew Road exit N to NAF. Clearly marked. Check in with Sun Security, Bldg 232, at front gate. RM: p-13, SP/21. NMC: Yuma, AZ, 60 mi E.

DESCRIPTION OF AREA: Located in the Imperial Valley of southern CA. Climate is most delightful during winter and early spring with daytime temperatures between 75 and 90. There is little rainfall except for occasional brief downpours during the summer. Full range of military facilities available on base.

SEASON OF OPERATION: Year round.

ELIGIBILITY: Active/Retired/DOD Civilians.

RESERVATIONS: No adv resv. Address: Recreation Services, Code 14, Naval Air Facility, El Centro, CA 92243-5001. Comm: 619-339-2481; ATVN: 958-8481.

CAMP FACILITIES:	NO UNITS	HOOKUPS	FEE
Mobile Homes, 2 bdrm	4		Call for Rates
Camper Spaces, 35' max	39 Hardstand	W/S/E (110)	$6 dly/35 wk/140 mo
Camper Spaces	15 Gravel	None	3.00 daily

SUPPORT FACILITIES:			
	Boat Rental	Chapel	Gas
	Golf*	Grill	Laundry (nearby)
	Picnic Area	Racquet Sports	Restrooms
	Sewage Dump Sta	Showers	Sports Fields
	Trailer Rental		
	*9-hole short course in El Centro		

ACTIVITIES:	Hunting (Dove, Sep)	Rec Equip Avail

RESTRICTIONS: Pets allowed; must be confined at all times (leash, cage, inside RV, etc). Pets will not be allowed on the running track or football field.

George Fam-Camp (CA70R4)

George Air Force Base, CA 92394-5000

Comm: 619-269-1110
ATVN: 353-1110

LOCATION: On base. From I-15 at Victorville, exit at Village Drive; follow signs. From US-395 at Adelanto, exit E on Air Base Road; 2 mi on L. RM: p-13, SJ/16. NMC: San Bernardino, 40 mi SE.

DESCRIPTION OF AREA: Located in beautiful southern California. Ski areas nearby. Los Angeles and beaches 1.5 hours' drive; 3 hours to Las Vegas. Full range of military facilities available on base.

SEASON OF OPERATION: Year round.

ELIGIBILITY: Active/Retired/DOD Civilians.

RESERVATIONS: Accepted with one day's adv payment. Address: Recreation Services, 831 CSG/SSRO, George Air Force Base, CA 92394-5000. Comm: 619-269-3233; ATVN: 353-3233.

CAMPING FACILITIES:	NO UNITS	HOOKUPS	FEE
Camper Spaces	7 Hardstand	W/S/E (110)	$5.00 daily

George Fam-Camp, Cont'd

SUPPORT FACILITIES:

Chapel	Gas	Golf
Grills	Picnic Area	Quick Shop
Rec Center	Sewage Dump Sta	Skeet/Trap Ranges

ACTIVITIES: Rec Equip Avail   Snow Skiing (nearby)

RESTRICTIONS: Pets allowed on leash no longer than 6 feet. 2-week limit. Open campfires are not permitted.

Lake Isabella Recreation Area (CAO2R4)
George Air Force Base, CA 92394-5000

Comm: 619-269-1110
ATVN: 353-1110

LOCATION: Off base. From US-395 take CA-178 W; R on CA-155 and travel lake shoreline for 3 mi to Rec Area. RM: p-12, SG/13. NMI: China Lake Naval Weapons Center, 40 mi E. NMC: Bakersfield, 45 mi SW.

DESCRIPTION OF AREA: Located on Lake Isabella Reservoir near Sequoia National Forest in South Central CA. Full range of military fac at China Lake NWC.

SEASON OF OPERATION: Year round.

ELIGIBILITY: Active/Retired/DOD Civilians.

RESERVATIONS: Required. Reservations for George AFB personnel taken for current month and next month; reservations for others taken by phone at least 2 weeks in advance or made in person at Outdoor Rec Office, Bldg 210, George AFB, with payment in full. Address: Outdoor Recreation Department, 831 CSG/SSRO, George AFB, CA 92394-5000. Comm: 619-269-3233/3480, ATVN: 353-3233/3480.

CAMP FACILITIES:	NO UNITS	HOOKUPS	FEE
Mobile Homes, 1 & 2 bdrm, furn exc linens, towels	7	W/S/E	$15-17 daily

SUPPORT FACILITIES:

Beach	Boat Rental	Food*
Chapel*	Golf*	Grills
Marina	Picnic Area	Playground
Restrooms	Showers	Trails

*In Kernville, 10 mi away

ACTIVITIES:

Boating	Fishing (lic)	Hiking
Hunting (lic)	Snow Skiing (DH)	Swimming
Water Skiing	White Water Rafting	

RESTRICTIONS: Pets allowed. Only the vehicle transporting the patrons to the campsite may be parked in camp area. No visitors' cars, boats, campers, tents, trailers, etc., are permitted in the camp. No open fires; briquettes ONLY in barbecue grills.

Lake Isabella Recreation Camp (CAO4R4)
Edwards Air Force Base, CA 93523-5000

Comm: 805-277-1110
ATVN: 527-1110

LOCATION: Off base. From US-395 take CA-178 W; R on CA-155 and travel lake shoreline for 10 mi to Rec Area. RM: p-12; SG/13. NMI: China Lake Naval Weapons Center, 40 mi E. NMC: Bakersfield, 45 mi SW.

DESCRIPTION OF AREA: Situated in Kern River Valley in Nevada mountains adjacent to Sequoia Natl Forest. Full range of mil fac at China Lake NWC.

SEASON OF OPERATION: Year round.

ELIGIBILITY: Active/Retired/Reserve on AD/DOD Civilians.

RESERVATIONS: Required. Address: Outdoor Recreation Office, Bldg 7211, Edwards AFB, CA 93523-5000. Comm: 805-277-2895; ATVN: 527-3546.

CAMP FACILITIES:	NO UNITS	HOOKUPS	FEE
Mobile Homes, 1 & 2 bdrm, furn exc linens, towels	7		$15-17 daily

SUPPORT FACILITIES:	Boat Rental Playground	Marina	Picnic Area

ACTIVITIES:	Fishing	Swimming	Water Skiing

RESTRICTIONS: Pets allowed. 2-night minimum on weekends.

Lake O'Neill Aquatic Park (CA65R4)

Marine Corps Base
Camp Pendleton, CA 92055-5001

Comm: 619-725-4111
ATVN: 365-4111
FTS: 725-4111

LOCATION: On base. Exit I-5 at Oceanside Harbor/Camp Pendleton. Enter main gate of base; NE on Vandegrift Blvd approx 8.5 mi. L at Naval Hospital road; R at entrance to campground. RM: p-13, SO/16. NMC: Oceanside, 10 mi SW.

DESCRIPTION OF AREA: 12-square-mile facility on northern side of Lake O'Neill. Southern side offers a large variety of recreational activities. Full range of military facilities available on base.

SEASON OF OPERATION: Year round.

ELIGIBILITY: Active/Retired/Active Reserve.

RESERVATIONS: Required, in person only: up to 5 wks in adv for AD at Camp Pendleton; up to 4 wks in adv for other AD; up to 3 wks in adv for Ret and Active Res. Payment required 1 wk in adv. Resv by mail not accepted. Address: Base Special Services, Marine Corps Base, Camp Pendleton, CA 92055-5001, ATTN: Lake O'Neill. Comm: 619-725-4241; ATVN: 365-4241; FTS: 725-4241.

CAMPING FACILITIES:	NO UNITS	HOOKUPS	FEE
Camper Spaces	40	W/E	$8.00 daily
Camper Spaces	20	W	6.00 daily
Tent Spaces	100	None	5.00 daily

SUPPORT FACILITIES:	Bicycle Route*	Boat Rental	Gas
	Grills	Mini Golf	Picnic Area
	Restrooms	Sewage Dump Sta	Showers
	Sports Eq Rntl	Sports Fields	

*Along coastline. Groups of 10 or more must get written permission to use route. Write JPAO, MCB, Camp Pendleton, CA 92055-5001 at least 45 days in adv.

ACTIVITIES:	Fishing	Horseshoes	Volleyball

RESTRICTIONS: Pets allowed on leash. Swimming in lake is prohibited.

Lake Tahoe Army Recreation Facilities
(CA73R4)
Presidio of San Francisco, CA 94129-5000

Comm: 415-561-2211
ATVN: 586-1110

LOCATION: Off post. Located at Lake Tahoe. Specific directions may be obtained from Outdoor Recreation at the address shown below. RM: p-10, NL/13. NMI: McClellan AFB, Sacramento, CA, 110 mi SW. NMC: Carson City, NV, 30 mi SE.

DESCRIPTION OF AREA: The Presidio has leased rental units in Lake Tahoe for year-round enjoyment. They are conveniently located for taking advantage of a wide range of mountain- and water-oriented recreational activities. Casinos are located within a few miles. Full range of military fac at McClellan AFB.

SEASON OF OPERATION: Year round.

ELIGIBILITY: Active/Retired/Reserve.

RESERVATIONS: Required with payment. Address: Outdoor Recreation, CRD, Bldg 667, Presidio of San Francisco, San Francisco, CA 94129-5206.Comm: 415-561-4324; ATVN: 586-4324. Write for additional info.

LODGING: All units are fully furn, including dishes, kitchen utensils, dishwasher, TV, washer and dryer, coffee pot, toaster and vacuum cleaner. NO bed linens, towels or wash cloths. Units sleep 8 to 12 persons.
    FEE: $50.00 daily, Sunday through Thursday
          70.00 daily, Friday, Saturday and any night preceding holiday

RESTRICTIONS: No pets allowed.

Lake Tahoe CG Recreation Facility
(CA24R4)
US Coast Guard Group, Yerba Buena Island
San Francisco, CA 94130-5000

Comm: 415-399-3413
FTS: 623-1413

LOCATION: Off base. Take I-80 to CA-89; S through Tahoe City; N on CA-28 to Lake Forest Blvd; R to USCG Station Lake Tahoe (marked). RM: p-10, NK/13. NMI: McClellan AFB, Sacramento, CA, 80 mi SW. NMC: Reno, NV, 30 mi NE.

DESCRIPTION OF AREA: Located at Coast Guard Station Lake Tahoe on SW shore of the beautiful lake. Much to do and see in nearby cities of Reno and Carson City. Many recreational activities avail on Lake Tahoe and surrounding Sierra Nevada mountains. Full range of military facilities avail at McClellan AFB.

SEASON OF OPERATION: Year round.

ELIGIBILITY: Active/Retired.

RESERVATIONS: Required, by application only. Resv accepted up to 50 days in adv and booked 42 days in adv. Address: Commander, USCG Group San Francisco, Yerba Buena Island, San Francisco, CA 94130-5000. Comm: 415-399-3413; FTS: 623-1413.

LODGING: Two A-Frame style cabins, each with two apartments, fully furnished; color TV; microwave ovens:

2-bdrm Apt, sleeps 9	$12-24 daily
1-bdrm Apt, sleeps 7	10-18 daily

Rates are the minimum rates and vary according to rank of sponsor. They are also based on number and age of occupants.

SUPPORT FACILITIES: There are no military facilities available but nearby commercial facilities offer marina, boat rental and boat launch facilities.

ACTIVITIES:

Boating	Fishing	Sailing
Skiing (DH&XC)	Swimming	Water Skiing

RESTRICTIONS: No pets allowed. 7-day limit, to include only 1 weekend.

Miramar RV Park (CAO7R4)
Miramar Naval Air Station, CA 92145-5000

Comm: 619-537-1011
ATVN: 577-1011

LOCATION: On base. 14 mi N of San Diego, 1 mi W of I-15. Take NAS Miramar exit. RM: p-15, K/24. NMC: San Diego, 14 mi S.

DESCRIPTION OF AREA: Beautiful area with many activities available and many special events. Sea World, zoo, museums and historical parks are all nearby. Full range of military facilities available on base.

SEASON OF OPERATION: Year round.

ELIGIBILITY: Active/Retired/DOD Civilians at NAS Miramar.

RESERVATIONS: Required up to 4 months in adv with $5 deposit. Address: Recreational Services Dept (Code 210), Naval Air Station Miramar, San Diego, CA 92145-5000. Comm: 619-537-4149, ATVN: 577-4149.

CAMP FACILITIES:	NO UNITS	HOOKUPS	FEE
Camper Spaces	15 Hardstand	W/S/E (30A)	$9.00 daily
	2 Hardstand	W/E	7.00 daily
	Overflow	W	5.00 daily

SUPPORT FACILITIES:

Archery	Gas	Golf
Grills	Jet Mart	Laundry
Picnic Area	Playground	Propane
Racquetball	Restrooms	RV Rental
Sewage Dump Sta	Showers	Tennis Courts

ACTIVITIES:

Boating	Fishing	Jogging
Rec Equip Avail	Scuba Diving	Softball
Swimming	Water Skiing	

RESTRICTIONS: One pet allowed per rental space; must be on leash at all times; spaces must be cleaned daily. 30-day limit.

Mission Gorge Campground (CA64R4)
San Diego Naval Station, CA 92136-5000

Comm: 619-235-1400
ATVN: 958-1400

LOCATION: Off base. Off Friar's Rd and Santo on Admiral Baker Rd, 1/2 mi E of I-15, 4 mi NE of downtown San Diego. RM: p-13, SP/17. NMI: San Diego NS, 11 mi SW. NMC: San Diego, 4 mi SW.

DESCRIPTION OF AREA: Campground is located in the midst of 44-acre picnic area & caters to families. Golf Crest RV Park is located N of campground, adjacent to the golf course and caters primarily to golfers. Full range of military facilities available at San Diego Naval Station.

SEASON OF OPERATION: Year round.

Mission Gorge Campground, Cont'd

ELIGIBILITY: Active/Retired.

RESERVATIONS: Recommended. **For campground**: Up to 60 days in adv for AD; 30 days for Ret: Full payment req. Address: Recreation Services, Mission Gorge Campground Reservations, Code 10, Box 15, Naval Station, San Diego, CA 92136-5000. Comm: 619-282-8481. **For Golf Crest**: Up to one year in adv with deposit of $50. Address: Recreation Services, Golf Crest RV Park Reservations, Code 10, Box 15, Naval Station, San Diego, CA 92136-5000. Comm: 619-281-0432.

CAMPING FACILITIES:	NO UNITS	HOOKUPS	FEE
Camper Spaces	24 Hardstand	W/E (110/220)	$ 7.00 daily
Camper Spaces	4	None	4.00 daily
RV Spaces at Golf Crest	14	W/S/E	14-17 daily

SUPPORT FACILITIES:			
	Golf	Grills	Picnic Area
	Playground	Sewage Dump Sta	Showers (at pool)
	Sports Fields	Swimming Pool	Tennis Courts

ACTIVITIES:	Basketball	Rec Equip Avail	Swimming

RESTRICTIONS: Pets allowed on leash in campground area only. Must keep noise down and clean up after pet. No tent camping.

Norton RV Park (CA69R4)
Norton Air Force Base, CA 92409-5235

Comm: 714-382-1110
ATVN: 876-1110

LOCATION: On base. From I-10 at Loma Linda, take Tippecanoe exit N to base approx 1.5 mi. Check in at Bldg 512, The Inland House. RM: p-15, E/24. NMC: San Bernardino, 3 mi NW.

DESCRIPTION OF AREA: Located in outskirts of San Bernardino, 60 mi from Los Angeles. Convenient base for enjoying varied desert and mountain sightseeing and recreation attractions. Full range of military facilities avail on base.

SEASON OF OPERATION: Year round.

ELIGIBILITY: Active/Retired.

RESERVATIONS: No adv resv. Address: 63 SVS/SVH, Norton Air Force Base, CA 92409-5235. Comm: 714-382-5531; ATVN: 876-5331/5332.

CAMPING FACILITIES:	NO UNITS	HOOKUPS	FEE
Camper Spaces	6 Hardstand	W/S/E (2A)	$5.00 daily
Camper Spaces	24	None	3.00 daily

SUPPORT FACILITIES:			
	Chapel	Gas	Golf
	Picnic Area	Racquetball	Shoppette
	Snack Bar	Sports Fields	Tennis Courts

ACTIVITIES:	Hiking	Sightseeing

RESTRICTIONS: No pets allowed. 7-day limit for RV spaces.

Petaluma Coast Guard Training Center (CA66R4)

Petaluma, CA 94952-5000

Comm: 707-765-7211
FTS: 623-7382

LOCATION: On base. Exit US-101 in Petaluma at Washington St (becomes Bodega Avenue); 11 mi W to Coast Guard Training Center. RM: p-10, NN/6. NMC: San Francisco, 40 mi S.

DESCRIPTION OF AREA: Located in beautiful Sonoma County. Campsites are near a small lake in a quiet rustic atmosphere. Full range of military fac on base.

SEASON OF OPERATION: Year round.

ELIGIBILITY: Active/Retired/DOT Civilians.

RESERVATIONS: Required, by application only, at least 60 days in advance. Address: USCG Training Center, Petaluma, CA 94952-5000, ATTN: Special Services Branch. Comm: 707-765-7348/7349; FTS: 623-7348

CAMPING FACILITIES:	NO UNITS	HOOKUPS	FEE
Camper Spaces	40	None	None
Tent Spaces	100	None	None

SUPPORT FACILITIES:			
	Camp Equip Rntl	Deli/Gas	Grills
	Mini Mart	Nature Trails	Picnic Area
	Racquetball	Restrooms	Tennis Courts

ACTIVITIES:			
	Basketball	Fishing	Horseshoes
	Jogging	Rec Equip Avail	Softball

RESTRICTIONS: Pets allowed on leash. No open fires. 2-week limit.

Point Mugu Recreation Area (CA11R4)

Point Mugu Naval Air Station, CA 93042-5000

Comm: 805-989-1110
ATVN: 351-1110

LOCATION: On base. 8 mi S of Oxnard and 40 mi N of Santa Monica on Coastal Highway, CA-1. RM: p-12, SL/11. NMC: Los Angeles, 50 mi SE.

DESCRIPTION OF AREA: Located along Pacific Ocean N of picturesque Point Mugu State Park and within easy driving distance of the world-famous tourist attractions in the Los Angeles area. Full range of military facilities on base.

SEASON OF OPERATION: Year round.

ELIGIBILITY: Active/Retired.

RESERVATIONS: Accepted with payment in full up to 30 days in adv (Pt Mugu AD: up to 60 days). Address: MWR Division, Code 6830, NAS Point Mugu, CA 93042-5000. Comm: 805-989-8770; ATVN: 351-8770.

CAMP FACILITIES:	NO UNITS	HOOKUPS	FEE
Cabins (sleep up to 5)	6		$ 15.00 daily
Motel Rooms w/kitchenette	12		8-12 daily
Camper Spaces	11 Hardstand	W/S/E	9 dly/55 wkly/ 108.00 biweekly
Camper Spaces	11 Overflow	None	4.00 daily
Tent Spaces	10 On Beach		3.00 daily

Point Mugu Rec Area, Cont'd

SUPPORT FACILITIES:	Beach	Chapel	Gas
	Golf	Laundry	Picnic Area
	Racquet Courts	Sewage Dump Sta	Skeet Range
	Sports Fields	Tennis Courts	

ACTIVITIES:	Bicycling	Fishing	Hunting (lic)
	Jogging	Racquetball	Swimming

RESTRICTIONS: Pets on leash allowed in camping areas only. 5-day limit for cabins and motel; 2 weeks for campsites. Fires allowed in fire rings only; all others must be approved by the NAS fire department. Scuba diving and surfing restricted to clubs only.

San Onofre Recreation Beach
(CA31R4)
Camp Pendleton Marine Corps Base
Camp Pendleton, CA 92055-5010

Comm: 619-725-4111
ATVN: 365-4111
FTS: 725-4111

LOCATION: On base. Exit I-5 on Basilone Rd 15 mi S of San Clemente. E to San Onofre Military Gate; 1.6 mi from gate turn R; road will take you to beach. RM: p-13, SN/15. NMI: Camp Pendleton, 17 mi SE. NMC: Oceanside, 15 mi SE.

DESCRIPTION OF AREA: Located along the Pacific Ocean in Southern California. Large variety of rec activities. Full range of military facilities on base.

SEASON OF OPERATION: Year round.

ELIGIBILITY: Active/Retired/Active Reserves.

RESERVATIONS: Up to 5 wks in adv for AD at Camp Pendleton; up to 4 wks in adv for AD stationed elsewhere; up to 3 wks for Ret and Active Res. Payment req 1 wk in adv. Resv by mail not acpt. Address: Base Special Services, Marine Corps Base, Camp Pendleton, CA 92055-5010, ATTN: San Onofre Beach. Comm: 619-725-7935; ATVN: 365-7935; FTS: 725-7935.

CAMP FACILITIES:	NO UNITS	HOOKUPS	FEE
Mobile Homes/Cottages	10		$23.00 dly (sumr)
			20.00 dly (winter)
Camper Spaces	80	W/E	8.00 daily
Camper & Tent Spaces	42	W	6.00 daily
Camper Spaces	8	None	4.00 daily

SUPPORT FACILITIES:	Beach	Bicycle Route*	Gas
	Golf	Picnic Area	Playground
	Restrooms	Sewage Dump Sta	Showers
	Sports Fields		

*Along coastline. Groups of 10 or more must get written permission to use route. Write JPAO, MCB, Camp Pendleton, CA 92055-5001 at least 45 days in adv.

A wide variety of camping, fishing, boating and skiing (water and snow) equipment is available for rent to active duty and retired military.

ACTIVITIES:	Rec Equip Avail	Surfing	Swimming

RESTRICTIONS: Pets on leash allowed on facility but not on beach. Swimming allowed only when lifeguards are on duty.

CALIFORNIA

Sharpe Army Travel Camp (CA63R4)
Sharpe Army Depot, CA 95331-5214

Comm: 209-982-2011
ATVN: 462-2011

LOCATION: On post. Off I-5 at Roth Rd; from CA-99 N, L on CA-120, N on Airport Way, L on Roth Rd to depot. RM: p-10, NO/10. NMC: Stockton, 10 mi N.

DESCRIPTION OF AREA: Located in the Delta Country (known for its 1000 mi of waterways). Oakwood Lake Resort within minutes. Easy drive to San Francisco, Lake Tahoe, Yosemite Natl Park, Great American Park and Sacramento. Limited military facilities available on post.

SEASON OF OPERATION: Year round.

ELIGIBILITY: Active/Retired.

RESERVATIONS: No adv resv. Address: Community Recreation Office, Sharpe Army Depot, Lathrop, CA 95331-5214. Comm: 209-982-2419; ATVN: 462-2419.

CAMPING FACILITIES:	NO UNITS	HOOKUPS	FEE
Camper Spaces	12 Gravel	W/S/E (110)	$7.00 daily

SUPPORT FACILITIES:			
	Boat Rental	Camp Equip Rntl	Chapel
	Consol Club	Grills	Laundry
	Picnic Area	Playground	PX
	Racquetball	Restrooms	Sewage Dump Sta
	Showers	Sports Fields	Swimming Pool(sumr)
	Tennis Courts		

ACTIVITIES: Recreation Equipment Available

RESTRICTIONS: Pets allowed on leash. No open fires. Firearms must be checked in to Security.

Travis Fam-Camp (CA68R4)
Travis Air Force Base, CA 94535-5000

Comm: 707-438-4011
ATVN: 837-1110

LOCATION: On base. From I-80 take Travis Airbase Parkway exit. Clearly marked. RM: p-10, NN/8. NMC: San Francisco, 45 mi SW.

DESCRIPTION OF AREA: Located in state's famed valley region near Sacramento at Fairfield. Major water sports centers of San Pablo Bay and Lake Berryessa are nearby. Full range of military facilities available on base.

SEASON OF OPERATION: Year round.

ELIGIBILITY: Active/Retired/DOD Civilians.

RESERVATIONS: No adv resv. Address: Crosswinds Recreation Center, Bldg 212, Travis AFB, CA 94535-5000. Comm: 707-438-5659/3076; ATVN: 837-5659/3076.

CAMPING FACILITIES:	NO UNITS	HOOKUPS	FEE
Camper Spaces	22 Hardstand	W/E (110)	$8.00 daily
Camper Spaces	12	None	3.00 daily
Tent Spaces	6 Open	None	3.00 daily

SUPPORT FACILITIES:			
	Camp Equip Rntl	Golf	Grills
	Laundry (nearby)	Picnic Area	Racquet Sports
	Restrooms	Sewage Dump Sta	Showers
	Snow Ski Rental	Sports Fields	Tennis Courts

Travis Fam-Camp, Cont'd

ACTIVITIES: Rec Equip Avail   Sightseeing

RESTRICTIONS: Pets allowed on leash; must not annoy others. Check in at Fam-Camp space 18-A during the hours 0830-1030 or 1530-1730 M-Sa. On Su and holidays, go directly to non-hookup area and manager will contact you on next working day.

Vandenberg Fam-Camp (CA67R4)
Vandenberg Air Force Base, CA 93437-5000

Comm: 805-866-1110
ATVN: 276-1110

LOCATION: On base. Located between Lompoc and Santa Maria. From US-101, W on CA-S20 to AFB. Check in with Billeting Office, Bldg 13005 (866-1844), for site number and lounge key. RM: p-12, SJ/7. NMC: Santa Maria, 17 mi N.

DESCRIPTION OF AREA: Space and missile center. Installation covers over 98,000 acres. Fam-Camp is situated about 3 mi from main base and provides unlimited sightseeing and recreational opportunities in nearby areas. Full range of military facilities available on base.

SEASON OF OPERATION: Year round.

ELIGIBILITY: Active/Retired/ DOD Civilians.

RESERVATIONS: No adv resv. Address: Fam-Camp, 4392 AEROSG/SSRO, PO Box 5938, Vandenberg AFB, CA 93437-5000. Comm: 805-866-8579; ATVN: 276-8579.

CAMPING FACILITIES:	NO UNITS	HOOKUPS	FEE
Camper Spaces	20 Hardstand	W/S/E	$8.00 daily
Camper Spaces	30 Hardstand	W/E	6.00 daily
Camper Spaces	19 Overflow		3.50 daily
Tent Spaces, fenced	15 Improved		3.50 daily

SUPPORT FACILITIES:			
	Camp Equip Rntl	Game Room	Gas
	Golf	Grills	Laundry
	Lounge	Picnic Area	Playground
	Racquetball	Restrooms	RV Parts Store
	Sewage Dump Sta	Showers	Skeet Range
	Snack Bar	Sports Fields	Tennis Courts
	Trails	Vending Machines	

ACTIVITIES: Hunting (lic)   Rec Equip Avail   Surf Fishing

RESTRICTIONS: Pets allowed; must comply with local license & leash laws. No Swimming.

COLORADO

Dillon Recreation Area (CO08R3)
Lowry Air Force Base, CO 80230-5000

Comm: 303-370-1110
ATVN: 926-1110

LOCATION: Off base. From I-70 at Dillon take US-6 S to Swan Mountain Rd (County Rd 1); W to Lowry campground. RM: p-16, G/10. NMI: Lowry AFB, 80 mi E. NMC: Denver, 80 mi E.

DESCRIPTION OF AREA: Located on Dillon Reservoir on 68 acres of wooded campground. Boating and fishing available within 1 mile of area. Full range of military facilities available at Lowry Air Force Base.

Dillon Rec Area, Cont'd

SEASON OF OPERATION: Memorial Day-Labor Day.

ELIGIBILITY: Active/Retired/DOD Civilians.

RESERVATIONS: Accepted. Address: Recreation Services, 3415 ABG/SSRR, Lowry AFB, CO 80230-5000, ATTN: Ticket & Tour. Comm: 303-370-2640; ATVN: 926-2640.

CAMPING FACILITIES:	NO UNITS	HOOKUPS	FEE
Camper & Tent Spaces	33	None	$3.00 daily

SUPPORT FACILITIES:	Grills	Picnic Area	Port-a-Potties
	Well Water		

ACTIVITIES:	Boating	Fishing (lic)

RESTRICTIONS: Pets allowed on leash.

Farish Memorial Fam-Camp (COO1R3)
USAF Academy, Colorado Springs, CO 80840-5000

Comm: 719-472-1818
ATVN: 259-3110

LOCATION: Off base. Off US-24, 6 mi NE of Woodland Park on Rampart Range Road. (Call manager at 303-687-9098 for additional information.) RM: p-16, I/13. NMI: US Air Force Academy, 38 mi E. NMC: Colorado Springs, 30 mi SE.

DESCRIPTION OF AREA: Located on 655 acres of magnificent woodland at an altitude of 9,150 feet in the Rocky Mountains. Wide range of mil fac on base.

SEASON OF OPERATION: Memorial Day-Labor Day.

ELIGIBILITY: Active/Retired/DOD Civilians.

RESERVATIONS: Required with deposit. Address: Farish Memorial Fam-Camp, PO Box 146, Woodland Park, CO 80866. Comm: 719-687-9098.

CAMP FACILITIES:	NO UNITS	HOOKUPS *	FEE
Sleeping Lodge	4 Rooms		$14-21 daily

Beds, stove, refrigerator furnished; bring bedding and cooking utensils. USAF Academy cadets have first priority during school year; then USAF Academy military and civilian employees.

Camper Spaces	24 Hardstand	E	$ 5.00 daily
Camper Spaces	11	None	4.00 daily
	*One local water hookup		

SUPPORT FACILITIES:	Grills	Grocery (small)	Picnic Area
	Playground	Rec Lodge	Snack Bar
	Stables	Trails	

ACTIVITIES:	Hiking	Horseback Riding Ice Skating

RESTRICTIONS: Pets allowed on leash. No sewage dump station. Fishing is restricted to USAF Academy personnel only. Because of rough roads and high altitude, campers over 20' are not advised to try to make it to the facility.

Lowry Fam-Camp (CO09R3)
Lowry Air Force Base, CO 80230-5000

Comm: 303-370-1110
ATVN: 926-1110

LOCATION: On base. From I-70 E of Denver, take I-225 S to 6th Ave; W 3 mi to Gate E of base at Dayton St. RM: p-16, F/13. NMC: Denver, 6 mi W.

DESCRIPTION OF AREA: Located in central section of state in metropolitan area of Denver. Convenient for enjoying Denver and Colorado Springs areas or for passing through to other Rockies or West Coast areas. Full range of military facilities available on base.

SEASON OF OPERATION: Year round.

ELIGIBILITY: Active/Retired/DOD Civilians on TDY orders to Lowry AFB.

RESERVATIONS: No adv resv. Report to space 20, Fam-Camp, for slot assignment 0800-2000 daily. Address: Recreation Services, 3415 ABG/SSRO, Lowry AFB, CO 80230-5000. Comm: 303-370-2888/3321; ATVN: 926-2888.

CAMPING FACILITIES:	NO UNITS	HOOKUPS	FEE
Camper Spaces (self-contained veh only)	20 Hardstand	W/S/E (110)	$8.00 daily
Camper Spaces (size ltd)		None	3.00 daily

SUPPORT FACILITIES:			
	Chapel	Golf	Grills
	Picnic Area	Playground	Sewage Dump Sta
	Sports Fields	Tennis Courts	

ACTIVITIES:	Racquetball	Recreation Equipment Available

RESTRICTIONS: Pets allowed on leash.

CONNECTICUT

-None-

DELAWARE

Fort Miles Recreation Area (DE02R1)
Fort George G. Meade, MD 20755-5071

Comm: 301-677-6261
ATVN: 923-6261

LOCATION: Off post. Located 1 mi from Lewes, DE. From DC/Baltimore area, take US-50 to MD-404; E to MD/DE-16; E to US-1; S to US-9 (Freeman Highway); E past Cape May Ferry. Look for sign where road divides; bear R to Ft Miles. RM: p-41, I/25. NMI: Dover AFB, DE, 40 mi NW; NMC: Dover, DE, 40 mi NW.

DESCRIPTION OF AREA: Located along Atlantic Ocean inside Cape Henlopen State Park, 6 mi N of Rehoboth Beach, DE. State camping area across the road from Fort Miles. Full range of military facilities available at Dover AFB.

SEASON OF OPERATION: 20 May-11 October.

ELIGIBILITY: Active/Retired/DOD Civilian employees of Ft Meade, Ft Indiantown Gap, Oakdale Support Center and Ft A P Hill.

Fort Miles Rec Area, Cont'd

RESERVATIONS: Required. Initial reservations (28 Mar-6 May) prioritized by category, serviced in person only. Payment in full req at time of resv. After initial resv period, eligibility limited to Active and Retired military. For complete information write: Community Recreation Div, ATTN: Ft Miles Reservation Office, Ft George G Meade, MD 20755-5071, ATTN: Ft Miles. Comm: 301-677-4945; ATVN: 923-4945.

LODGING:	NO UNITS	FEE
Mobile Homes, 3 bdrm	20	$33-46 daily*
Apartments, 2 bdrm	Total	20-38 daily
Apartments, 3 bdrm	of 19	30-41 daily
Family Duplex, 1 bdrm	1	17-28 daily
Dorm Unit, sleeps to 14	1	48-72 daily

    *Additional $3.00 daily for unit with screened porch/privacy fence.

Equipped with dishes, kitchen utensils, pots, refrigerator, stove, grill. Patrons supply items such as towels, soap, hangers, detergent, etc.

SUPPORT FACILITIES:

Beach	Bicycle Rental	Boat Rental
Fast Food*	Fishing Eq Rntl	Golf*
Grills	Laundry	Marina*
Picnic Area	Playground	PX (small)
Rec Hall	Restrooms	Showers
Sports Fields*	Tennis*	Trails
*Nearby		TV Room

ACTIVITIES:

Bingo	Boat Trips/fee	Fishing
Jogging	Rec Equip Avail	Volleyball

RESTRICTIONS: No pets allowed. User fee of $5 per carload for authorized personnel who are not registered patrons/guests. No firearms allowed. Use of RVs, campers and tents is not authorized. Patrons may bring TV sets but good reception cannot be assured.

DISTRICT OF COLUMBIA

-None-

FLORIDA

Avon Park Recreation Area (FL29R1)
Avon Park Air Force Range, FL 33825-5000

Comm: 813-452-4114
ATVN: 968-1110-EX-114

LOCATION: On base. From US-27 at Avon Park take FL-64 E 10.5 mi to AFR. RM: p-21, N/12. NMC: Orlando, 70 mi N.

DESCRIPTION OF AREA: Situated on the shores of Lake Arbuckle within two hours of all major Florida attractions, e.g., Disney World, Sea World, Busch Gardens. Limited military fac on base; full range of fac at MacDill AFB, 95 mi NW.

SEASON OF OPERATION: Year round.

ELIGIBILITY: Active/Retired/DOD Civilians in the area (space available only).

Avon Park Rec Area, Cont'd

RESERVATIONS: Resv req: 30 days in adv for Fam-Camp and mobile homes (4-14 day stay); 15 days in adv for mobile homes (1-3 day stay). $18 dep req for mobile homes. Address: 56 CSS/SS, Avon Park AF Range, FL 33825-5000, ATTN: Reservation Clerk. Comm: 813-452-4128/4287; ATVN: 968-1110-EX-287/128.

CAMP FACILITIES:	NO UNITS	HOOKUPS	FEE
Mobile Homes, 2 bdrm*	5		$18.00 daily
Camper Spaces	13 Hardstand	W/S/E (30A)	9.00 dly/50 wkly
Tent Spaces	4	None	2.00 daily

*A/C; furn except bedding (sgl beds), towels and personal items.

SUPPORT FACILITIES:			
	Boat Rental	Camp Equip Rntl	Golf (nearby)
	Grills	Laundry	Multi-Purpose Court
	Nature Trail	Picnic Area	Playground
	Racquetball/resv	Rec Equip Rntl	Restrooms
	Sewage Dump Sta/fee		Tennis Court

ACTIVITIES:			
	Fishing	Hunting	Sightseeing
	Swimming	Water Skiing	

RESTRICTIONS: No pets allowed in mobile homes, marina or beach areas. Pets allowed on leash in Fam-Camp area. Occupants must clean up mobile homes. No open fires. Regulations available at Range for restricted hunting.

Coon's Creek Recreation Area (FL23R1)

MacDill Air Force Base, FL 33608-5000

Comm: 813-830-1110
ATVN: 968-1110

LOCATION: On base. I-275 to exit 23B, Dale Mabry Highway (US-92). South approx 5 mi to main gate. RM: p-20, Q/4. NMC: Tampa, 5 mi N.

DESCRIPTION OF AREA: Located on S end of installation in coastal peninsula area approx 2 mi from main base area. Recreation Area consists of Fam-Camp, marina, beach, snack bar and pavilions. Fresh water lakes nearby, nature trail and an abundance of natural flora and fauna. Full range of military fac on base.

SEASON OF OPERATION: Year round.

ELIGIBILITY: Active/Retired/DOD Civilians.

RESERVATIONS: Required Oct-Apr. Address: Coon's Creek Recreation Area, PO Box 6825, MacDill AFB, FL 33608-5000. Include self-addressed envelope. Comm: 813-830-4982/4983/3864; ATVN: 968-4982/4983/3864.

CAMPING FACILITIES:	NO UNITS	HOOKUPS	FEE
Camper Spaces	144 Hardstand	W/E (some 220)	$7.00 daily
Camper Spaces	30	None	3.00 daily
Tent Spaces	Open	None	3.00 daily

SUPPORT FACILITIES:			
	Bait	Beach	Boat Launch
	Boat Rental	Equipment Rntl	Golf
	Grills	Ice	Laundry
	Marina	Nature Trail	Pavilions
	Picnic Area	Playground	Propane
	Restrooms	Sewage Dump Sta	Showers
	Snack Bar	Sports Fields	Swimming Pools
	TV/Game Room		

Coon's Creek Rec Area, Cont'd

ACTIVITIES:
Fishing   Jogging   Sailing
Swimming   Windsurfing

RESTRICTIONS: Pets allowed on short leash or in RV; owner must clean up after pet. Pets without complete and current immunizations are not allowed on MacDill AFB and Recreation Area. No open campfires.

Destin Army Infantry Center
Recreation Area (FLO1R1)
Fort Benning, GA 31905-5065

Comm: 404-544-2011
ATVN: 784-2011

LOCATION: Off post. In Destin, FL. US-231 S to Panama City, FL; US-98 W to 3d traffic light in Destin; R to area. Or I-10 to FL-85; S to Fort Walton Beach; US-98 E to Destin; L to area. RM: p-21, X/5. NMI: Eglin AFB, FL, 25 mi N. NMC: Pensacola, FL, 40 mi W.

DESCRIPTION OF AREA: Located on 15-acre site on Choctawhatchee Bay in Destin, FL. Sandy beach. Gulf of Mexico fishing and swimming areas approx 1 mi from recreation area. Full range of military facilities available at Eglin AFB.

SEASON OF OPERATION: Year round.

ELIGIBILITY: Active/Retired/DOD Civilians at Fort Benning.

RESERVATIONS: Required. Address: Community Recreation Div, PO Box 53323, ATTN: Destin Rec Area, Ft Benning, GA 31905-5226. Comm: 404-545-4155; ATVN: 835-7680.

CAMP FACILITIES:	NO UNITS	HOOKUPS	FEE
Cottages, 3 bdrm	Total		$37-46 daily*
Cottages, 2 bdrm	of 15		33-42 daily*
Motel	10 Units		20-25 daily
Camper Spaces	32	W/S/E	8.00 daily
Tent & Camper Spaces	37 Primitive	None	6.00 daily

*Includes immediate family only. Additional fee for guests.
Off-season rates available 1 November-31 March.

SUPPORT FACILITIES:
Beach   Boat Slip Rental   Boat Launch
Boat Rental   Camper Svc Ctr   Grills
Grocery   Laundry   Marina
Picnic Area   Playground   Restrooms
Sewage Dump Sta   Showers   Snack Bar
Water Sports Equipment Rental

ACTIVITIES:
Boating   Deep-Sea Fishing   Fishing
Rec Equip Avail   Swimming

RESTRICTIONS: No pets allowed.

Eglin Fam-Camp (FL25R1)
Eglin Air Force Base, FL 32542-5000

Comm: 904-882-6668
ATVN: 872-1110

LOCATION: On base. From I-10 at Crestview take FL-85 S to Niceville. Take John Simms Blvd to East Gate. RM: p-21, W/5. NMC: Pensacola, 40 mi W.

DESCRIPTION OF AREA: Located on the northern coast of the Gulf of Mexico in Ft Walton area off Choctawhatchee Bay. Fam-Camp is situated adjacent to beach.

Eglin Fam-Camp, Cont'd

Beautiful forested areas and fresh water lakes also nearby. Full range of military facilities available at Eglin AFB.

SEASON OF OPERATION: Year round.

ELIGIBILITY: Active/Retired.

RESERVATIONS: No adv resv. Address: Recreation Services, 3201 ABG/SSRO, Eglin AFB, FL 32542-5000. Comm: 904-882-5058.

CAMPING FACILITIES:	NO UNITS	HOOKUPS	FEE
Camper Spaces	22 Hardstand	W/E	$5.00 daily
Tent Spaces	10	None	2.50 daily

SUPPORT FACILITIES:			
	Beach	Boat Launch	Boat Rental
	Chapel	Gas	Golf
	Grills	Laundry	Marina
	Picnic Area	Restrooms	Sewage Dump Sta
	Shoppette	Showers	Sports Fields
	Trails		

ACTIVITIES:	Hunting	Jogging	Rec Equip Avail

RESTRICTIONS: Pets allowed.

Lake Fretwell Recreation Area
(FL24R1)
Cecil Field Naval Air Station, FL 32215-5000

Comm: 904-778-5675
ATVN: 860-5675

LOCATION: On base. Take Normandy Blvd (FL-228) exit off I-295; W to main gate. Rec area approx 2 mi from gate. RM: p-20, D/10. NMC: Jacksonville, 13 mi NE.

DESCRIPTION OF AREA: Located at Lake Fretwell. Full range of military facilities available on base.

SEASON OF OPERATION: Year round.

ELIGIBILITY: Active/Retired.

RESERVATIONS: Accepted up to 30 days in adv. Address: MWR Dept, PO Box 109, Bldg 200, NAS Cecil Field, FL 32215-5000. Comm: 904-778-6112; ATVN: 860-6112.

CAMPING FACILITIES:	NO UNITS	HOOKUPS	FEE
Camper Spaces	4 Hardstand	W/E (110/220)	$ 6 dly/35 weekly
			60 biweekly
Tent Spaces	Only on or adjacent to camper spaces		

SUPPORT FACILITIES:			
	Boat Rental	Gas	Grills
	Picnic Area	Playground	Restrooms
	Sewage Dump Sta	Showers	Sports Fields
	Tennis Courts	Trails	

ACTIVITIES:	Hiking	Racquetball	Rec Equip Avail

RESTRICTIONS: Pets allowed on leash.

Space-A Travel Newsletter
(Space-A Air . . . Space-A RV & Camping . . . Space-A Temporary Military Lodging)

FREE COPIES FOR PURCHASERS of THIS BOOK

"TRAVEL ON LESS PER DAY.... THE MILITARY WAY"

We'd like to acquaint you with our travel newsletter, Military Living's R&R Report. It gives late breaking info on Space-A air travel, new info on military camping and rec areas, and temporary military lodging plus informative and helpful reader trip reports.

We'll send you two free copies (a $4.00 value) if you will send $1.00 to cover the cost of postage and handling.

To get your copies, send your name and address and $1.00 to:
Military Living R&R (Dept. SA)
Box 2347
Falls Church, VA 22042

Hanna Park
Jacksonville, Florida

We have it all at the Beach!

Camping • Fishing
Picnicking • Swimming

- 450 acres of fun and relaxation
- 300 wooded campsites with full hookups
- 1.5 miles sandy beach
- playground area
- ocean and fresh water fishing
- laundry and facilities
- country store
- Good Sampark club member
- City owned and operated
- Located next door to Mayport Naval Station

For further information write:
Hanna Park and Campground
500 Wonderwood Road
Jacksonville, Florida 32233
(904) 249-4700 — 249-2316

Registration Hours:
8 a.m. to Sunset

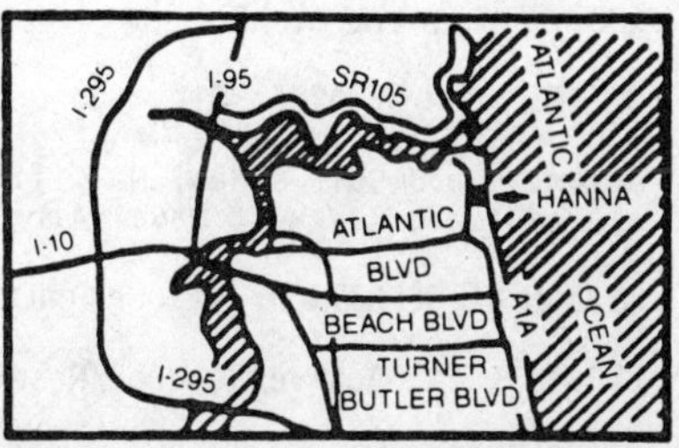

Lake Pippin, Maxwell/Gunter
Recreation Area (FL12R1)
Maxwell Air Force Base, AL 36112-5000

Comm: 205-293-1110
ATVN: 875-1110

LOCATION: Off base. Near Niceville, FL. From I-10 at Crestview take FL-85 S through Eglin AFB to Niceville. Take FL-20 E approx 6.5 mi to sign for Maxwell/Gunter Recreation Area. RM: p-21, W/5. NMI: Eglin AFB, FL, 15 mi N. NMC: Pensacola, FL, 25 mi W.

DESCRIPTION OF AREA: Located on Choctawhatchee Bay on northern coast of Gulf of Mexico. Lovely wooded site on beach. Within easy driving of Pensacola, Panama City and Ft Walton beach and fishing attractions. Easy access to full range of military facilities available at Eglin Air Force Base.

SEASON OF OPERATION: Year round.

ELIGIBILITY: Active/Retired/DOD Civilians at Maxwell/Gunter AFB.

RESERVATIONS: Required. Must be made in person at Maxwell AFB with payment in full. Patrons must have receipt. Address: Recreation Center, Bldg 834, Maxwell AFB, Montgomery, AL 36112-5000. Comm: 205-293-5496.

CAMPING FACILITIES:	NO UNITS	HOOKUPS	FEE
Mobile Home, A/C, furn except linens	30		$22-24 daily
Camper Spaces	16 Hardstand	W/E	6.00 daily
Tent Spaces	30		5.00 daily

SUPPORT FACILITIES:			
	Beach	Boat Rental	Gas
	Laundry	Playground	Picnic Area/fee
	Restrooms	Sewage Dump Sta	Showers

ACTIVITIES:	Fishing	Swimming	Water Skiing

RESTRICTIONS: Limit of 2 pets. Pets must be on short leash at all times and must not be left unattended. Pets not permitted in beach, picnic or swimming areas at any time.

Marathon Recreation Cottages (FL28R1)
United States Coast Guard, 7th CG District
Miami, FL 33130-5000

Comm: 305-536-5850
FTS: 536-5850

LOCATION: On base. Exit US-1 on Florida Keys at mile marker 48 in Marathon. Check in with OD, Coast Guard Station, 1800 Overseas Highway. RM p-21, Y/13. NMC: Miami, 111 mi NE.

DESCRIPTION OF AREA: Situated on Vaca Key in the heart of the Florida Keys. Topography is similar to that of islands in the eastern Caribbean. Beaches on Atlantic and Gulf sides. No military facilities available on base. Full range available at Key West Naval Air Station on Boca Chica Key, 40 mi S.

SEASON OF OPERATION: Year round.

ELIGIBILITY: Active/Retired/Reserve.

RESERVATIONS: Required, by application only, with $25 adv payment, at least 6 wks in adv. Address: Commander (ps), 7th CG District, 51 SW First Ave, Miami, FL 33130-5000, ATTN: Cottage Reservations. Comm:305-536-5850; FTS: 536-5850.

Marathon Rec Cottages, Cont'd

LODGING: Two cottages with 2 dbl beds, slp 4 adults.
One cottage with 3 dbl & 2 sgl beds, slp 8 adults.
FEE: $5.00 daily

All cottages fully furnished and A/C; CTV. Cots may be available; parties of more than four should bring sleeping bags.

SUPPORT FACILITIES:

Boat Dock	Boat Rental	Fishing Tackle
Rec Equip Avail at Homestead AFB in Miami		

ACTIVITIES:

Basketball	Boating	Fishing
Hiking	Swimming	Volleyball

RESTRICTIONS: No pets allowed. 12-day limit, to include only one weekend.

Mystic Lake Fam-Camp (FL22R1)

Homestead Air Force Base, FL 33039-5000

Comm: 305-257-8011
ATVN: 791-0111

LOCATION: On base. From Florida Turnpike (US-1), take Homestead exit E. Approx 2.5 mi to base. RM: p-21, V/16. NMC: Miami, 30 mi NE.

DESCRIPTION OF AREA: Located on installation with Biscayne Bay on one side and Everglades National Park on the other. Fam-Camp is adjacent to Mystic Lake. A new Fam-Camp with 57 sites and full hookups is scheduled for completion in 1988. Full range of military facilities available on base.

SEASON OF OPERATION: Year round.

ELIGIBILITY: Active/Retired.

RESERVATIONS: Accepted by mail with a $9.50 deposit. Written resv can be made up to 60 days in adv; telephone resv will be accepted up to 7 days in adv. Address: CBF/SSRO, Outdoor Recreation, Bldg 665, Homestead AFB, FL 33039-5000. Comm: 305-257-8949; ATVN: 791-8949.

CAMPING FACILITIES:	NO UNITS	HOOKUPS	FEE
Camper Spaces	15 Hardstand	W/S/E (110)	$9.50 daily

SUPPORT FACILITIES:

Boat Rental	Gas	Golf
Laundry	Marina	Picnic Area
Rec Center	Skeet Range	Sports Fields

ACTIVITIES: Recreation Equipment Available

RESTRICTIONS: Pets must be controlled at all times.

Oak Grove Trailer Park (FL09R1)

Pensacola Naval Air Station, FL 32508-5000

Comm: 904-452-0111
ATVN: 922-0111

LOCATION: On base. I-10 to US-29; S to Pensacola; take Navy Blvd directly to Naval Air Station. RM: p-21, X/3. NMC: Pensacola, 8 mi E.

DESCRIPTION OF AREA: Located in wooded area across from Naval Aviation Museum along a 1.5 mi Gulf of Mexico beachfront with historic lighthouse in center. Old Ft Pickens can be viewed from along beach. Full range of mil fac on base.

Oak Grove Trailer Park, Cont'd

SEASON OF OPERATION: Year round.

ELIGIBILITY: Active/Retired.

RESERVATIONS: Required up to 31 days in adv with one day's deposit. Address: Oak Grove Park Recreation Dept, NAS Pensacola, FL 32508-5000. Comm: 904-452-2535; ATVN: 922-2535.

CAMP FACILITIES:	NO UNITS	HOOKUPS	FEE
Efficiency Apartments*	4		$15.00 daily
Apartments, 2 bdrm*	2		20.00 daily
Mobile Homes, 2 bdrm*	11		20.00 daily
Camper Spaces	45	W/E	5.00 daily
Tent Spaces	15	None	2.00 daily

*Furnished, except TV.

SUPPORT FACILITIES:			
	Boat Launch	Boat Rental	Camp Equip Rntl
	Marina	Picnic Area	Rec Equip Rntl
	Restrooms	Sailing Facility	Sewage Dump Sta
	Showers		

ACTIVITIES:	Boating	Fishing	Swimming

RESTRICTIONS: No pets allowed in apartments or mobile homes; allowed on leash in camping area.

Orlando Travel Trailer Park (FL21R1)
Orlando Naval Training Center, FL 32813-5000

Comm: 305-646-4111
ATVN: 791-4111

LOCATION: On base. At the NTC Annex, S Orlando. I-4 to FL-528 (toll road) exit; E to Tradeport Road exit; R on Tradeport Road to Express St; R, and follow signs. RM: p-20, K/12. NMC: Orlando, 12 mi S.

DESCRIPTION OF AREA: Minutes away from Magic Kingdom and EPCOT Center, Sea World, Circus World, Church St Station, Wet n Wild. Busch Gardens, Cypress Gardens and Silver Springs within driving distance. Mil fac avail at NTC Annex.

SEASON OF OPERATION: Year round.

ELIGIBILITY: Active/Retired.

RESERVATIONS: Accepted only for Active Duty on PCS and TAD orders; others first come, first served. Address: Recreational Services, Travel Trailer Park, 3480 W 8th St, Orlando, FL 32812. Include self-addressed, stamped envelope. Comm: 305-857-2120.

CAMPING FACILITIES:	NO UNITS	HOOKUPS	FEE *
Camper Spaces	38 Hardstand	W/S/E	$8.50 dly/50 wkly
Camper Spaces	13 Grass	W/E	7.00 dly/40 wkly
Camper Spaces	10 Overflow	None	3.00 dly/18 wkly
Tent Spaces	15 Primitive	None	3.00 dly/18 wkly

*When NTC Orlando Rec Services equipment is utilized: 5.50 dly/30 wk/70 mo

SUPPORT FACILITIES:			
	Camper Rental	Chapel	Gas
	Golf	Grills (hard-	Laundry
	Picnic Area	stand site)	Playground
	Restrooms	Sewage Dump Sta	Showers

Orlando Travel Trailer Park, Cont'd

ACTIVITIES: Recreation Equipment Available

RESTRICTIONS: Pets allowed on leash; must not annoy others; must not be left alone in park; must use designated walking area.

Panama City NCSC Outdoor
Recreation Center (FLO7R1)
Comm: 904-234-4100
Panama City Naval Coastal Systems Center, FL 32407-5000   ATVN: 436-4100

LOCATION: On base. Located on US-98 at the foot of the Hathaway Bridge in Panama City Beach. RM: p-21, X/7. NMI: Tyndall AFB, 35 mi E. NMC: Panama City, adjacent.

DESCRIPTION OF AREA: Panama City Beach is considered one of the world's most beautiful beaches because of the brilliant white sand and emerald waters of the Gulf of Mexico. Water sports (jet skiing, sailing, boating, swimming, etc) attract tourists to the area. Limited military facilities available on base; full range available at Tyndall Air Force Base.

SEASON OF OPERATION: Year round.

ELIGIBILITY: Active/Retired/Reserve/DOD Civilians at NCSC.

RESERVATIONS: Required. Address: Recreation Services, Naval Coastal Systems Center, Panama City, FL 32407-5000. For campers/boats, call the Marina 904-234-4402 or write to address above. List dates/times of arrival. A refundable cleaning deposit of $30 is required to hold a camper reservation.

CAMPING FACILITIES:	NO UNITS	HOOKUPS	FEE
Travel Trailers, slp 4-6	8 Hardstand	W/S/E	$17-19 daily
Camper Spaces	4	W/E	7.50 daily
Boat Slips	13 Wet		60-70 monthly
Boat Slips	28 Dry		35-45 monthly

SUPPORT FACILITIES:			
	Beach	Boat Ramp	Boat Rental
	Camper Rental	Camp Equip Rntl	Consol Mess
	Exchange	Gas	Golf Driving Range
	Grills	Grocery (nearby)	Gym
	Ice	Laundry (nearby)	Marina
	Pavilion	Picnic Area	Playground
	Racquetball	Restrooms	Showers
	Sports Eq Rntl	Sports Fields	Swimming Pool
	Tennis Courts	Trails	Vending Machines

ACTIVITIES:			
	Bicycling	Boating	Canoe Trips
	Fishing	Rafting	Rec Equip Avail
	Sailing	Scuba Diving	Snorkeling
	Swimming	Tours	Water Skiing
	Windsurfing		

RESTRICTIONS: No pets allowed. Certification tests for boat rental given on Fridays or by scheduled appointment.

Rucker Florida Recreation Area (FL10R1)
Fort Rucker, AL 36362-5000

Comm: 205-255-6181
ATVN: 558-1110

LOCATION: Off post. Near Niceville, FL. From I-10 at Crestview take FL-85 S through Eglin AFB to Niceville. E on FL-20. Located between Niceville and Freeport. RM: p-21, W/5. NMI: Eglin AFB, 15 mi NW. NMC: Pensacola, 30 mi W.

DESCRIPTION OF AREA: Located on Choctawhatchee Bay in the Ft Walton area of Florida's northern Gulf of Mexico coast about 100 mi from Ft Rucker. Sandy beach. Easy access to full range of military facilities at Eglin AFB.

SUPPORT FACILITIES: Year round.

ELIGIBILITY: Active/Retired/NG/Reserve/DOD Civilians.

RESERVATIONS: Required, with one night's deposit: 60 days in adv for all AD; 45 days in adv for Retired, NG, Res and DOD employees. Address: Rec Center, ITT Office, PO Drawer 189, Ft Rucker, AL 36362-5000. Comm: 205-255-5816.

CAMP FACILITIES:	NO UNITS	HOOKUPS	FEE
Mobile Homes, 2 bdrm*	15		$30-35 daily**
Mobile Homes, 3 bdrm*	3		40-45 daily**
Travel Trailers, sleep 2	3		6.00 dly/30 wkly
Camper Spaces	20 Hardstand	W/E	5.00 dly/25 wkly
Tent Spaces		None	3.00 daily

*Mobile homes are air-conditioned and completely furnished.
**Reduced rates available 1 October-30 April.

SUPPORT FACILITIES:			
	Beach	Boat Launch	Boat Rental
	Conv Store	Fast Food (near)	Game Room
	Gas	Ice	Laundry
	Marina	Picnic Area	Restrooms
	Sewage Dump Sta	Showers	Vending Machines

ACTIVITIES:	Fishing	Rec Equip Avail	Water Skiing

RESTRICTIONS: No pets allowed.

Tyndall Fam-Camp (FL26R1)
Tyndall Air Force Base, FL 32403-5225

Comm: 904-283-1110
ATVN: 523-1110

LOCATION: On base. US-231 S to Panama City; US-98 E to base. Fam-Camp .25 mi on R after crossing Dupont Bridge. RM: p-21, Y/8. NMC: Panama City, 11 mi W.

DESCRIPTION OF AREA: Located on the coast of the Gulf of Mexico with the Gulf on one side and East Bay on the other. Some sites have water views; all are larger than normal and shaded by oak trees with Spanish moss. Bird-watching is excellent. Water sports attract many tourists to the area. Full range of military facilities available on base.

SEASON OF OPERATION: Year round.

ELIGIBILITY: Active/Retired/DOD Civilians.

RESERVATIONS: No adv resv for campsites; resv for cottages accepted up to 60 days in adv. Address: Fam-Camp, Tyndall AFB, FL 32403-5225. Comm: 904-283-2798; ATVN: 523-2798.

Tyndall Fam-Camp, Cont'd

CAMPING FACILITIES:	NO UNITS	HOOKUPS	FEE
Cottages, 2 bdrm, furn	3		CALL
Camper Spaces	9 Hardstand	W/S/CTV/E (30A)	
Camper Spaces	12 Hardstand	W/CTV/E (30A)	FOR
Camper Spaces being added	40		
Tent Spaces	8 Cleared		RATES
Adequate overflow parking available, some with W/E.			

SUPPORT FACILITIES:			
	Archery	Beach	Boat Rental
	Camp Equip Rntl	Chapel	Gas, LP Gas
	Golf	Grills	Laundry
	Marina	Mini Golf	Nature Trail
	Picnic Area	Quick Shop	Racquetball
	Restrooms	Sewage Dump Sta	Showers
	Shuffleboard	Skeet Range	Snack Bar
	Sports Fields	Tennis Courts	Water Sports Equip

ACTIVITIES:	Fishing (lic)	Hunting (lic)	Swimming

RESTRICTIONS: Maximum of two domestic pets allowed on leash.

GEORGIA

Gordon Recreation Area (GAO4R1)
Fort Gordon, GA 30905-5283

Comm: 404-791-0110
ATVN: 780-0110

LOCATION: Off post. Off GA-47 N of Leah. From I-20 W of Augusta, take GA-47 or GA-104 N to Leah. Signs clearly mark entrance. RM: p-22, G/12. NMI: Ft Gordon, 25 mi S. NMC: Augusta, 25 mi SE.

DESCRIPTION OF AREA: Located on an 814-acre site at Clarks Hill Reservoir on Georgia-South Carolina line. Ideal for wide range of outdoor activities in fresh-water lakes and rivers of area. Savannah about 120 mi SE. Easy access to full range of military facilities at Ft Gordon.

SEASON OF OPERATION: Year round. Marina closed November through March.

ELIGIBILITY: Active/Retired/DOD Civilians.

RESERVATIONS: Accepted only for mobile homes and cabins for a min of 2 nights; 1 night's deposit required 7 days in advance. Address: Ft Gordon Rec Area, PO Box 67, Appling, GA 30802. Comm: 404-541-1057.

CAMP FACILITIES:	NO UNITS	HOOKUPS	FEE
Cabins, 3 bdrm	8		$40.00 daily
Mobile Homes, 3 bdrm	6		35.00 daily
Camper Spaces	60 Hardstand	W/S/E (110)	7.00 daily
Camper Spaces	30	W/E	6.00 daily
Tent Spaces	50	None	4.00 daily

SUPPORT FACILITIES:

Boat Launch	Bath House	Beach
Boat Rental*	Boat Sheds	Camp Equip Rntl
Country Store	Marina	Picnic Area
Playground	Restrooms	Sewage Dump Sta
Showers	Snack Bar**	Trails
TV Room		

*Ft Gordon boating safety card required
**Summer months only

ACTIVITIES: Fishing (lic)   Hiking   Swimming

RESTRICTIONS: No pets in cabins, mobile homes or swimming area. Allowed on leash in other areas; owners must clean up after pets. Firearms, bows and arrows, explosives, fireworks and all sporting devices capable of causing death or injury are prohibited.

Grassy Pond Recreation Area (GA06R1)
Moody Air Force Base, GA 31699-5000

Comm: 912-559-4211
ATVN: 460-1110

LOCATION: Off base. From I-75 S of Valdosta, take exit 2; W on GA-376 (Clyattville Road). Watch for signs to rec area. RM: p-23, S/9. NMI: Moody AFB, 23 mi N. NMC: Valdosta, 15 mi N.

DESCRIPTION OF AREA: Located on a fresh-water lake near Georgia/Florida line. Area situated in rolling, wooded terrain. Full range of military facilities available at Moody Air Force Base.

SEASON OF OPERATION: Year round.

ELIGIBILITY: Active/Retired/DOD Civilians.

RESERVATIONS: Required. Address: Recreation Services, Grassy Pond, Rte 3, Box 10, Lake Park, GA 31636-5000. Comm: 912-559-5840; ATVN: 460-5840.

CAMP FACILITIES:	NO UNITS	HOOKUPS	FEE
Cabins	7	W/S/E	$20.00 daily
Camper Spaces	4	W/S/E	5.00 daily
Tent Spaces	Many	None	2.00 daily

SUPPORT FACILITIES:

Boat Launch	Boat Rental	Concession
Paddle Boats	Picnic Area	Playground
Rec Room	Rec Equip Rntl	Tackle/Bait
TV Room		

ACTIVITIES: Boating   Fishing   Nature Trail

RESTRICTIONS: No pets allowed in cabins; leash required in other areas.

Holbrook Pond Army Travel Camp (GA19R1)
Fort Stewart, GA 31314-5000

Comm: 912-767-1110
ATVN: 870-1110

LOCATION: On post. From US-17 or I-95 take Ft Stewart exit; take G-144 W to Outdoor Recreation Area sign. Turn L to Outdoor Recreation Service Center to check in. RM: p-23, M/14. NMC: Savannah, 45 mi NE.

Holbrook Pond Army Travel Camp, Cont'd

DESCRIPTION OF AREA: Located in Holbrook Pond area. Full range of military facilities available on post, approx 6 miles away.

SEASON OF OPERATION: Year round.

ELIGIBILITY: Active/Retired/NG on AD/DOD Civilians at Ft Stewart and Hunter AAF

RESERVATIONS: Accepted up to 30 days in adv; payment required. Address: Community Recreation Division (AFZP-PAR), Outdoor Recreation, Bldg 361, Ft Stewart, GA 31314-5000. Comm: 912-767-2717; ATVN: 870-2717.

CAMPING FACILITIES:	NO UNITS	HOOKUPS	FEE
Camper Spaces	20 Hardstand	W/E (some 220)	$5.00 daily
Tent Spaces	20 Primitive	Central Fresh W	2.50 daily

SUPPORT FACILITIES:			
	Boat Rental	Camper Rental	Camp Equip Rntl
	Conv Store	Gas	Golf
	Grills	Ice	Laundry
	Off-Rd Veh Area	Picnic Area	Restrooms
	Sewage Dump Sta	Showers	Sports Fields
	Trails	Vending Machines	

ACTIVITIES:	Boating	Hiking	Hunting (lic)

RESTRICTIONS: Pets allowed on leash or physically restrained at all times. Firearms check-in required at Pass and Permit Office, Bldg 8091.

Lake Allatoona Army Recreation Area
(GAO5R1)
Fort McPherson, GA 30330-5000

Comm: 404-752-3113
ATVN: 572-1110

LOCATION: Off post. From I-75 N of Atlanta, take exit 122 E. Follow signs for approx 3 mi to entrance on L. RM: p-22, F/4. NMI: Dobbins AFB and Atlanta NAS, 15 mi S. NMC: Atlanta, 43 mi S.

DESCRIPTION OF AREA: Located on 99-acre site at Lake Allatoona reservoir. Full range of beach and water activities. Conveniently situated for sightseeing in Atlanta and surrounding area, including Stone Mountain Memorial State Park. Full range of military facilities at Ft McPherson in Atlanta.

SEASON OF OPERATION: Year round.

ELIGIBILITY: Active/Retired/Reserve/NG/DOD Civ at Ft McPherson and Ft Gillem.

RESERVATIONS: Accepted with deposit. AD at Forts McPherson and Gillem have priority to make resv during first 10 days of any month and 3 succeeding months; all others may make resv for same period after 10th day. Address: Army Recreation Area, 40 Old Sandtown Rd, Cartersville, GA 30120. Comm: 404-974-3413.

CAMP FACILITIES:	NO UNITS	HOOKUPS	FEE *
Cabins, 1 bdrm**	8		$26.00 daily
Cabins, 2 bdrm**	14		31.00 daily
Motel**	8 Units		20.00 daily
Apartment,3 bdrm**	1		40.00 daily
Camper Spaces	6	W/E	7.00 daily
RV Spaces	13	W/S/E	7.00 daily
Tent Spaces	18	W/E	4.00 daily

GEORGIA

Lake Allatoona Army Rec Area, Cont'd

*Off-season rates available 1 Nov-1Apr.
**A/C; furnished, including TV, bed linens, pots, pans, dishes and kitchen
  utensils. Bring towels, extra blankets, can opener, soap, detergent.

SUPPORT FACILITIES:	Bath House	Beach	Boat Launch
	Fishing Pier	Grills	Grocery
	Laundry	Marina	Mini Golf
	Picnic Area	Playground	Rec Hall
	Restrooms	Sewage Dump Sta	Showers
	Sports Fields	Tennis Courts	Trails

Scheduled improvements include: 12 cabins, new bath house, game room and nature
trail.

ACTIVITIES:	Boat Tours	Boating	Fishing (lic)
	Swimming	Water Skiing	

RESTRICTIONS: No pets allowed. Motorcycles, minibikes, all terrain vehicles and
motor carts are prohibited. No open fires. 7-day limit 1 Apr-31 Oct. Check in
1700 to closing. Family members under 18 must be accompanied by authorized
adult sponsor to use the area.

Lake Allatoona NAS Recreation Center (GAO1R1)

Atlanta Naval Air Station, Marietta, GA 30060-5000

Comm: 404-429-5503
ATVN: 925-5503

LOCATION: Off base. On Lake Allatoona, 40 mi NW of Atlanta off I-75. RM:
p-22, F/4. NMI: NAS Atlanta, Marietta, 20 mi SE. NMC: Atlanta, 40 mi SE.

DESCRIPTION OF AREA: Located near Lake Allatoona reservoir. Ideal spot for
many outdoor rec activities. Wide range of military facilities at NAS Atlanta.

SEASON OF OPERATION: Cabins: Year round; Campgrounds: 1 April-31 October.

ELIGIBILITY: Active/Retired/Reserve/DOD Civilians.

RESERVATIONS: Required for cabins only. Address: MWR Office, Naval Air Station Atlanta, Marietta, GA 30060-5000; Comm: 404-421-5502. Rec area, Comm:
404-974-6309.

CAMP FACILITIES:	NO UNITS	HOOKUPS	FEE
Cabins, 1 bdrm*	2		$17.00 daily
Cabins, 2 bdrm*	4		24.00 daily
Cabins, 3 bdrm*	1		32.00 daily
RV Camper Spaces	13	W/E	5.00 daily
Tent Spaces	3	None	3.00 daily

*Furnished, including TV, dishes, pots and pans; bring linens.

SUPPORT FACILITIES:	Beach	Boat Launch	Boat Rental
	Marina	Picnic Areas	Playgrounds
	Restrooms	Sewage Dump Sta	Showers

ACTIVITIES:	Boating	Fishing	Swimming

RESTRICTIONS: No pets allowed. 14-day limit for RV spaces.

Lakeside Fam-Camp (GA18R1)
Dobbins Air Force Base, GA 30069-5000

Comm: 404-421-5000
ATVN: 925-1110

LOCATION: On base. From I-75, S of Marietta, exit to GA-280. W 1.5 mi to AFB. Entrance is on US-41 S. RM: p-24, B/1. NMC: Atlanta, 15 mi S.

DESCRIPTION OF AREA: Offers many recreation and leisure activities. Conveniently located for sightseeing in Atlanta and surrounding area. Ltd military facilities available on base; wide range available at Atlanta NAS, adjacent and to the E of Dobbins AFB.

SEASON OF OPERATION: Year round..

ELIGIBILITY: Active/Retired/Reserve/DOD Civilians.

RESERVATIONS: No adv resv. Address: Recreational Services, 94 CSG/SSR, Bldg 537, Dobbins AFB, GA 30069-5000. Comm: 404-421-5262/5716; ATVN: 925-5262/5716.

CAMPING FACILITIES:	NO UNITS	HOOKUPS	FEE
Camper and Tent Spaces	16 Hardstand	W/E	$6.00 daily
		W	5.00 daily

SUPPORT FACILITIES:			
	Beach	Chapel	Fast Food*
	Gas*	Grills	Grocery*
	Lakeside Lounge	Picnic Area	Playground
	Racquetball	Rec Center	Restrooms
	Sewage Dump Sta	Showers	Snack Bar
	Sports Fields	Tennis Courts	
	*Nearby		

ACTIVITIES:			
	Horseshoes	Jogging	Rec Equip Avail
	Volleyball		

RESTRICTIONS: Pets allowed on leash. No swimming or fishing allowed.

Robins Fam-Camp (GAO7R1)
Robins Air Force Base, GA 31098-5000

Comm: 912-926-1001
ATVN: 468-1001

LOCATION: On base. From US-129 take GA-247 E at Warner Robins to AFB. RM: p-22, L/8. NMC: Macon, 16 mi N.

DESCRIPTION OF AREA: Fam-Camp is situated at SE corner of installation adjacent to Luna Lake. Very rustic setting surrounded by trees. Full range of military facilities available on base.

SEASON OF OPERATION: Year round.

ELIGIBILITY: Active/Retired/DOD Civilians.

RESERVATIONS: Not required. Address: Outdoor Recreation (SSRO), Bldg 1305, Robins AFB, GA 31098-5000. Comm: 912-926-4500; ATVN: 468-4500.

CAMPING FACILITIES:	NO UNITS	HOOKUPS	FEE
Camper Spaces	16	W/E	$5.00 daily
Tent Spaces	12	None	4.00 daily

SUPPORT FACILITIES:			
	Bicycle Path	Chapel	Gas
	Golf	Picnic Areas	Playground
	Rec Equip Rntl	Restrooms	Showers

Robins Fam-Camp, Cont'd

ACTIVITIES: Bicycling   Fishing   Hiking

RESTRICTIONS: None.

Uchee Creek Recreational Area (GA2OR1)

Fort Benning, GA 31905-5000

Comm: 404-544-2011
ATVN: 784-2011

LOCATION: On post. Located on S side of Columbus. Accessible from US-80, I-185, US-27 and US-280. Clearly marked. RM: p-22, L/3. NMC: Columbus, 18 mi NW.

DESCRIPTION OF AREA: The geography and climate are ideal for most outdoor activities. National Infantry Museum on post. Full range of mil fac on post.

SEASON OF OPERATION: Year round.

ELIGIBILITY: Active/Retired/DOD Civilians.

RESERVATIONS: Accepted. Address: Community Recreation Division, P O Box 53323, Ft Benning, GA 31905-5226, ATTN: Uchee Creek Rec Area. Comm: 404-545-4155/7680; ATVN: 835-4155/7680.

CAMPING FACILITIES:	NO UNITS	HOOKUPS	FEE
Camper & Tent Spaces	34	W/E	$5.00 daily

SUPPORT FACILITIES:			
	Boat Launch	Boat Rental	Chapel
	Fishing Pier	Gas	Golf
	Ice	Marina	Picnic Area
	Quick Shop	Restrooms	Sewage Dump Sta
	Snack Bar	Sports Fields	Stables
	Vending Machines		

ACTIVITIES: Fishing (lic)   Hunting (lic)   Rec Equip Avail

RESTRICTIONS: Pets allowed.

IDAHO

Mountain Home Fam-Camp (IDO3R4)

Mountain Home Air Force Base, ID 83648-5000

Comm: 208-828-2111
ATVN: 857-1110

LOCATION: On base. From I-84, take ID-67 12 mi SW to base. RM: p-25, N/4. NMC: Boise, 50 mi NW.

DESCRIPTION OF AREA: Located in open country surrounded by mountains, close to Snake River. Sun Valley approx 100 mi NE. Ideal base for many sightseeing and recreational activities in area. Full range of military facilities on base.

SEASON OF OPERATION: Year round; no showers in winter.

ELIGIBILITY: Active/Retired.

RESERVATIONS: No adv resv. Address: 366 CSG/SVH, Mountain Home AFB, ID 83648-5000. Comm: 208-828-6451; ATVN: 857-6451.

Mountain Home Fam-Camp, Cont'd

CAMPING FACILITIES:

	NO UNITS	HOOKUPS	FEE
Camper Spaces	12 Hardstand	W/S/E	$6.00 daily
Tent Area	10	None	3.00 daily

SUPPORT FACILITIES:

Chapel	Golf	Grills
Ice	Picnic Area	Playground
Rec Equip Rntl	Restrooms	Sewage Dump Sta
Showers (sumr)	Skeet/Trap	Stables
	Range (nearby)	

ACTIVITIES:

Fishing	Hunting	Sightseeing
Snow Skiing (nearby)		(ghost towns)

RESTRICTIONS: Pets allowed.

Strike Dam Recreation Area (IDO2R4)
Mountain Home Air Force Base, ID 83648-5000

Comm: 208-828-2111
ATVN: 857-1110

LOCATION: Off base. From I-84 take ID-67 SW to Marina. RM: p-25, O/3. NMI: Mountain Home AFB, 27 mi NE. NMC: Boise, 60 miles N.

DESCRIPTION OF AREA: Situated along Snake River and surrounded by mountains. Full support for water sports and picnic activities. Full range of military facilities available at Mountain Home AFB.

SEASON OF OPERATION: 15 April-Labor Day.

ELIGIBILITY: Active/Retired/DOD Civilians.

RESERVATIONS: One day in adv. Address: 366 CSG/SSRO, ATTN: Strike Dam Recreation Area, Bldg 2800, Mountain Home AFB, ID 83648-5000. Comm: 208-834-2723.

CAMPING FACILITIES: Available at Mountain Home AFB; no camping facilities at rec area.

SUPPORT FACILITIES:

Boat Docks	Boat Launch	Boat Rental
Fishing Tackle	Golf (on base)	Grills
Laundry	Marina	Picnic Area
Playground	Quick Shop	Restrooms
Sewage Dump Sta	Snack Bar	Sports Fields
Water Sports Equipment Rental		

ACTIVITIES:

Boating	Fishing	Jet Skiing
Pontoon Boat/26'	Swimming	Water Skiing

RESTRICTIONS: No pets allowed. Day use only.

Thank you for showing this book to a friend!

ILLINOIS

Chanute Fam-Camp (IL1OR2)
Chanute Air Force Base, IL 61868-5225

Comm: 217-495-1110
ATVN: 862-1110

LOCATION: On base. Take US-45 or I-57 to Rantoul-Chanute AFB exit (US-136). Ask gate guard for map and directions to Fam-Camp. RM: p-26, K/14. NMC: Champaign, 15 mi S.

DESCRIPTION OF AREA: Located approx 125 mi S of Chicago in densely populated Urbana-Champaign area. Fam-Camp is in open terrain. Base has recreation area with a fishing lake. Full range of military facilities available on base.

SEASON OF OPERATION: March-October.

ELIGIBILITY: Active/Retired/DOD Civilians.

RESERVATIONS: Accepted. Address: Tradewinds Recreation Center, 3345 ABG/SSRO, Chanute AFB, IL 61868-5225. Comm: 217-495-3444; ATVN: 862-3444.

CAMPING FACILITIES:	NO UNITS	HOOKUPS	FEE
Camper Spaces	10 Hardstand	W/E (30A)	$5.00 daily
Camper Spaces	20 Grass	E	4.00 daily
Tent Spaces	10	None	2.00 daily

SUPPORT FACILITIES:		
Chapel	Gas	Golf
Laundry	Picnic Area	Quick Stop
Racquet Sports	Restrooms	Sewage Dump Sta
Showers	Sports Fields	Skeet/Trap Ranges
Tennis Courts		

ACTIVITIES:		
Fishing	Recreation Equipment Available	

RESTRICTIONS: Pets allowed on leash.

Scott Fam-Camp (IL09R2)
Scott Air Force Base, IL 62225-5225

Comm: 618-256-1110
ATVN: 576-1110

LOCATION: On base. Take exit 19 S from I-64. At 2d traffic light, turn L to base. Ask gate guard for directions to Gateway Recreation Center (open 1000-2200). RM: p-27, S/8. NMC: St Louis, MO, 20 mi W.

DESCRIPTION OF AREA: Located E of St Louis metropolitan area near O'Fallon. Camp is situated in a wooded area adjacent to base lake and was completely redone in the summer of 1985. Full range of military facilities on base.

SEASON OF OPERATION: Year round.

ELIGIBILITY: Active/Retired/Reserve/DOD Civilians.

RESERVATIONS: Required with 1 night's deposit. Address: Rec Services, 375 ABG/SSRR, Scott AFB, IL 62225-5225. Comm: 618-256-5919; ATVN: 576-5919.

CAMPING FACILITIES:	NO UNITS	HOOKUPS	FEE
Camper Spaces	12 Gravel	W/E (110/220)	$6.00 daily

Scott Fam-Camp, Cont'd

SUPPORT FACILITIES:	Chapel	Gas	Golf
	Grills	Picnic Area	Racquet Sports
	Restrooms	Sewage Dump Sta	Shoppette
	Skeet/Trap Range	Sports Fields	Snack Bar (nearby)
	Stables (boarding by resv)		Tennis Courts

ACTIVITIES:	Fishing (base permit req)	Rec Equip Avail

RESTRICTIONS: Pets allowed on leash.

INDIANA

Delaware Campground (IN04R2)
Fort Benjamin Harrison, IN 46216-5040

Comm: 317-546-9211
ATVN: 699-1110

LOCATION: On post. I-465 E to Ft Harrison exit 40; E on 56th St. OR take IN-67/US-36 (Pendleton Pike) exit 42 to Post Rd; N to Ft Harrison. Check in at Outdoor Rec Office 0900-1800; other hours at Bldg 560, Campground office. RM: p-30, M/11. NMC: Indianapolis, 10 mi SW.

DESCRIPTION OF AREA: Located in Delaware Recreation Area which also contains Delaware Lake and Duck Pond (picnic area). Located on N end of post between Shafter Ave and Lee Rd. Full range of military facilities available on post.

SEASON OF OPERATION: 1 May-30 Nov. No water or sewage when weather turns cold.

ELIGIBILITY: Active/Retired/DOD Civilians.

RESERVATIONS: Accepted. Address: Outdoor Recreation, Bldg 435, Ft Benjamin Harrison, IN 46216-5040. Comm: 317-542-4862.

CAMPING FACILITIES:	NO UNITS	HOOKUPS	FEE
Camper Spaces	20	W/S/E	$6.00 daily
Camper Spaces (700 area)	Overflow	E	4.00 daily
Tent Spaces	5 Primitive	None	3.00 daily

SUPPORT FACILITIES:	Chapel	Gas	Gazebo/fireplace
	Golf	Grills	Paddle Boat Rntl
	Pavilions	Picnic Area	Playground
	Restrooms	Sewage Dump Sta	Showers
	Physical Fitness Facility offers racquet sports.		

ACTIVITIES:	Jogging	Rec Equip Avail	Swimming

RESTRICTIONS: Pets allowed on leash; owner must clean up after pets. Cars, campers and motorcycles must be kept on concrete, blacktop or gravel. Quiet hours after 2300.

IOWA

-None-

KANSAS

Kiernan/Smith Marina, Travel Camp and Beach (KSO5R3)
Fort Riley, KS 66442-6416

Comm: 913-239-3911
ATVN: 856-1110

LOCATION: Off post. From US-77 N of Junction City, take KS-82 W for 1 mi. RM: p-35, E/18. NMI: Fort Riley, 14 mi SE. NMC: Manhattan, 40 mi SE.

DESCRIPTION OF AREA: Located on the N end of Milford Lake NW of installation near Wakefield. Many points of interest, including Eisenhower Museum, historic Ft Riley and old Abilene town. A variety of water-oriented activities is avail. There are also many public camping and rec areas around Milford Lake. Marina and ITT office on post can supply most necessary outdoor equipment. Full range of military facilities available on post.

Moon Lake, a large recreation area on post, has large areas for group outings. It is complete with picnic tables, grills, canoeing, fishing and an enclosed pavilion and storage area. For more information call the Outdoor Recreation Center at 856-239-6189.

SEASON OF OPERATION: Year round. Reduced hours: 1 October-31 March.

ELIGIBILITY: Active/Retired/DOD Civilians.

RESERVATIONS: Accepted up to 30 days in adv, with payment, for pontoon boats and mobile homes. Address: Hq, 1st Inf Division (M) & Ft Riley, Ft Riley, KS 66442-6416, ATTN: AFZN-CA-MS, Marina. Comm: 913-239-6451; ATVN: 856-6451. (Marina) Comm: 913-239-4478/9611; ATVN: 856-4478/9611/9670. (Mobile Homes) Comm: 913-239-4478; ATVN: 856-4478.

CAMP FACILITIES:	NO UNITS	HOOKUPS	FEE
Mobile Homes, 2 bdrm, A/C	5		$25.00 daily
Camper Spaces	10 Hardstand	W/E	6.00 daily
Tent & Camper Spaces	30 Wilderness	None	2.00 daily

SUPPORT FACILITIES:

Boat Ramp	Boat Rental	Boat Slip Rntl
Camp Equip Rntl	Golf (on post)	Grills
Laundry	Marina	Picnic Area
Playground	Restrooms	Showers
Snack Bar	Water Sports Equipment Rental	

ACTIVITIES:

Boating	Fishing/fee(lic)	Hiking
Hunting (lic)	Rec Equip Avail	Windsurfing

Cross Country Skiing avail through Outdoor Rec Section during winter months.

RESTRICTIONS: Pets are allowed in travel camp but not in trailers or on boats. All personnel renting a boat MUST have a Ft Riley Boating License (Fee: $1.00) prior to renting.

Leavenworth RV Park (KSO1R3)
Fort Leavenworth, KS 66027-5000

Comm: 913-684-5337
ATVN: 552-5337

LOCATION: On post. From I-70 take US-73 N to Leavenworth. Ft Leavenworth is adjacent to city of Leavenworth. RM: p-35, D/23. NMC: Kansas City, 30 mi SE.

DESCRIPTION OF AREA: Situated on the west bank of the Missouri River. Full range of military facilities available on post.

Leavenworth RV Park, Cont'd

SEASON OF OPERATION: Year round. 1 May-15 August: Use limited to AD on PCS orders in and out of Ft Leavenworth.

ELIGIBILILTY: Active/Retired.

RESERVATIONS: Accepted only for AD on PCS orders. AD on PCS orders have priority at all times; others Space-A 16 Aug-30 Apr. Address: Billeting Office, Bldg 695-B-2, Hoge Barracks, Ft Leavenworth, KS 66027-5000. Comm: 913-651-9522; ATVN: 552-4091.

CAMPING FACILITIES:	NO UNITS	HOOKUPS	FEE
Camper Spaces	12 Hardstand	W/S/E	$4.00 daily

SUPPORT FACILITIES:	Picnic Area	Playground	Sewage Dump Sta

ACTIVITIES:	Golf	Rec Equip Avail	Tennis

RESTRICTIONS: Pets are not allowed in TML facilities on post.

KENTUCKY

Camp Carlson Army Travel Camp (KYO3R2)
Fort Knox, KY 40121-5000

Comm: 502-624-1181
ATVN: 464-0111

LOCATION: On post. From N, exit from I-64 or I-71 in Louisville to I-264 (Watterson Expressway); exit to US-31W; S to Ft Knox. From S, exit from I-65 at Elizabethtown/Ft Knox to US-31W N to Ft Knox. Campground is 2.5 mi W on US-60. RM: p-36, J/10. NMC: Louisville, 30 mi N.

DESCRIPTION OF AREA: Full range of outdoor activities avail. Patton Museum on post. Abraham Lincoln birthplace among nearby national historical sites. Full range of military facilities available 5 miles from camp.

SEASON OF OPERATION: Year round.

ELIGIBILITY: Active/Retired/DOD Civilians.

RESERVATIONS: Required for cottages and cabins. Address: Community Recreation Division, 1468A Third Street, Camp Carlson, Ft Knox, KY 40121-5000. Comm: 502-624-4836; ATVN: 464-4836.

CAMP FACILITIES:	NO UNITS	HOOKUPS	FEE
Family Cottages	4		$18.00 daily
Youth Cabins, 18 bunks ea	4		3.00 per bunk dly
Mobile Homes, 32'	2		18.00 daily
Camper Spaces	25 Hardstand	W/E	7.00 daily
Camper Spaces	10	None	5.50 daily
Tent Spaces	25 Improved	None	5.50 daily

SUPPORT FACILITIES:			
	Archery	Bait	Boat Rental
	Camper Rental	Chapel	Gas
	Golf	Grills	Gun Ranges
	Ice	Laundry	Marina
	Picnic Area	Playground	Restrooms
	Sewage Dump Sta	Showers	Sports Fields
	Tennis Courts	Trails	TV/Game Room
	Vending Machines		

Camp Carlson Army Travel Camp, Cont'd

ACTIVITIES: Fishing (lic)   Hunting (lic)   Rec Equip Avail

RESTRICTIONS: Pets allowed on leash.

Eagles' Rest Travel Camp (KYO4R2)
Fort Campbell, KY 42223-5000

Comm: 502-798-2151
ATVN: 635-2151

LOCATION: On post. From I-24 S of Hopkinsville take Fort Campbell exit; S on ALT US-41 to Gate 1; Lee Rd to stop light; L on Woodlawn Dr; R on Lafayette Rd to camp. RM: p-36, P/3. NMC: Clarksville TN, 5 mi SE.

DESCRIPTION OF AREA: Beautiful scenic area offering great fishing, other water sports and many other activities. Full range of military facilities on post.

SEASON OF OPERATION: Year round.

ELIGIBILITY: Active/Retired/DOD Civilians.

RESERVATIONS: Accepted. Address: Community Recreation Div, Outdoor Rec Br, Ft Campbell, KY 42223-5000, ATTN: AFZB-PA-CR-O. Comm: 502-798-3126; ATVN: 635-3126

CAMPING FACILITIES:	NO UNITS	HOOKUPS	FEE
Camper Spaces	25	W/E	$5.00 daily

SUPPORT FACILITIES:			
	Boat Rental	Chapel	Food Vending
	Gas	Golf	Laundry
	Picnic Area	Playground	Restrooms
	Showers	Snack Bar	Sewage Dump Sta

ACTIVITIES:			
	Bicycling	Boating	Fishing
	Hiking	Hunting	Rec Equip Avail

RESTRICTIONS: Pets allowed on leash.

Fletchers Fork Travel Camp (KYO5R2)
Fort Campbell, KY 42223-5000

Comm: 502-798-2151
ATVN: 635-2151

LOCATION: On post. Off ALT US-41 near intersection with I-24; clearly marked. RM: p-36, P/3-4. NMC: Clarksville TN, 12 mi S.

DESCRIPTION OF AREA: Located adjacent to Land between the Lakes area, between Clarksville TN and Hopkinsville KY. Tennessee Valley Authority manages an extensive reservoir complex on Tennessee River along KY-TN line. Unlimited water recreation opportunities. Equipment rental center can supply outdoor recreation equipment for a wide variety of activities. Full range of military facilities available on post.

SEASON OF OPERATION: Year round.

ELIGIBILITY: Active/Retired/DOD Civilians.

RESERVATIONS: Accepted with $5 deposit. Address: Community Recreation Division, Outdoor Rec Br, Ft Campbell, KY 42223-5000, ATTN: AFZB-PA-CR-O, Army Travel Camp. Comm: 502-798-3126/5590; ATVN: 635-3126/5590.

CAMPING FACILITIES:	NO UNITS	HOOKUPS	FEE
Camper Spaces	40 Gravel	W/E (110)	$5.00 daily

Fletchers Fork Travel Camp, Cont'd

SUPPORT FACILITIES:	Boat Launch	Boat Rental	Fishing Pier
	Golf	Grills	Laundry
	Nature Center	Picnic Area	Playground
	Rec Room/Video	Restaurant	Restrooms
	Sewage Dump Sta	Showers	Sports Fields
	Stables	Tennis Courts	Vending Machines

ACTIVITIES:	Boating	Fishing (lic)	Hunting (lic)
	Jogging	Rec Equip Avail	

RESTRICTIONS: Pets allowed on leash.

LOUISIANA

Barksdale Fam-Camp (LA09R2)
Barksdale Air Force Base, LA 71110-5000

Comm: 318-456-2252
ATVN: 781-1110

LOCATION: On base. From I-20 E of Bossier City, take Barksdale exit. From US-71 enter base S of Bossier City. RM: p-38, A/13. NMC: Shreveport, 3 mi SW.

DESCRIPTION OF AREA: Camp is situated in alternatingly open and wooded areas shaded by many oaks and hickories. Toledo Bend, Caddo, Cross and Bistineau Reservoir lakes conveniently located for variety of water-oriented recreation. Full range of military facilities available on base.

SEASON OF OPERATION: Year round.

ELIGIBILITY: Active/Retired/DOD Civilians.

RESERVATIONS: No adv resv. Address: Billeting Office, PO Box 28, Barksdale AFB, LA 71110-5000. Comm: 318-456-3091; ATVN: 781-3091.

CAMPING FACILITIES:	NO UNITS	HOOKUPS	FEE
Camper Spaces	12 Hardstand	W/S/E	$4.00 daily
Tent Spaces	Many	None	2.50 daily

SUPPORT FACILITIES:	Boat Launch	Boat Rental	Chapel
	Gas	Golf	Grocery Store
	Laundry	Picnic Area	Playground
	Rec Equip Rntl	Restrooms	Showers

ACTIVITIES:	Boating	Fishing (lic)	Hiking
	Hunting (lic)		

RESTRICTIONS: Pets allowed on leash. No swimming.

Cotile Recreation Area (LA02R2)
England Air Force Base, LA 71311-5000

Comm: 318-448-2100
ATVN: 683-2100

LOCATION: Off base. W of Alexandria in Boyce. From England AFB, take LA-496 (Hot Wells Rd) to LA-1200. Rec area is off LA-1200. Check in on base at Rec Center, Bldg 1211. (England AFB can be reached via LA-1 or LA-28 from Alexandria.) RM: p-38, 5/F. NMI: England AFB, 11 mi E. NMC: Alexandria, 15 mi E.

LOUISIANA
Cotile Rec Area, Cont'd

DESCRIPTION OF AREA: Rec area is in 20 acres of pine woods by Cotile Lake in S central section of state. Screened pavilion furnished with tables and chairs overlooks lake. Each trailer has picnic table and grill. Full range of military facilities available at England AFB.

SEASON OF OPERATION: Year round.

ELIGIBILITY: Active/Retired/Reserve/NG/DOD Civilians at England AFB.

RESERVATIONS: Accepted for mobile homes. Address: Recreation Center, 23 CSG/ SSRR, England AFB, LA 71311-5000. (Resv) Comm: 318-793-8871; (Info) Comm: 318- 448-2503.

CAMP FACILITIES:	NO UNITS	HOOKUPS	FEE
Mobile Homes, 2 bdrm	8		$15.00 daily
Camper Spaces	6		4.00 daily
Tent Spaces	Open		None

SUPPORT FACILITIES:			
	Boat Launch	Boat Rental	Camp Equip Rntl
	Grills	Ice	Kitchen Equip Rntl
	Laundry	Marina	Picnic Area
	Quick Shop(near)	Playground	Restrooms
	Snack Bar		

ACTIVITIES:	Fishing (lic)		Rec Equip Avail

RESTRICTIONS: Pets allowed on leash.

New Orleans NAS Campground (LAO8R2)
New Orleans Naval Air Station, LA 70143-4000

Comm: 504-393-3011
ATVN: 363-3011

LOCATION: On base. From BUS US-90 S of New Orleans, take LA-23 S to Belle Chasse. RM: p-38, J/11. NMC: New Orleans, 10 mi N.

DESCRIPTION OF AREA: Campground is located just minutes from the famous French Quarter and downtown New Orleans. Wide range of military facilities on base.

SEASON OF OPERATION: Year round.

ELIGIBILITY: Active/Retired/DOD Civilians.

RESERVATIONS: Required with deposit. Address: Recreation Services, Bldg 308, NAS, New Orleans, LA 70143-4000. Comm: 504-393-3448; ATVN: 363-3448.

CAMPING FACILITIES:	NO UNITS	HOOKUPS	FEE
Camper Spaces	17 Hardstand	W/E	$ 5.00 dly/50 wkly
Camping Trailers	4		15.00 dly/50 wkly

SUPPORT FACILITIES:			
	Chapel	Gas	Golf
	Grills	Laundry (nearby)	NEX Branch
	Picnic Area	Restrooms	Sewage Dump Sta
	Showers	Skeet Range	Sports Fields
	Swimming Pool	Tennis Courts	

ACTIVITIES:	Hunting	Jogging	Swimming
	Rec Equip Avail		

RESTRICTIONS: Pets allowed.

New Orleans NSA RV Park (LA03R2)
New Orleans Naval Support Activity, LA 70142-5000

Comm: 504-361-2011
ATVN: 485-2011

LOCATION: On base. On W bank of Mississippi; from I-10 take Canal Street-Mississippi River Bridge exit; R on Clairborne Ave; R at Gretna exit. Take Gen DeGaulle E exit after passing over bridge and turn left at Shirley Drive, which leads to NSA. Report to Officers' Housing by RV Park. RM: p-38, J/11. NMC: New Orleans, adjacent to base.

DESCRIPTION OF AREA: Attractions along the Mississippi River include boat cruises, zoo cruise, bus tours, plantations, museums and historic homes. The famous New Orleans French Quarter and Bourbon Street are nearby. Full range of military facilities available on base, many within walking distance.

SEASON OF OPERATION: Year round.

ELIGIBILITY: Active/Retired/DOD Civilians.

RESERVATIONS: No adv resv. Address: Naval Support Activity, Bldg 128, New Orleans, LA 70142-5000. Comm: 504-361-2269; ATVN: 485-2269, FTS: 686-2269.

CAMPING FACILITIES:	NO UNITS	HOOKUPS	FEE
Camper Spaces	16 Hardstand	W/E (some 220)	$5.00 daily

SUPPORT FACILITIES:			
	Boat Rental	Camp Equip Rntl	Chapel
	Gas	Mini Mart	Picnic Area
	Playground	Racquetball	Rec Equip Avail
	Sewage Dump Sta	Sports Fields	Tennis Courts

ACTIVITIES:	Fishing	Sightseeing	Tours

RESTRICTIONS: Pets allowed. 30-day limit.

NOTE: Discount tickets, tour info and a free gift available at ITT Office, Bldg 706. Hours: Tu-F 1000-1700, Sa 0900-1400, closed Su-M. Snack Bar at Bowling Center, Bldg 722, open 7 days a week.

Toledo Bend Recreation Site (LA04R2)
Fort Polk, LA 71459-5000

Comm: 318-535-2911
ATVN: 863-1110
FTS: 528-1110

LOCATION. Off post. Take US-171 N from Leesville; W on LA-111 at Anacoco; bear R onto LA-392. Turn N on LA-191; L at Army Travel Camp sign. RM: p-38, G/4. NMI: Fort Polk, 45 mi SE. NMC: Alexandria, 60 mi NE.

DESCRIPTION OF AREA: Toledo Bend is the largest man-made lake in the South and 5th largest in the country. Excellent fishing and swimming area. Campsite is located on 26 acres of wooded land. Major renovation is in progress to make this the most modern recreation area in the US Army. Hodges Gardens and Fort Jesup offer sightseeing opportunities. Full range of military fac on post.

Fort Polk also operates the **Alligator Lake Recreation Site** on LA-469 just north of North Fort. It covers approx 20 acres along a man-made lake. Ample space for picnicking and all sorts of sports. The lake itself offers paddle boating and some good fishing. Community Recreation Division operates a check-out center where boats, campers, camping equipment, fishing equipment rnt1, scuba gear and water skis can be rented. Equipment can be reserved in advance by calling Comm: 318-535-5332/5350.

LOUISIANA
Toledo Bend Rec Site, Cont'd
SEASON OF OPERATION: Year round.

ELIGIBILITY: Active/Retired/DOD Civilians at Fort Polk.

RESERVATIONS: Accepted up to 30 days in adv. Address: Toledo Bend Recreation Site, HCR 65 Box 75, Florien, LA 71429. Comm: 318-565-4235; ATVN: 863-2842.

CAMP FACILITIES:	NO UNITS	HOOKUPS	FEE
Mobile Homes, 2 bdrm*	12	W/S/E	$15.00 daily
Camper Spaces, 33 ft	15 Hardstand	W/E (110)	4.00 daily
Tent Spaces	8 Wilderness	None	2.00 daily

*Furnished; linens can be rented.

SUPPORT FACILITIES:			
	Beach	Boat Launch	Boat Rental
	Cabanas	Fishing Eq Rntl	Fishing Pier
	Grills	Jet Skis	Marina
	Party Barges	Pavilions	Picnic Areas
	Playground	Rec Equip Rntl	Restrooms
	Sewage Dump Sta	Showers	Vending Machines

ACTIVITIES:			
	Boating (lic)	Fishing	Horseshoes
	Hunting (lic)	Swimming	Volleyball

RESTRICTIONS: Pets allowed on leash.

MAINE

Dow Pines Recreation Area (MEO3R1)
Loring Air Force Base, ME 04751-5000

Comm: 207-999-1110
ATVN: 920-1110

LOCATION: Off base. From I-95 exit E to Bangor/Brewer and cross the bridge spanning the Penobscot River. After crossing bridge, turn L on ME-9 and travel approx 30 mi to Aurora. Watch for the Dow Pines Rec Area sign (approx .25 mi past "Mace's" Store); L for 7 mi to rec area. RM: p-39, E/9. NMI: Winter Harbor Naval Security Group Activity, 45 mi SE. NMC: Bangor, 38 mi W.

DESCRIPTION OF AREA: Dow Pines is located on 375-acre reservation which boasts excellent fishing, hiking and scenic vistas second to none. Included in this area are Great Pond and King Pond. Wide range of mil fac at Winter Harbor.

SEASON OF OPERATION: Year round.

ELIGIBILITY: Active/Retired/Reserve/DOD and NAF Civilians at Loring AFB.

RESERVATIONS: Required for cabins; accepted for other facilities. Deposit of 1 day's rent required. Address: Recreation Services, 42 CSG/SSRR, Loring AFB, ME 04751-5000. Comm: 207-999-2382/2646; ATVN: 920-2382.

CAMP FACILITIES:	NO UNITS	HOOKUPS	FEE
Lodges	2	Kitchen/Bath	$32.00 & up daily
Cabins	5	Kitchen/Bath	27.00 & up daily
Dorm (no heat) small grps	1	Showers	2 per person dly
Camper Spaces	18	W/E	5 dly+.50 ea pers
Tent Spaces	5	None	2 dly+.50 ea pers

Dow Pines Rec Area, Cont'd

SUPPORT FACILITIES:	Beach	Boat Launch	Boat Rental
	Conv S(seasonal)	Grills	Grocery (nearby)
	Ice	Laundry	Marina
	Picnic Area	Rec Center	Restrooms
	Sewage Dump Sta	Showers	Snack Bar
	TV/Game Room	Winter Sports	Equipment Rental

ACTIVITIES:	Fishing (lic)	Hiking	Ice Fishing
	Rec Equip Avail	Skiing	Swimming

RESTRICTIONS: Pets allowed on leash. No hunting and no firearms allowed. All open fires must be authorized by the manager. All persons using boats and motors must be briefed on safety.

Malabeam Lake and Fam-Camp Area (MEO5R1)

Loring Air Force Base, ME 04571-5000

Comm: 207-999-1110
ATVN: 920-1110

LOCATION: On base. Take I-95 to Houlton, exit to US-1; N to Caribou. AFB is 1 mi N of ME-89 and ME-223 intersection. Clearly marked. Enter West Gate from Sawyer Rd. During duty hrs check in at MWR Equipment Checkout, Bldg 7610; after hrs, at Billeting, Bldg 250. RM: p-39, B/17. NMC: Caribou, 3 mi SW.

DESCRIPTION OF AREA: The camping area is located approx 10 miles from Canadian border. **In addition to the spaces listed below, there are a limited number of unimproved spaces at Green Pond and Chapman Pit.** All three areas offer trout fishing and have moose running wild. Full range of military facilities on base.

SEASON OF OPERATION: 1 May-1 November.

ELIGIBILITY: Active/Retired/DOD and NAF Civilians.

RESERVATIONS: Accepted. Address: Recreation Services, 42 CSG/SSRO, Loring AFB, ME 04751-5000. Comm: 207-999-2432/2501; ATVN: 920-2432/2501; after duty hours (Billeting Office) Comm: 207-999-2227.

CAMPING FACILITIES:	NO UNITS	HOOKUPS	FEE
Camper Spaces	9 Hardstand		$10.00 daily
Camper Spaces	10	None	4.00 daily
Tent Spaces	8 Improved & Wilderness		4.00 daily

SUPPORT FACILITIES:	Archery	Chapel	Golf
	Gas	Laundry	Picnic Area
	Racquet Sports	Rec Center	Restrooms
	Sewage Dump Sta	Showers	Snack Bar
	Sports Fields	Trails	

ACTIVITIES:	Fishing (lic)	Hunting (lic)	Rec Equip Avail

RESTRICTIONS: Pets allowed on leash.

Rocky Lake (MEO1R1)

Cutler Naval Communications Unit
East Machias, ME 04630-5000

Comm: 207-259-8218
ATVN: 476-7218

LOCATION: Off base. From US-1 in East Machias, take ME-191 SE approx 7 mi to installation. Obtain directions, map and equipment from Rec Services. RM: p-39, F/12. NMI: NAVCOMMU Cutler, 30 mi S. NMC: Bangor, 100 mi NW.

DESCRIPTION OF AREA: Wooded inland area in eastern corner of Maine about 10 mi off Atlantic Coast. Very rustic. Wide range of military fac at NCU Cutler.

SEASON OF OPERATION: Year round, road conditions permitting.

ELIGIBILITY: Active/Retired.

RESERVATIONS: Required: up to 3 wks in adv for AD; up to 2 wks for Retired. Address: Recreational Services, Naval Communications Unit Cutler, East Machias, ME 04630-5000. Comm: 207-259-8218, ATVN: 476-7218.

CAMPING FACILITIES: Rustic 3-room cabin. Gas lights, stove and refrigerator; wood heat. **No running water, indoor sanitary facilities or electricity.**
<u>FEE:</u> $12.50 daily - 15 May-15 Sep
9.50 daily - 16 Sep-14 May

ACTIVITIES:	Fishing	Hunting (lic)	Ice Skating
	Jogging	Skiing (XC)	

RESTRICTIONS: Pets allowed. Fire permits required.

Sprague's Neck (ME02R1)

Cutler Naval Communications Unit
East Machias, ME 04630-5000

Comm: 207-259-8218
ATVN: 476-7218

LOCATION: On base. From US-1 in East Machias, take ME-191 S approx 7 mi to installation. Obtain directions, map and equipment from Rec Services. RM: p-39, F/12. NMC: Bangor, 100 mi W.

DESCRIPTION OF AREA: Located in a wooded section in eastern corner of Maine, overlooking rugged Atlantic Coast in Machias Bay area. Very rustic. Wide range of military facilities available at Naval Cummunications Unit Cutler.

SEASON OF OPERATION: Year round, road conditions permitting.

ELIGIBILITY: Active/Retired.

RESERVATIONS: Required. Address: Recreation Services, Naval Communications Unit Cutler, East Machias, ME 04630-5000. Comm: 207-259-8218/8284; ATVN: 476-7218/7284.

CAMPING FACILITIES:	<u>NO UNITS</u>	<u>HOOKUPS</u>	<u>FEE</u>
Camper Spaces	4	None	$ 1.00 daily
Rustic, 4-rm log cabin. Lights, stove,		15 May-15 Sep	12.50 daily
refrigerator; wood heat. **Running water**		16 Sep-14 May	9.50 daily
& indoor sanitary fac 15 May-15 Sep.			

SUPPORT FACILITIES:	Firearms Ranges	Gas	Grills
	Gym	Laundry	Picnic Area
	Racquetball	Rec Equip Rntl	Sports Fields
	Tennis Courts	Trails	

ACTIVITIES:	Fishing	Hiking	Hunting (lic)
	Ice Skating	Jogging	Skiing (XC)

RESTRICTIONS: Pets allowed. Fire permits required.

Winter Harbor Recreation Area (MEO4R1)
Winter Harbor NSGA, ME 04693-5000

Comm: 207-963-5534
ATVN: 476-9011

LOCATION: On base. From I-95 at Bangor, take ALT US-1 S to Ellsworth; take US-1 N (traveling E) approx 20 mi to ME-186; S to Winter Harbor. Installation is 6 mi from Winter Harbor. Stop at Quarter Deck for directions. RM: p-39, G/9. NMC: Bangor, 45 mi NW.

DESCRIPTION OF AREA: Rec area is located on Schoodic Point and is part of Acadia Natl Park on Maine's rugged Atlantic Coast. Many nature trails, ponds and lakes within easy driving distance. Wide range of military fac on base.

SEASON OF OPERATION: Campsites: May-September; Mobile Homes: Year round.

ELIGIBILITY: Active/Retired/DOD Civilians.

RESERVATIONS: Reservations accepted up to 30 days in advance. Address: Recreation Services, Naval Security Group Activity, Winter Harbor, ME 04693-5000. Comm: 207-963-5537; ATVN: 476-9287/9288.

CAMP FACILITIES:	NO UNITS	HOOKUPS	FEE
Mobile Homes, furnished	5		$22.00 daily
Camper Spaces	6	W/E	8.00 daily
Camper & Tent Spaces	4	None	5.00 daily

SUPPORT FACILITIES:			
	Camp Equip Rntl	Chapel	Gas
	Golf (local)	Grills	Gym
	Marina	Picnic Area	Playground
	Racquetball	Restrooms	Showers
	Tennis Courts	Trailer Rental	Vending Machines
	Water & Winter Sports Equipment Rental		

ACTIVITIES:			
	Boating	Fishing	Hiking
	Hunting (lic)	Snow Skiing	Water Skiing

RESTRICTIONS: No pets allowed.

MARYLAND

Andrews Fam-Camp (MD15R1)
Andrews Air Force Base, MD 20331-5000

Comm: 301-981-1110
ATVN: 858-1110

LOCATION: On base. E of Washington, DC. From I-95 (east portion of Capital Beltway I-495), exit 7, S to Allentown Road. Proceed to base. Report to Rec Center, Bldg 1442. RM: p-41, I/16. NMC: Washington DC, 12 mi NW.

DESCRIPTION OF AREA: Aerial gateway to Washington DC, home of "Air Force One," the President's aircraft. There is much to do in the way of entertainment, i.e., monuments, parks, museums, restaurants, theaters, zoo, etc. Full range of military facilities available on base.

SEASON OF OPERATION: Year round.

ELIGIBILITY: Active/Retired/DOD Civilians at Andrews AFB.

RESERVATIONS: Required. Address: Recreation Center, 1776 ABW/SSRR, Andrews AFB, MD 20331-5000. Comm: 301-981-6560.

MARYLAND
Andrews Fam-Camp, Cont'd

CAMPING FACILITIES:	NO UNITS	HOOKUPS	FEE
Camper Spaces	12	W/S/E	$8.00 daily
Tent Spaces	50	None	2.00 daily

SUPPORT FACILITIES:			
	Chapel	Gas	Golf
	Grills	Picnic Area	Playground
	Racquetball	Rec Center	Restrooms
	Sewage Dump Sta	Showers	Skeet Range
	Snack Bar	Sports Fields	

ACTIVITIES: Fishing (base permit req)   Rec Equip Avail

RESTRICTIONS: Pets are allowed; owner is responsible for animal.

Annapolis Fam-Camp (MD16R1)
United States Naval Academy/Annapolis Naval Station
Annapolis, MD 21402-5058

Comm: 301-267-6100
ATVN: 281-0111
FTS: 930-0111

LOCATION: On base. 35 mi NE of Washington DC. S of US-50/301; off MD-648.
RM: p-41, G/18. NMC: Annapolis in city limits near city dock.

DESCRIPTION OF AREA: Scenic and historic Annapolis offers a walking tour of the
Naval Academy Museum, city dock area, and much more. Full range of military
facilities available at US Naval Academy and Naval Station.

SEASON OF OPERATION: 1 March-1 December.

ELIGIBILITY: Active/Retired.

RESERVATIONS: No adv resv. Address: Recreational Services, Bldg 89, Naval
Station, Annapolis, MD 21402-5054. Comm: 301-267-3580; ATVN: 281-2518.

CAMPING FACILITIES:	NO UNITS	HOOKUPS	FEE
Camper Spaces	10 Hardstand	W/E	$7.00 daily
Group Camping	1 Primitive		.70 per camper

SUPPORT FACILITIES:			
	Beach	Bicycle Rental	Boat Rental
	Camp Equip Rntl	Chapel	Gas
	Golf (Academy)	Grills	Marina
	Mini Mart	Picnic Area	Playground
	Racquetball	Rec Center	Restrooms
	Sewage Dump Sta	Showers	Sports Fields
	Swimming Pools	Tennis Courts	

ACTIVITIES: Crabbing   Fishing   Rec Equip Avail

RESTRICTIONS: Pets allowed on leash. No swimming.

Goose Creek/West Basin Recreation Area (MDO3R1)
Patuxent River Naval Air Station, MD 20670-5409

Comm: 301-863-3000
ATVN: 356-3000

LOCATION: On base. From US-301, MD-5 or MD-4 SE to MD-235. Follow MD-235 to
Lexington Park and Naval Air Station. RM: p-41, L/18. NMC: Washington DC,
65 mi NW.

Goose Creek/West Basin Rec Area, Cont'd

DESCRIPTION OF AREA: There are two campgrounds, at Goose Creek and West Basin, available to military personnel. The Naval Air Station offers a wide range of recreational facilities and a full range of support facilities.

SEASON OF OPERATION: Camping area closes in winter.

ELIGIBILITY: Active/Retired/Reserve.

RESERVATIONS: Required. Address: Recreational Services, Naval Air Station, Bldg 458, Patuxent River, MD 20670-5423. Comm: 301-863-3508; ATVN: 356-3508. Ask for a recreation guidebook.

CAMPING FACILITIES:	NO UNITS	HOOKUPS	FEE
Camper Spaces	14 Hardstand	W/E	$ 6.00 daily
Camper & Tent Spaces	50	None	4.00 daily

Rental trailers, furn, slp 4, NO bathrooms
17' trailers	18.00 daily
15' trailers	12.50 daily

SUPPORT FACILITIES:			
	Archery	Beach	Boat Launch
	Boat Rental	Camp Equip Rntl	Gas
	Golf	Laundry	Marina
	Picnic Area	Playground	Racquetball
	Rec Center	Sewage Dump Sta	Skeet/Trap Range
	Sports Eq Rntl	Sports Fields	Stables
	Tennis Courts	Trails	

ACTIVITIES:			
	Crabbing	Fishing (lic)	Hunting
	Jogging	Swimming	Water Skiing

RESTRICTIONS: No pets allowed.

Ritchie Outdoor Recreation Center
(MD17R1)
Fort Ritchie, MD 21719-5010

Comm: 301-241-1300
ATVN: 277-1300
DC Area Line: 878-1300

LOCATION: On post. Traveling N from Washington DC, take I-270 W to US-15; N to Thurmont; then MD-550 W to post. RM: p-40, B/12. NMC: Hagerstown, 16 mi SW.

DESCRIPTION OF AREA: Historic Civil War sites surround the area. Close to Appalachian Trail. Several snow ski areas within short drives. Lake on post offers fishing, swimming and boating. This is a recreation center; no camping facilities are available. Full range of military facilities on post.

SEASON OF OPERATION: Year round.

ELIGIBILITY: Active/Retired/DOD and NAF Civilians at Ft Ritchie.

RESERVATIONS: Address: Outdoor Recreation Center, Bldg 834, ATTN: ASNJ-P-CF-R, Fort Ritchie, MD 21719-5010. Comm: 301-878-4186; ATVN: 277-4186.

SUPPORT FACILITIES:			
	Bowling	Camp Equip Rntl	Fishing Tackle
	Gas	Golf	Pavilions
	Picnic Area	Playground	Pool/Beach
	Rec Equip Rntl	Skeet Range	Sports Fields
	Tennis Courts	Watercraft Rntl	

ACTIVITIES:

Boating	Fishing	Horseshoes
Ice Skating	Snow Skiing	Swimming

RESTRICTIONS: No pets in picnic or swimming areas.

Solomons Navy Recreation Center (MDO5R1)

Solomons, MD 20688-0147

Comm: 301-863-9074
301-326-4216
ATVN: 356-3566
DC Area Line: 261-2816

LOCATION: On base. On the Patuxent River. From US-301 take MD-4 SE to Solomons; OR take MD-5 SE to MD-235, then MD-4 NE to Solomons. RM: p-41, L/18. NMI: Patuxent River NAS, 10 mi S. NMC: Washington DC, 65 mi NW.

DESCRIPTION OF AREA: Located in southern Maryland on the delta where Patuxent River meets Chesapeake Bay. Rustic and relaxing area that has retained its natural beauty. Campground and facilities encompass approx 260 acres with extensive frontage on river. Only Navy facility dedicated solely to recreation. Historic waterfront community. Local points of interest include Calvert Marine Museum, Cliffs of Calvert, Oyster Fleet, St Marys City, Battle Creek Cypress Swamp, Naval Air Test & Evaluation Museum, area festivals, Point Lookout State Park and many other historical sites. Full range of mil fac at Patuxent NAS.

SEASON OF OPERATION: Year round.

ELIGIBILITY: Active/Retired/Reserve.

RESERVATIONS: Required. Address: Navy Recreation Center, PO Box 147, Solomons, MD 20688-0147. Comm: 301-326-4216, 301-863-9074; DC Metro Area: 261-2816.

CAMP FACILITIES:	NO UNITS	HOOKUPS	FEE
Camper Spaces	96	W/S/E	$8.00 daily
Camper Spaces	151	W*/E	7.00 daily
Camper Spaces	5	E	6.00 daily
Tent Spaces	7 Group Sites	None	1.00 ea pers dly/ 10.00 minimum
Tent/Camper Spaces	50	None	4.00 daily

*No water in winter

Apartments, Bungalows & Cottages, 1-5 bdrm (max 3 persons per bdrm), A/C, bath, kitchenette, utensils. Linens can be rented from the resv office. No soap, TV or telephones. FEE:

	E1-E5	E6-E9	Officers
1 Bedroom	$ 8.00	$12.00	$17.00
2 Bedroom	10.00	14.00	19.00
3 Bedroom	12.00	16.00	21.00
4 Bedroom	14.00	18.00	23.00
5 Bedroom	16.00	20.00	25.00

All lodging units and campsites have grill and picnic table.

SUPPORT FACILITIES:

Beach	Boat Launch	Boat Rental
Boat Slip Rental	Camper Rental	Camping & Sports
Conv Store	Fun/Fitness Ctr	Equip Rental
Fish/Crab Pier	Gas	Golf Driv Range
Grills	Ice	Marina
Miniature Golf	Party Pavilion	Picnic Area

Solomons Navy Rec Ctr, Cont'd

Playground	Rec Center	Restrooms
Sewage Dump Sta	Showers	Special Event Prog
Swimming Pools	Tennis Courts	Video Arcade

ACTIVITIES:

Basketball	Bicycling	Boating
Duck Hunting	Fishing (lic)	Horseshoes
Swimming	Volleyball	Windsurfing

RESTRICTIONS: Pets are not allowed in lodging units; must have proof of shots and be registered at Reservation and Information Center; must be on leash and under positive control. Open fires prohibited except in group site areas where fire rings are provided.

MASSACHUSETTS

Cape Cod Vacation Apartments (MA1OR1)
Coast Guard Air Station
Otis Air National Guard Base, MA 02542-5000

Comm: 617-968-5300*
ATVN: 557-5300
FTS: 829-5300

LOCATION: On base.Take Mass Military Reservation exit off MA-28; S on Connley Avenue approx 2 mi to Bourne gate. RM: p-45, M/22. NMC: Boston, 50 mi NW.

DESCRIPTION OF AREA: Situated on Cape Cod, a famous New England vacation area. Limited military facilities available on base; wide range available at South Weymouth Naval Air Station, 40 mi NW.

SEASON OF OPERATION: Year round.

ELIGIBILITY: Active/Retired/Reserve.

RESERVATIONS: Req, by application obtained by telephone only: up to 90 days in adv for AD on PCS; up to 60 days in adv for AD on TDY or TAD; up to 30 days in adv for all others. Resv for categories other than PCS may be cancelled up to 2 wks in adv if lodging is req for AD on PCS. Advance payment and cleaning/damage deposit req. Address: Temporary Quarters, Bldg 5204, Otis ANGB, MA 02542-5024. Comm: 617-968-5461*; FTS: 829-5461.

LODGING:	NO UNITS	FEE **
Single Rooms, furn	3	$ 7.00-27.00 daily
Efficiency Units, furn	22	9.00-32.00 daily
Townhouse Apartments, 2 bdrm, slp 6	4	11.00-37.00 daily
2 dbl beds & bunk bed; furn		

**Rates vary, depending on rank and duty status.

SUPPORT FACILITIES:

Boat Rental	Fishing Tackle	Golf
Laundry	Picnic Area	Playground

ACTIVITIES:

Boating	Fishing	Rec Equip Avail
Swimming		

RESTRICTIONS: No pets allowed. 2-week limit.

*Effective 16 Jul 88, the area code will be changed to 508.

Cuttyhunk Island Recreation Facility (MAO4R1)

Coast Guard Air Station •
Otis Air National Guard Base, MA 02542-5000

Comm: 617-968-5300*
ATVN: 557-5300
FTS: 829-5300

LOCATION: Off base. A former CG lifeboat station on Cuttyhunk Island. From I-195 or MA-6 at New Bedford, S to State Pier (near Elm St). Transportation to the island is via Cuttyhunk Boat Lines M/V ALERT. RM: p-45, O/19. NMI: Otis AFB, 35 mi E. NMC: New Bedford, 17 mi N.

DESCRIPTION OF AREA: The dwelling site is located about 17 mi S off the coast of New Bedford and just W of Martha's Vineyard. It is approximately 300 yards from the ferry landing and is within easy walking distance of the local community. As the community is very small and depends on ferry service for delivery of supplies, prices will be understandably higher than on the mainland. A small grocery store is available on the island, but visitors are advised to bring adequate food supplies to meet most of their needs during their stay.

SEASON OF OPERATION: Year round.

ELIGIBILITY: Active CG/Retired CG.

RESERVATIONS: Req, by application only, with adv payment. Resv for summer season (Jun-Sep) must be made prior to 1 May; all other seasons as early as possible. The Coast Guard advises us that the facility is being considered for closing by GSA and there are always more requests (in the First Coast Guard District alone) than can be approved. Address: Temporary Quarters, Bldg 5204, Otis ANGB, MA 02542-5024. Comm: 617-968-5461*; FTS: 829-5461.

LODGING:

	FEE: **
One 3-bdrm apartment, furn; kit, bath; no TV	$180-280 weekly
One 2-bdrm apartment, furn; kit, bath; no TV	200-300 weekly

**Rates vary, depending on rank.

SUPPORT FACILITIES:

Bicycle Rental	Boat Rental	Boat Launch
Fishing Pier	Laundry	Nature Trails
Picnic Area	Playground	Rec Room

ACTIVITIES:

Boating	Fishing	Hiking
Swimming		

RESTRICTIONS: It is recommended that pets not be brought. If brought, they must be kept on leash; owner must clean up after pets. 1-week limit (Sat-Sat) in summer; in other seasons partial-week stays are allowed, based on ferry schedule. Preference is given to patrons desiring to stay a full week. Ferry runs daily 15 Jun-15 Sep, twice a week other months.

*Effective 16 Jul 88, the area code will be changed to 508.

Fourth Cliff Recreation Area (MAO2R1)

Hanscom Air Force Base, MA 01731-5000

Comm: 617-861-4441
ATVN: 478-4441

LOCATION: Off base. I-95 or I-93 to MA-3, approx 10 mi S of Boston; S to exit 12; MA-139 E to Marshfield. 1.5 mi to Furnace St; turn L. Continue to "T" intersection; turn L on Ferry St. Stay on Ferry St to Sea St; R over South River Bridge; L on Central Ave and proceed to gate. RM: p-45, H/20. NMI: South Weymouth NAS, 15 mi NW. NMC: Boston, 30 mi N.

Fourth Cliff Rec Area, Cont'd

DESCRIPTION OF AREA: Rec area is 56-acre seaside resort situated high on a cliff on the tip of a small peninsula overlooking the Atlantic Ocean on one side and scenic North River on the other. Easy access to Boston, Cape Cod, Martha's Vineyard, Nantucket Islands and a host of recreational activities. Wide range of military facilities available at S Weymouth Naval Air Station.

SEASON OF OPERATION: Memorial Day-Columbus Day weekend. 6 Cabins: Year round. Self-contained trailers can be accommodated year round.

ELIGIBILITY: Active/Retired/Reserve on AD/DOD Civilians at Hanscom AFB.

RESERVATIONS: Required with payment in full. Address: Fourth Cliff Recreation Area, PO Box O, Humarock, MA 02047. (Resv) Comm: 617-837-9269; (Info) Comm: 617-837-6785.

CAMP FACILITIES:	NO UNITS	HOOKUPS	FEE
Cabins, furn, 1-3 bdrm	18		$30-50 daily*
Camper Spaces	11 Hardstand	W/E (30A)	9.00 daily
		None	7.00 daily
Other veh used as sleeping			7.00 daily
quarters & parked overnight			
Tent Spaces	Unimproved	None	4.00 daily

*Off-season: $39.00 daily

SUPPORT FACILITIES:	Beach	Grills	Ice
	Laundry	Picnic Area	Rec Hall
	Restrooms	Sewage Dump Sta	Showers
	Snack Bar		

ACTIVITIES:	Fishing (lic)	Horseshoes	Rec Equip Avail

RESTRICTIONS: Pets are not allowed inside any cabins. In other areas, they must be leashed or tied at all times and must not annoy others. No open fires. Firearms and/or hunting equipment, to include all projectile-firing apparatus, are not allowed. Swimming at Fourth Cliff is prohibited due to possibility of strong undertows. A public beach is located 1 mi S in Humarock. Children will not be left unattended. Wildlife will not be captured, killed or harrassed in any way. Check in 1400-2000 daily. Call desk clerk at 617-834-9191 to make arrangements for other hours. **No checking in after 2300.**

Hanscom Fam-Camp (MA08R1)
Hanscom Air Force Base, MA 01731-5000

Comm: 617-377-4441
ATVN: 478-4441

LOCATION: On base. From I-95, exit to MA-4/225; W for .5 mi to L on Hartwell Ave; R on McGuire Rd to end. RM: p-45, E/17. NMC: Boston, 20 mi SE.

DESCRIPTION OF AREA: Located in wooded section of base 6 mi from Concord Bridge (site of the shot heard round the world) and other Revolutionary War historical sites. Easy drive to Boston and the cultural and social world of the city known as the "Hub of the Universe." Full range of military facilities on base.

SEASON OF OPERATION: 1 May-31 October.

ELIGIBILITY: Active/Retired/DOD Civilians at Hanscom AFB.

RESERVATIONS: Accepted for AD only. Address: Recreational Services, ABG/SSRA, ATTN: Fam-Camp, Hanscom AFB, Bedford, MA 01731-5000. Comm: 617-377-4670. For info (off-season only), Comm: 617-837-6785.

MASSACHUSETTS

Hanscom Fam-Camp, Cont'd

CAMPING FACILITIES:	NO UNITS	HOOKUPS	FEE
Camper Spaces	19 Hardstand	W/S/E	$8.00 daily
Camper Spaces	21 Hardstand	W/E	7.00 daily
Tent Spaces	17	None	4.00 daily

SUPPORT FACILITIES:		
Conv Store	Gas	Laundry
Picnic Area	Restrooms	Sewage Dump Sta
Showers		

ACTIVITIES:		
Rec Equip Avail	Sightseeing	

RESTRICTIONS: Pets allowed on leash.

Robbins Pond Travel Camp (MA01R1)
Fort Devens, MA 01433-5000

Comm: 617-796-3911*
ATVN: 256-3911

LOCATION: On post. N of Worcester, from I-190 E on MA-2, or I-495 W on MA-2, to Jackson Gate. Jackson St to R on Patton Rd; bear L to Queenstown Rd; R on El Caney St. Check in at Outdoor Rec. RM: p-45, D/14. NMC: Boston, 35 mi SE.

DESCRIPTION OF AREA: Located on Robbins Pond with sandy beach extending from water's edge to shaded area. Natural habitat for wild ducks and geese which may be fed. Several domestic animals at stables for petting and children's enjoyment. Full range of military facilities available on post.

SEASON OF OPERATION: 15 April-15 October.

ELIGIBILITY: Active/Retired/DOD Civilians.

RESERVATIONS: Accepted 30 days in advance with half of total rental. Address: Outdoor Recreation, Morale Support Activities, Box 18, Ft Devens, MA 01433-5180. Comm: 617-796-3255*; ATVN: 256-3255.

CAMPING FACILITIES:	NO UNITS	HOOKUPS	FEE
Camper Spaces	14 Hardstand	W/E	$6.00 daily
Camper Spaces	10	None	4.00 daily
Tent Spaces	6		3.00 daily

SUPPORT FACILITIES:		
Beach	Boat Rental	Camp Equip Rntl
Chapel	Conv Store	Gas
Golf	Grills	Laundry
Picnic Area	Playground	Restrooms
Sewage Dump Sta	Showers	Snack Bar
Sports Fields	Stables	Tennis Courts

ACTIVITIES:		
Hunting	Racquetball	Rec Equip Avail

RESTRICTIONS: Pets allowed on leash; owner must clean up after pet. Open fires permitted in grills and fireplaces only.

*Effective 16 Jul 88, the area code will be changed to 508.

MICHIGAN

Point Betsie Recreation Cottage (MIO4R2)
Coast Guard Group, Muskegon, MI 49441-1089

Comm: 616-352-9151

LOCATION: Off base. From US-131 N of Grand Rapids take MI-115 NW to Frankfort; N on MI-22 for 5 mi. Sign in and get cottage key at CG Sta at W end of Main St in Frankfort. RM: p-46, M/5. NMI: Traverse City Air Station, 45 mi E. NMC: Muskegon, 100 mi S.

DESCRIPTION OF AREA: Located in NW Michigan on eastern shores of Lake Michigan S of Sleeping Bear Dunes Natl Lakeshore. Crystal Lake and Betsie Bay resorts nearby. Full range of military facilities avail at Traverse City Air Station.

SEASON OF OPERATION: Year round.

ELIGIBILITY: Active/Retired/Reserve.

RESERVATIONS: Req by phone: 60 days in adv for CG Active; 40 days for others. Address: Officer In Charge, USCG Station Frankfort, Box 192, Frankfort, MI 49635-0192. Comm: 616-352-9151. Adv payment for cottage is sent to: Commander, USCG Group Muskegon, Fulton Ave & Bluff St, Muskegon, MI 49441-1089, ATTN: Morale Officer. Comm: 616-789-7508 **(Do not call this number for reservations.)**

LODGING: One Cottage, 2 bdrm, slp 6. Fully furnished, including kitchen utensils, bed linens and blankets.
    <u>FEE:</u> $10.00 daily

SUPPORT FACILITIES: There are no support facilities at the cottage. The following facilities are nearby or within a short driving distance.

	Boat Launch	Boat Rental	Rec Equip Rntl
ACTIVITIES:	Boating	Fishing	Hunting
	Skiing (DH&XC)	Swimming	Water Skiing

RESTRICTIONS: No pets allowed. No telephone at cottage.

Wurtsmith Air Force Beach and Fam-Camp (MIO5R2)
Wurtsmith Air Force Base, MI 48753-5000

Comm: 517-739-2011
ATVN: 623-1110

LOCATION: Off base. From Oscoda, N on US-23; L on F-41 to Van Etten Lake. Check in at Wurtsmith AFB Billeting Office. RM: p-47, N/14. NMI: Wurtsmith AFB, 1.5 mi S. NMC: Bay City, 65 mi SW.

DESCRIPTION OF AREA: Located in an area of woods and open meadows overlooking Van Etten Lake. Surrounded by thousands of acres of national forests. Full range of military facilities available on base.

SEASON OF OPERATION: 15 May-15 October.

ELIGIBILITY: Active/Retired/DOD Civilians.

RESERVATIONS: No adv resv. Address: 379 SVS/SVH, Bldg 1600, Wurtsmith AFB, MI 48753-5000. Comm: 517-747-6033/6562; ATVN: 623-6033/6562.

MICHIGAN
Wurtsmith Air Force Beach & Fam-Camp

CAMPING FACILITIES:	NO UNITS	HOOKUPS	FEE
Camper Spaces	6	W/S/E	$4.00 daily
Tents	Open		1.00 daily

SUPPORT FACILITIES:			
	Beach	Boat Launch	Boat Rental
	Boat Storage	Gas	Grill
	Laundry (nearby)	Party Pavilions	Picnic Area
	Playground	Restrooms	Sewage Dump Sta
	Showers	Snack Bar	

ACTIVITIES:	Fishing	Swimming	Water Skiing

RESTRICTIONS: Pets allowed on leash. No pets allowed on beach.

MINNESOTA

-None-

MISSISSIPPI

Keesler Marina (MSO5R2)
Keesler AFB, MS 39534-5000

Comm: 601-377-1110
ATVN: 868-1110

LOCATION: On base. From I-10 take I-110 S; Bayview Dr W to Forest Ave; L 2 blocks to Meadows; R to gate. RM: p-52, P/5, 10. NMC: Biloxi, 2 mi E.

DESCRIPTION OF AREA: Mississippi Gulf Coast holds a wealth of history. In Biloxi tours are available daily at Beauvoir, the home of Jefferson Davis. Marina located off Ploesti Drive on Back Bay offers a park, boating and fishing. Full range of military facilities available on base.

SEASON OF OPERATION: Year round.

ELIGIBILITY: Active/Retired/DOD Civilians.

RESERVATIONS: Required. Address: Recreation Services, 3380 ABG/SSROM, Keesler AFB, MS 39534-5225. Comm: 601-377-3160/3186; ATVN: 868-3160/3186.

CAMPING FACILITIES:	NO UNITS	HOOKUPS	FEE
Camper Spaces	20	W/S/E (110)	$7.00 daily
		W/E (110)	5.00 daily

SUPPORT FACILITIES:			
	Beach	Boat Rental	Camp Equip Rntl
	Chapel	Fishing Eq Rntl	Gas
	Golf	Grills	Laundry (nearby)
	Marina	Picnic Area	Playground
	Quik Shop(near)	Showers	Snack Bar
	Sports Fields	Swimming Pool	Tennis Courts
	Trailer Rental		

ACTIVITIES:			
	Bicycling	Boating	Fishing (lic)
	Hiking	Jogging	Rec Equip Avail
	Swimming		

RESTRICTIONS: No open fires on beach without city approval.

Sardis Lake Recreation Area (MSO6R2)
Blythville Air Force Base, AR 72317-5000

Comm: 501-762-7000
ATVN: 637-1110

LOCATION: Off base. Near Oxford, MS. From I-55 in northern MS, take MS-6 E towards Oxford. Travel approx 9 mi to John W Kyle State Park sign; L for .7 mi to Pat's Bluff/Cole's Point sign; R 4.3 mi; R on paved road to gate. RM: p-52, C/8. NMI: Memphis NAS, Millington, TN, 88 mi NW. NMC: Memphis, TN, 68 mi NW.

DESCRIPTION OF AREA: Sardis Lake, located on the Little Tallahatchie River, has approx 58,500 acres of surface area. It ranks high among the nation's famous parks, monuments and recreation areas and is Mississippi's favorite playground. Excellent fishing (crappie, bass, catfish). 341-acre campsite is in heavily wooded area. Full range of military facilities at Memphis Naval Air Station.

SEASON OF OPERATION: Year round.

ELIGIBILITY: Active/Retired/Reserve/DOD Civilians.

RESERVATIONS: None required. Address: Outdoor Recreation, 97 CSG/SSRO, Blytheville AFB, AR 72317-5000. Comm: 501-762-7264; ATVN: 721-7264.

CAMPING FACILITIES:	NO UNITS	HOOKUPS	FEE*
Camper/Tent Spaces, 30'	108 Gravel	W/S/E (110) +RV A/C plug	$4 dly/24 wk/75 mo 6 dly/36 wk/125 mo
Tent Spaces	Primitive		None

*Half-price November-March

SUPPORT FACILITIES:			
	Archery	Bait Shop	Beaches
	Boat Launch/near	Canoe Rental	Country Store
	Fire Ring	Grills	Picnic Area
	Rec Equip Rntl	Restrooms	Showers
	Sewage Dump Sta	Tent Rental	

ACTIVITIES:			
	Boating	Fishing	Hiking
	Swimming		

RESTRICTIONS: Small pets allowed on leash.

MISSOURI

Lake of the Ozarks Recreation Area (MOO1R2)
Fort Leonard Wood, MO 65473-5000

Comm: 314-368-0113
ATVN: 581-0110
FTS: 270-0110

LOCATION: Off post. From I-70 at Columbia, take US-54 SW to Linn Creek area; L at County Rd A for 6 mi to Freedom; L on Lake Rd A-5 for 4.7 mi to travel camp. From I-44 NE of Springfield, MO-7 NW to Richland; R on County Rd A and travel 19.8 mi to Freedom; R on Lake Road A-5 4.7 mi to travel camp. RM: p-55, J/14. NMI: Ft L Wood, 50 mi SE. NMC: Jefferson City, 40 mi NE.

DESCRIPTION OF AREA: Located on Grand Glaize Arm of the Lake of the Ozarks in the center of a State Wildlife Refuge. Situated on 360-acre reserve with excellent fishing and beautiful scenery. Nearby attractions include Osage Beach, Ozark Caverns, musical shows, theme park, water slides, helicopter rides, etc. Historical and recreational points of interest surround the area. Full range of military facilities available at Ft Leonard Wood.

MISSOURI
Lake of the Ozarks Rec Area, Cont'd

SEASON OF OPERATION: First weekend in April-last weekend in October.

ELIGIBILITY: Open to all military-connected ID card holders, to include: Medal of Honor recipients and family members; members of ARNG & USAR; Academy and ROTC cadets on active duty for training; DOD, APF and NAF civilians; military personnel of foreign nations and their family members; paid members of American Red Cross and other such organizations when assigned to and serving with the Armed Forces and family members; surgeons under contract to DOD components during the period of their contracts.

RESERVATIONS: Accepted starting 2d week in March with adv payment. Address: Ft Leonard Wood LORA, Route 1, Box 380, Linn Creek, MO 65052. Comm: 314-346-5640.

CAMP FACILITIES:	NO UNITS	HOOKUPS	FEE
Mobile Homes, 3 bdrm*	Total		$30-34 daily
Mobile Homes, 2 bdrm*	of 42		26-28 daily
Camper Spaces	16 Hardstand	W/E (110)	8.00 daily
Tent & Camper Spaces	20	None	4.00 daily

*Furnished except bedding and towels.

SUPPORT FACILITIES:			
	Beach	Boat Rental	Boat/RV Storage
	Grills	Laundry	Marina
	Pavilion	Picnic Area	Playground
	PX	Restrooms	Sewage Dump Sta
	Shoppette	Showers	Water Sprts Eq Rntl

ACTIVITIES:			
	Fishing (lic)	Swimming	Water Skiing

Special events are scheduled throughout the summer.

RESTRICTIONS: Pets must be on leash or under voice control and have all shots (tags displayed); owner responsible for damage caused by pet. No open fires.

MONTANA

Malmstrom Fam-Camp (MTO1R3)
Malmstrom Air Force Base, MT 59402-5000

Comm: 406-731-9990
ATVN: 632-1110

LOCATION: On base. From I-15 take 10th Ave S exit to AFB. RM: p-57, P/22. NMC: Great Falls, 2 mi W.

DESCRIPTION OF AREA: Situated in open terrain surrounded by Little Belt range of the Rockies. Full range of military facilities available on base.

SEASON OF OPERATION: 15 Apr-15 Oct, depending on weather for hookups. Year round for no-hookup service.

ELIGIBILITY: Active/Retired.

RESERVATIONS: No adv resv. Address: Recreation Services, Malmstrom AFB, MT 59402-5000. Comm: 406-731-3394; ATVN: 632-3394.

CAMPING FACILITIES:	NO UNITS	HOOKUPS	FEE
Camper Spaces	10	W/S/E	$7.00 daily
Camper & Tent Spaces	5	None	5.00 daily

Malmstrom Fam-Camp, Cont'd

SUPPORT FACILITIES:	Chapel	Gas	Picnic Area
	Restrooms	Sewage Dump Sta	Showers (Arena)

ACTIVITIES:	Rec Equip Avail	Swimming	Tennis

Outdoor Rec has ongoing programs such as fishing, floating, backpacking, etc.

RESTRICTIONS: Parking spaces will not be assigned until 0800; renewals will not be accepted after 0800.

St. Mary's Recreation Camp (MT02R3)
Malmstrom Air Force Base, MT 59402-5000

Comm: 406-731-9990
ATVN: 632-1110

LOCATION: Off base. On US-89, 3 mi N of Glacier Natl Park entrance in St Mary. RM: p-56, B/7. NMI: Malmstrom AFB, 165 mi SE. NMC: Great Falls, 160 mi SE.

DESCRIPTION OF AREA: Situated at lower end of St Mary Lake in the NW corner of the state about 30 mi from Canada; beautiful wooded, mountainous terrain. Area is leased from Blackfoot Indian Tribe. Full range of military facilities avail at Malmstrom Air Force Base.

SEASON OF OPERATION: 1 June-15 September.

ELIGIBILITY: Active/Retired/DOD Civilians.

RESERVATIONS: Req up to 45 days in adv with payment. Address: Rec Services, 341 CSG/SSRO, Malmstrom AFB, MT 59402-5000. Comm: 406-731-3263; ATVN: 632-3263.

CAMP FACILITIES:	NO	UNITS	HOOKUPS	FEE
Mobile Homes, 3 bdrm	10			$22-40 daily
Mobile Homes, 2 bdrm	5			18.00 daily
Tent, bungalow, slp 4, refr, hotplate, heater	8		W/E (110)	10.00 daily*
RV Spaces	10		W/E (110)	12.00 daily*
Tent Spaces		Open	None	5.00 daily
Travel Trailer Rental				
17'				12.00 daily
18'				20.00 daily
24'				22.00 daily

*No charge to bona fide volunteers.

SUPPORT FACILITIES:	Boat Rental**	Laundry	Marina
	Playground	Rec Center	Restrooms
	Sewage Dump Sta	Showers	

**Malmstrom AFB Boat Safety Certificate required or successful completion of safety test given by Camp Supervisor or his attendant.

ACTIVITIES:	Boating (lic)	Fishing (lic)	Hiking
	Rec Equip Avail		

RESTRICTIONS: Pets allowed on leash; owner must clean up after pets. 14-day limit. No swimming. RV's cannot be used in auto parking spaces or adjacent to mobile homes without paying the $12 RV fee and obtaining approval of the Camp Supervisor. **As a minimum, you must provide your bedding, food, warm clothing, utensils, pots and pans. No electric blankets.**

NEBRASKA

Offutt Fam-Camp (NEO1R3)
Offutt Air Force Base, NE 68113-5000

Comm: 402-294-1110
ATVN: 271-1110

LOCATION: On base. From I-80 in Omaha, take US-73/75 S to Bellevue. E on NE-131 to Mission St; R on Hancock St for 1.5 mi; L to base lake. RM: p-59, L/24. NMC: Omaha, 8 mi N.

DESCRIPTION OF AREA: Located near state's eastern boundary with Iowa. Strategic Air Command Headquarters. Surrounding area open farm country. Full range of military facilities available on base.

SEASON OF OPERATION: Year round; 8 November-31 March: Electric only.

ELIGIBILITY: Active/Retired/DOD Civilians at Offutt AFB.

RESERVATIONS: Required. Address: Billeting Office, 3902 ABW/SSR, Offutt AFB, NE 68113-5000. Comm: 402-294-3671.

CAMPING FACILITIES:	NO UNITS	HOOKUPS	FEE
Camper Spaces	10 Hardstand	W/S/E (110)	$4.50 daily
		E	3.00 daily
Tent Spaces	Wilderness		None

SUPPORT FACILITIES:			
	Archery	Boat Launch	Boat Rental
	Chapel	Gas	Golf
	Grills	Grocery(nearby)	Gym (on base)
	Marina	Picnic Area	Playground
	Racquetball	Restrooms	Skeet/Trap Ranges
	Sports Fields	Stables	Tennis Courts

ACTIVITIES:	Boating	Fishing (lic)	Hunting (lic)
	Rec Equip Avail		

RESTRICTIONS: Pets allowed on leash.

NEVADA

Nellis Fam-Camp (NVO4R4)
Nellis Air Force Base, NV 89191-5000

Comm: 702-643-1800
ATVN: 682-1800

LOCATION: On base. From I-15 N of Las Vegas, exit Craig Rd to Las Vegas Blvd to main gate. Clearly marked. Check in at Rec Center, Bldg 555. RM: p-60, N/10, 3. NMC: Las Vegas, 8 mi SW.

DESCRIPTION OF AREA: Located in desert Southwest with mountains on one side and Lake Mead National Recreation Area on the other. Easy drive to Grand Canyon. Las Vegas attractions nearby. Full range of military facilities avail on base.

SEASON OF OPERATION: Year round.

ELIGIBILITY: Active/Retired/DOD Civilians.

RESERVATIONS: Accepted up to 90 days in adv. Address: Recreation Services, 554 CSG/SSRR, Nellis AFB, NV 89191-5000. Comm: 702-652-5014; ATVN: 682-5014.

Nellis Fam-Camp, Cont'd

CAMPING FACILITIES:

	NO UNITS	HOOKUPS	FEE
Camper Spaces	16 Hardstand	W/E	$6.50 daily
Tent Spaces	8	None	3.00 daily

SUPPORT FACILITIES:

Boat Rental	Chapel	Gas
Golf	Grills	Laundry
Picnic Area	Racquetball	Restrooms
Sewage Dump Sta	Shoppette	Showers
Sports Fields		

ACTIVITIES:

Boating	Fishing	Rec Equip Avail
Snow Skiing	Swimming	

RESTRICTIONS: Pets allowed on leash; must have complete and current immunizations; must not be left unattended; owner must clean up after pets. 14-day limit per month. No open fires.

NEW HAMPSHIRE

Peverly Pond Recreation Area (NHO3R1)

Pease Air Force Base, NH 03803-5000

Comm: 603-430-0100
ATVN: 852-1110

LOCATION: On base. From I-95 near Portsmouth, take Spaulding Turnpike N, then follow signs to main gate. Base is at intersection of Newington Rd. Check in at Outdoor Recreation, Bldg 85. RM: p-61, 0/12. NMC: Portsmouth, 3 mi NE.

DESCRIPTION OF AREA: Campsite is situated along beautiful Upper Peverly Pond; Lower Peverly Pond is for recreational water activities and family picnicking. The entire seacoast area is of historical interest. New Hampshire's mountain and lake regions are within easy driving distance. Upper Peverly Pond is stocked with trout yearly; well-stocked Bass Pond is located 1.5 mi from camping area. Full range of military facilities available on base.

SEASON OF OPERATION: 15 April-last weekend in September.
Closed during NH hunting season (Oct-Nov).

ELIGIBILITY: Active/Retired/DOD Civilians.

RESERVATIONS: Recommended. Address: 509 CSG/SSRO, Pease AFB, NH 03803-5000.
Comm: 603-430-2509; ATVN: 852-2509.

CAMPING FACILITIES:

	NO UNITS	HOOKUPS	FEE
Camper Spaces	16 Gravel	None	$4.00 daily
Tent Spaces	16 Improved	None	4.00 daily

SUPPORT FACILITIES:

Archery	Beach (summer)	Boat Landing
Boat Rental	Chapel	Elec Motor Rntl
Gas	Golf	Grills
Picnic Area	Playground	Racquet Sports
Rec Equip Rntl	Restrooms/nearby	Showers/nearby
Skeet Rg/shotgun	Ski Rental	Snack Bar
Sports Fields		

ACTIVITIES:

Fishing (lic)	Hunting (lic)	Swimming

RESTRICTIONS: Pets allowed. No gas motors allowed on pond. No open fires; pits for cooking are provided at each site.

NEW JERSEY

Barnegat Recreation Cottage (NJO6R1)
Maintenance and Logistics Command Atlantic
Governors Island, NY, NY 10004-5098

Comm: 212-668-7032
FTS: 664-7032

LOCATION: Off base. On tip of Long Beach Island, NJ. Exit 63 off the Garden State Pkwy; NJ-72 E to Ship Bottom; R (S) 5 mi to Long Beach. RM: p-63, S/13. NMI: Ft Dix and McGuire AFB, 40 mi NW. NMC: Atlantic City, 30 mi SW.

DESCRIPTION OF AREA: Converted Coast Guard station near beautiful beach between Barnegat Bay and Atlantic Ocean. Full range of military facilities available at Ft Dix and McGuire AFB.

SEASON OF OPERATION: 20 May-18 September.

ELIGIBILITY: Active/Retired/Reserve.

RESERVATIONS: Required, by application only, with payment in full, starting 18 Apr for CG and 16 May for other AD. Address: Commander (ps), Maintenance and Logistics Command Atlantic, Governors Island, New York, NY 10004-5098. Comm: 212-668-7032/7717; FTS: 664-7032.

LODGING: 4-apartment beach house; community kitchen and dining room; fully furnished except bed linens, towels and pans.
<u>FEE:</u> $20-30 daily; $2 for each additional person over age of 12.

SUPPORT FACILITIES:	Beach	Laundry	Picnic Area
ACTIVITIES:	Fishing	Swimming	

RESTRICTIONS: No pets allowed. 7-day limit, to include only one weekend. No campers/trailers allowed in the area.

Brindle Lake Travel Camp (NJO4R1)
Fort Dix, NJ 08640-5111

Comm: 609-562-1011
ATVN: 944-1110
FTS: 484-1110

LOCATION: On post. Take exit 7 off NJ Turnpike; S on NJ-68, which leads to post. L on Wrightstown/Cookstown Rd to Hockamick Rd to Brindle Lake Rd. Check in at Bldg 9905 at Brindle Lake (first Bldg when you enter) or Bldg 5201 on post (corner of Maryland Ave and 8th St). RM: p-63, 0/10. NMC: Trenton, 20 mi NW.

DESCRIPTION OF AREA: Wooded site located on a 30-acre lake 7 mi from main area of post. Full range of military facilities available on post.

SEASON OF OPERATION: Year round.
Boating: Memorial Day weekend-Labor Day weekend, Tu-Su.

ELIGIBILITY: Active/Retired/DOD Civilians.

RESERVATIONS: Accepted. Address: Outdoor Recreation, Bldg 5201, Ft Dix, NJ 08640-5110. Comm: 609-562-2358/2830; ATVN: 944-2358/2830; FTS: 484-2358/2830.

CAMPING FACILITIES:	NO UNITS	HOOKUPS	FEE
Camper & Tent Spaces	10	None	$4.00 daily

Brindle Lake Travel Camp, Cont'd

SUPPORT FACILITIES:

Boat Rental	Camp Equip Rntl	Fishing Equip Rntl
Grills	Picnic Areas	Port-a-Potties

ACTIVITIES:

Boating	Firearms Ranges	Fishing (lic)
Rec Equip Avail		

RESTRICTIONS: Pets allowed on leash; owner must clean up after pets.

Lake Denmark Recreation Area
(NJO2R1)
Picatinny Arsenal
Dover, NJ 07806-5000

Comm: 201-724-4021
ATVN: 880-4021

LOCATION: On post. I-80 to NJ-15; N 1 mi to post on R. Security ID check required. RM: p-62, E/10. NMC: Dover, 2 mi S.

DESCRIPTION OF AREA: Situated in picturesque area in northern New Jersey. Full range of military facilities available on post.

SEASON OF OPERATION: Late May-1 October.

ELIGIBILITY: Active/Retired.

RESERVATIONS: Required. Address: Community Recreation Branch, Bldg 3050, Picatinny Arsenal, Dover, NJ 07806-5000, ATTN: Trailer Park Manager. Comm: 201-724-4014; ATVN: 880-4014; FTS 724-4186.

CAMP FACILITIES:	NO UNITS	HOOKUPS	FEE
Mobile Homes, 2 & 3 bdrm*	9		$7.00-16.00 daily
Camper Spaces	2	W/E (110/220)	7.00 daily
		None	5.00 daily

*Furnished, including dishes, pots & pans; linens on request. No TV or towels.

SUPPORT FACILITIES:

Boat Rental	Chapel	Grills
Gym & Weightroom	Laundry	Picnic Area
Restrooms	Showers	Softball Field

ACTIVITIES:

Fishing (lic)	Hunting

RESTRICTIONS: Pets allowed; must be under control at all times. Security ID check required.

McGuire Fam-Camp (NJO7R1)
McGuire AFB, NJ 08641-5000

Comm: 609-724-1110
ATVN: 440-0111

LOCATION: On base. New Jersey Turnpike to exit 7; S on NJ-68 and follow signs to McGuire AFB through Gate 1. Report to Recreation Center, Bldg 25-01. RM p-63, O/10. NMC: Trenton, 15 mi NW.

DESCRIPTION OF AREA: Small, cozy campground set on 3.5 acres of beautiful trees and fields. Weekend campfires and activities. Surrounding areas have many U-PICK farms with fresh vegetables and fruits. Full range of military facilities available on base.

SEASON OF OPERATION: 15 April-15 October.

ELIGIBILITY: Active/Retired/Reserve/DOD Civilians.

McGuire Fam-Camp, Cont'd

RESERVATIONS: Accepted with deposit. Address: Fam-Camp, 438 ABG/SSRR, McGuire AFB, NJ 08641-5000. Comm: 609-724-2176; ATVN: 440-2176.

CAMPING FACILITIES:	NO UNITS	HOOKUPS	FEE
Camper Spaces	6 Hardstand	W/E (110/220)	$6.00 daily
Tent Spaces	5 Improved	E	2.00 daily

SUPPORT ACTIVITIES:			
	Chapel	Gas	Golf
	Grills	Picnic Area	Playground
	Quik Shop	Rec Center	Restrooms
	Sewage Dump Sta	Showers	Sports Fields
	Trails		

ACTIVITIES:	Hiking	Recreation Equipment Available

RESTRICTIONS: Small pets allowed on leash. No wood fires.

Wildwood Campground (NJ12R1)

USCG Electronics Engineering Center
Wildwood, NJ 08260-0060

Comm: 609-729-8926
FTS: 346-7226

LOCATION: On base. From Garden State Parkway take exit 4. E on NJ-47 to Wildwood; S on Pacific Ave to Wildwood Crest and into Lower Township. RM: p-63, Z/8. NMC: Atlantic City, 45 mi N.

DESCRIPTION OF AREA: Situated along 2 mi of superb beach on peninsula in SE New Jersey. Many water sports available. Wide range of military fac (including BX, gas and commissary) at Cape May Coast Guard Training Center, 5 mi S.

SEASON OF OPERATION: Memorial Day through Labor Day.

ELIGIBILITY: Active/Retired.

RESERVATIONS: Required at least 30 days in adv. Address: Commanding Officer (AP), USCG EECEN, Wildwood, NJ 08260-0060. Comm: 609-729-8912; FTS 346-7212.

CAMPING FACILITIES:	NO UNITS	HOOKUPS	FEE
Camper Spaces	8	W/E	$6.00 daily
Tent Spaces	8	None	4.00 daily

SUPPORT FACILITIES:			
	Beach	Beach Hut	Restrooms
	Sewage Dump Sta	Showers	Sports Fields

ACTIVITIES:	Jogging	Rec Equip Avail	Swimming

RESTRICTIONS: No pets allowed. 10-day limit.

NEW MEXICO

Holloman Fam-Camp (NMO6R3)
Holloman Air Force Base, NM 88330-5000

Comm: 505-479-6511
ATVN: 867-1110

LOCATION: On base. 10 mi SW of Alamogordo off US-70. Turn L immediately inside main gate on Mesquite Road. Fam-Camp is on left near entrance. RM: p-70, K/6. NMC: El Paso, TX, 90 mi S.

DESCRIPTION OF AREA: Situated on open, semi-arid terrain with few trees, but surrounded by shrubs. Nearby: Space Center Hall of Fame, Planetarium, zoo, White Sands National Park, horse racing and winter sports. Full range of military facilities available on base.

SEASON OF OPERATION: Year round.

ELIGIBILITY: Active/Retired/DOD Civilians.

RESERVATIONS: Resv accepted. Address: Holloman Fam-Camp, Bldg 598, 833 CSG/SSRO, Holloman AFB, NM 88330-5000. Comm: 505-479-7476; ATVN: 867-7476.

CAMPING FACILITIES:	NO UNITS	HOOKUPS	FEE
Camper Spaces	12 Hardstand	W/S/E	$8.00 daily

SUPPORT FACILITIES:			
	Chapel	Gas	Golf
	Laundry	Picnic Area	Playground
	Racquet Sports	Rec Center	Restrooms
	Showers	Swimming Pool	Trails

ACTIVITIES: Rec Equip Avail Snow Skiing (29 mi)

RESTRICTIONS: Pets allowed.

Kirtland Fam-Camp (NMO7R3)
Kirtland Air Force Base, NM 87117-5000

Comm: 505-844-0011
ATVN: 244-0011

LOCATION: On base. From I-40 E of Albuquerque take Exit 164; S on Wyoming Blvd to AFB. Check in at Rec Center, Bldg 20155, 0900-0100, F-Sa; 0900-2200 Su-Th. RM: p-70, Q/11. NMC: Albuquerque, adjacent to base.

DESCRIPTION OF AREA: Situated in a desert area with few trees around. Sandia and Manzano mountains are E of base. Sandia Crest Recreation Area and aerial tram nearby. Full range of military facilities available on base.

SEASON OF OPERATION: Year round.

ELIGIBILITY: Active/Retired.

RESERVATIONS: Accepted for PCS, TDY and medical personnel only. Address: Recreational Director/SSR, 1606 ABW/SS, Kirtland AFB, NM 87117-5000. Comm: 505-844-5420; ATVN: 244-5420.

CAMPING FACILITIES:	NO UNITS	HOOKUPS	FEE
Camper Spaces	20 Hardstand	W/S/E	$7.50 daily
		W	4.00 daily
		None	2.00 daily
Tent Spaces	Many	None	2.00 daily

NEW MEXICO
Kirtland Fam-Camp, Cont'd

SUPPORT FACILITIES: Chapel   Gas   Golf
                           Picnic Area   Playground   Sewage Dump Sta

ACTIVITIES: Hiking   Outdoor Sports

RESTRICTIONS: Pets allowed on leash. No generators after 1800.

Lake Conchas Recreation Area
(NMO1R3)
Cannon Air Force Base, NM 88103-5000

Comm: 505-784-3311
ATVN: 681-1110

LOCATION: Off base. Off NM-104 NW of Tucumcari. RM: p-70, E/10. NMI: Cannon
AFB, 115 mi SE. NMC: Clovis, 120 mi SE.

DESCRIPTION OF AREA: Scenic rec area on Lake Conchas in NE New Mexico. Offers
many water activities. Full range of military facilities avail at Cannon AFB.

SEASON OF OPERATION: 1 February-31 October.

ELIGIBILITY: Active/Retired/DOD Civilians.

RESERVATIONS: Required: 30 days in advance for Cannon AFB personnel; 2 weeks in
adv for others. Address: Lake Conchas Rec Area, 27 TFW/PA, Cannon AFB, NM
88103-5128. Comm: 505-868-2444, ATVN: 681-2795.

CAMPING FACILITIES:	NO UNITS	HOOKUPS	FEE
Mobile Homes	13		$20-25 daily
Camper Spaces	3 Hardstand	W/E	7.00 daily
Camper Spaces	15 Hardstand	W	7.00 daily
Camper Spaces	Unlimited	None	5.00 daily

SUPPORT FACILITIES: Boat Rental   Laundry   Playground
                           Restrooms   Showers   Snack Bar

ACTIVITIES: Boating   Fishing   Skiing

RESTRICTIONS: Pets allowed on leash; owners liable for any damage done by
pets. No swimming.

Volunteer Park Travel Camp Site
(NMO8R3)
White Sands Missile Range, NM 88002-5035

Comm: 505-678-2121
ATVN: 258-2121

LOCATION: On post. On US-70 E of Las Cruces. Entry to installation controlled
by Mil Police; visitor pass required. RM: p-70, L/6. NMC: Las Cruces, 25 mi SW.

DESCRIPTION OF AREA: Many outdoor sports to be found within a 100-mi radius.
To the E is Cloudcroft ski area; horse racing at Ruidoso Downs; and the Apache
Indian Reservation with Ski Apache, a first-class ski area, and the Inn of the
Mountain Gods, a resort of international repute. El Paso, where you can cross
the border into Mexico, is to the S. To the N are Caballo and Elephant Butte
Lakes featuring state-operated recreational areas with RV facilities, boating,
water skiing, fishing and swimming. Full range of military facilities on post.

Tours to Trinity Site, the location of the world's first nuclear explosion, are
conducted on the first Sa in Apr and first Sa in Oct. Arrangements may be made
through the Public Affairs Office, Bldg 122. Comm: 505-678-1134/1135/1700.

Volunteer Park Travel Camp Site, Cont'd

SEASON OF OPERATION: Year round. Closed W, Su and half-day Sa.

ELIGIBILITY: Active/Retired/DOD Civilians.

RESERVATIONS: Required. Address: White Sands Missile Range, NM 88002-5035, ATTN: STEWS-DP-AR. Comm: 505-678-1713; ATVN: 258-1713.

CAMPING FACILITIES:	NO UNITS	HOOKUPS	FEE
Camper Spaces	8 Hardstand	W/E	$4.00 dly/24 wkly

SUPPORT FACILITIES:			
	Archery	Boat Rental	Camper Rental
	Chapel	Fishing Tackle	Fitness Trail
	Gas	Golf (9 holes)	Grills
	Gym (on post)	Laundry (nearby)	Off-Road Trails
	Outside Light	Pavilion	Picnic Area
	Rec Ctr (nearby)	Rec Equip Rntl	Restrooms
	Sewage Dump Sta	Skeet/Trap Rg	Sports Fields
	Tennis Courts	(Shotgun only)	

ACTIVITIES:	Fishing	Hiking	Hunting (lic)*
	*Special hunts only		

RESTRICTIONS: Pets allowed on leash.

NEW YORK

Griffiss Fam-Camp (NY15R1)
Griffiss Air Force Base, NY 13441-5000

Comm: 315-330-1110
ATVN: 587-1110

LOCATION: On base. N of Rome on NY-46. Entrance on Chestnut, Floyd and E Domonick St. Fam-Camp at W end of base on Perimeter Rd by golf course. RM: p-66, EK/8. NMC: Rome, adjacent.

DESCRIPTION OF AREA: Located in densely populated Rome-Utica area. Oneida Lake, with many recreational areas, nearby. Full range of military facilities on base.

SEASON OF OPERATION: 15 May-15 October.

ELIGIBILITY: Active/Retired/DOD Civilians.

RESERVATIONS: No adv resv. Address: Billeting Office, 416 CSG/SVH, Bldg 704, Griffiss AFB, NY 13441-5000. Comm: 315-330-4391; ATVN: 587-4391.

CAMPING FACILITIES:	NO UNITS	HOOKUPS	FEE
Camper Spaces	10	W/E (120/240)	$4.00 daily

SUPPORT FACILITIES:			
	Chapel	Gas	Golf
	Picnic Area	Playground	Rec Equip Rntl
	Restrooms	Sewage Dump Sta	

ACTIVITIES:	Fishing	Swimming	Tennis

RESTRICTIONS: 7-day limit, then space available.

Remington Pond Recreation Area (NY14R1)
Fort Drum, NY 13602-5000

Comm: 315-772-6900
ATVN: 341-6011

LOCATION: On post. From I-81 at Watertown, take exit 48; NY-3 NE to gates 1, 2 or 3. RM: p-66, EF/7. NMC: Watertown, 9 mi SW.

DESCRIPTION OF AREA: Beautiful area offering every recreational pursuit. Many tourist attractions such as Sackets Harbor Battleground (site of the War of 1812), Thousand Islands, Lake Ontario, Canada, Dry Hill ski area and white-water rafting. Full range of military facilities available on post.

SEASON OF OPERATION: 1 April-30 November.

ELIGIBILITY: Active/Retired.

RESERVATIONS: Accepted. Address: Outdoor Rec Rental, Bldg T-1001, Fort Drum, NY 13602-5000, ATTN: AFZS-PA-CRD. Comm: 315-772-5169; ATVN: 341-5169; FTS: 775-5169. Ask for monthly calendar.

CAMPING FACILITIES:	NO UNITS	HOOKUPS	FEE
Camper & Tent Spaces	6 Wilderness	None	$5.00 daily

SUPPORT FACILITIES:			
	Beach	Boat Rental	Chapel
	Dock (floating)	Gas	Golf Driv Range
	Grills	Paddle Boats	Pavilions
	Picnic Area	Rec Equip Rntl	Restrooms
	Showers	Vending Machines	

ACTIVITIES:			
	Fishing (lic)	Hunting (lic)	Swimming
	Tours	Windsurfing	

RESTRICTIONS: Pets allowed on leash. 14-day limit. No motorized boats permitted.

Round Pond Recreation Area (NY04R1)
United States Military Academy
West Point, NY 10996-5000

Comm: 914-938-4011
ATVN: 688-1110

LOCATION: Off post. 5 mi W of West Point on NY-293. Exit 17 from I-87; follow US-6 E to NY-293; continue E to rec area. RM, p-67, EV/14. NMI: US Military Academy, 5 mi E. NMC: New York City, 50 mi SE.

DESCRIPTION OF AREA: Located on Academy property in a rocky, wooded area near the old Ramapo mines. A delightful place with a natural spring-fed pond. Full range of military facilities available at US Military Academy.

SEASON OF OPERATION: 15 April-15 November.

ELIGIBILITY: Active/Retired/DOD Civilians residing on post.

RESERVATIONS: Required: 30-60 days in adv for AD; 14 days in adv for Retired. Address: Physical Activity Branch, Bldg 622, West Point, NY 10996-5000. Comm: 914-938-2503; ATVN: 688-2503. Ask for parking instructions.

Round Pond Rec Area, Cont'd

CAMP FACILITIES:	NO UNITS	HOOKUPS	FEE
Mobile Homes, 3 bdrm	6	E	$12-18 daily
Travel Trailers	3	E	10.00 daily
Camper Spaces	25	E	4.50 daily
Tent Spaces	50	None	2.00 daily

SUPPORT FACILITIES:			
	Boat Rental	Hiking Trail	Marina
	Picnic Area	Rental Center	Playground
	Restrooms	Scout Camping	Sewage Dump Sta
	Showers		
	Community House and Cabin for groups can be rented.		

ACTIVITIES: Fishing (lic) Rec Equip Avail Swimming

RESTRICTIONS: Pets allowed on leash in camp area only. Quiet after 2230.

Seneca Army Depot Lakeshore Travel Camp (NY13R1)
Seneca Army Depot, Romulus, NY 14541-5000

Comm: 607-869-5110
ATVN: 489-5110

LOCATION: On post. Seneca is located 12 mi S of Geneva on NY-96A. RM: p-69, WF/21. NMC: Rochester, 50 mi NW.

DESCRIPTION OF AREA: Located in the center of New York's Finger Lakes Region. Seneca Lake, the lake-trout capital of the world, is approximately 42 mi long and 2 mi wide and is the largest of the Finger Lakes. The area offers some of the best fishing and hunting in the country. Full range of mil fac on post.

SEASON OF OPERATION: Year round.

ELIGIBILITY: Active/Retired.

RESERVATIONS: Required for mobile homes; accepted for campsites. Address: Seneca Army Depot, ATTN: SDSSE-PER (Travel Camp), Romulus, NY 14541-5001. Comm: 607-869-1211; ATVN: 489-5211.

CAMP FACILITIES:	NO UNITS	HOOKUPS	FEE
Mobile Homes	19		$18.00 daily
Camper Spaces	6	W/E	7.50 daily
Camper Spaces	2	E	5.00 daily
Tent Spaces	Many	None	5.00 daily

SUPPORT FACILITIES:			
	Boat Launch	Boat Rental	Chapel
	Gas	Laundry	Marina
	Picnic Area	Playground	Restrooms
	Sewage Dump Sta	Showers	

ACTIVITIES:			
	Fishing	Rec Equip Avail	Snow Skiing
	Swimming	Water Skiing	

RESTRICTIONS: No pets allowed in mobile homes.

Thayer Hotel (NYO5R1)
United States Military Academy
West Point, NY 10996-5000

Comm: 914-938-2632
914-446-4731
800-247-5047
ATVN: 688-2632

LOCATION: On post. 11 mi S of Newburgh off I-87 or US-9W. Bldg 674 on installation. RM: p-67, EU/14. NMC: New York City, 50 mi S.

DESCRIPTION OF AREA: Historic US Military Academy on the Hudson River. The hotel is operated under direction of Superintendent, US Military Academy. Full range of military facilities available at US Military Academy.

SEASON OF OPERATION: Year round.

ELIGIBILITY: Open to the public.

RESERVATIONS: Preferred. Address: Hotel Thayer, West Point, NY 10996-0016. Comm: 914-446-4731; ATVN: 688-2632.

LODGING: The Hotel Thayer has 210 guest rooms in addition to dining rooms and facilities for groups. Renovations in 1981 of all guest rooms; newly furnished in 1986. Desk operation: 24 hours daily.

FEE:	
Single	$ 49.00-54.00 daily
Double	64.00-70.00 daily
Family Room, 3-6 persons	110.00 daily
Suites	85.00-140.00 daily

SUPPORT FACILITIES: The Academy has a full range of support and recreational facilities available. Snow skiing from 15 Dec-1 Mar, weather permitting.

ACTIVITIES: Many sightseeing and entertainment opportunities at the Academy and in nearby towns/cities. Golf, tennis, and swimming in pool in season.

RESTRICTIONS: No pets allowed.

NORTH CAROLINA

Cape Hatteras Coast Guard Recreation Area (NCO9R1)
Fifth Coast Guard District, Portsmouth, VA 23704-5004

Comm: 804-398-6475
FTS: 827-9475

LOCATION: On base. From US-158 or US-64, take NC-12 to Buxton, NC (approx 40 mi S of Nags Head). Check in with USCG Group OOD. RM: p-73, G/26. NMI: Located at Buxton, NC, CG Group. NMC: Elizabeth City, NC, 110 mi NW.

DESCRIPTION OF AREA: On the Outer Banks of NC in the Cape Hatteras National Seashore. Beautiful bathing beach and ocean fishing. Site of famous Wright brothers' first airplane flight, 50 mi N. Beach is 100 yards from facility. A sick bay with a corpsman is available for medical emergencies. Full range of military facilities available at Norfolk Naval Base, VA, 150 mi NW.

SEASON OF OPERATION: Year round.

ELIGIBILITY: Active/Retired/Reserve.

Cape Hatteras CG Rec Area, Cont'd

RESERVATIONS: Required with adv payment: 30-90 days in adv by mail. Address: Commander (aps), Fifth Coast Guard District, 431 Crawford St, Portsmouth, VA 23704-5004; Comm: 804-398-6475; FTS: 827-9475. Rec Area, Comm: 919-995-5881.

CAMPING FACILITIES: Available through National Park Service and KOA. Fees range from $8.00 up.

LODGING: All rooms are air-conditioned.

8 Units	Sleep 3 w/rollaway avail, comm kitchen	$15.00 daily
1 Suite	Sleeps 6, kitchen, color TV	22.00 daily
1 VIP Suite (E7+)	Sleeps 6, kitchen	30.00 daily

SUPPORT FACILITIES:

Beach	Chapel	Commissary
Exchange	Grills	Laundry (nearby)
Picnic Area	Sports Fields	Snack Bar (nearby)
Tennis Courts	Trails	Theater (summer)

There are marinas in Hatteras Inlet area, 11 mi S. Sunfish, surfboards, jet skis, fishing gear, and most items for water sports can be rented in the area.

ACTIVITIES:　　　　　Fishing　　　　Water Sports

RESTRICTIONS: No pets allowed. 7-day limit Jun-Aug. No open fires allowed. Kennels are located in general area. If pets are found in rooms, patron will be asked to leave and/or charged with cost of spraying rooms. This is a seasonal area for shops, stores, etc; many close during winter months.

Cherry Point MWR Fam-Camp
(NCO4R1)
Cherry Point Marine Corps Air Station, NC 28533-4297　　Comm: 919-466-1110　ATVN: 582-1110

LOCATION: On base. On NC-101, E of US-70, between New Bern and Morehead City. Upon arrival call Special Services Officer at 466-4232 (Station Duty Officer after hours) for additional info. RM: p-73, I/21. NMC: Jacksonville, 45 mi SW.

DESCRIPTION OF AREA: Located near Neuse Waterway and Outer Banks area; surrounded by Croatan National Forest. Fam-Camp within walking distance of full range of military facilities available on base.

SEASON OF OPERATION: Year round.

ELIGIBILITY: Active/Retired.

RESERVATIONS: Accepted 30 days in adv. Address: ITT Director, Postal Service Center 4297, Marine Corps Air Station, Cherry Point, NC 28533-4297. Comm: 919-466-2197; ATVN: 582-2197.

CAMP FACILITIES:	NO UNITS	HOOKUPS	FEE
Mobile Homes, 2 bdrm	5		$12.00 daily
Camper Spaces	50 Hardstand	W/S/E (110/220)	7.00 daily
Tent Spaces/Duck Pond Area	Wilderness	None	

Cherry Point MWR Fam-Camp, Cont'd

SUPPORT FACILITIES:

Boat Rental	Camper Rental	Camp Equip Rntl
Chapel	Gas	Golf
Grills	Laundry	Marina
Picnic Area	Pig Cooker Rntl	Racquetball
Sewage Dump Sta	Skeet Range	Snack Bar
Sports Fields	Stable	Tennis Courts

ACTIVITIES: Arts/Crafts   Fishing (lic)   Hunting (lic)

RESTRICTIONS: Small pets allowed on leash. There is usually a waiting list for the mobile homes as they are used for temporary housing. Boat rental available at Slocum Creek Marina only; permits must be obtained from Recreation Dept.

Fisher Fam-Camp (NC13R1)

Fort Fisher Air Force Station, NC 28449-5000

Comm: 919-458-8251
ATVN: 652-2212

LOCATION: On base. On US-421 S of Wilmington go through Carolina and Kure Beaches to Ft Fisher AFS. RM: p-73, M/18. NMC: Wilmington, 20 mi NW.

DESCRIPTION OF AREA: Ft Fisher is located on Pleasure Island. Its history dates back to before the Civil War. Beaches are within walking distance; parks, fishing and museums nearby. Wide range of military facilities avail on base.

SEASON OF OPERATION: Year round.

ELIGIBILITY: Active/Retired/DOD Civilians.

RESERVATIONS: Accepted only for AD and retired military. Address: 701 RADS, Ft Fisher AFS, NC 28449-5000. Comm: 919-458-8251-EX-263; ATVN: 652-2212-EX-263.

CAMPING FACILITIES:	NO UNITS	HOOKUPS	FEE
Camper Spaces	9 Hardstand	W/S/E (110)	$10.00 daily

SUPPORT FACILITIES:

Boat Launch	Camp Equip Rntl	Fishing Pier
Picnic Area	Racquetball	Rec Center
Restrooms	Sewage Dump Sta	Sports Fields
Swimming Pool	Tennis Courts	TV/Game Room

ACTIVITIES: Fishing   Rec Equip Avail   Swimming

RESTRICTIONS: Pets allowed on leash.

New River Recreation Beach Areas (NCO7R1)

New River Marine Corps Air Station
Jacksonville, NC 28545-5000

Comm: 919-451-6197
ATVN: 484-1110

LOCATION: On base. Off US-17 S of Jacksonville. RM: p-73, J/19. NMC. Jacksonville, 2 mi NE.

DESCRIPTION OF AREA: Situated along New River. Offers water sports, recreational and picnic areas. Wide range of military facilities available on base.

SEASON OF OPERATION: Year round.

ELIGIBILITY: Active/Retired.

New River Rec Beach Areas, Cont'd

RESERVATIONS: Accepted. Address: Recreation Area, Marine Corps Air Station, New River, Jacksonville, NC 28545-5000. Comm: 919-451-6578; ATVN: 484-6578; FTS: 919-451-6578.

CAMPING FACILITIES:	NO UNITS	HOOKUPS	FEE
Camper Spaces, max 20', self-contained veh	6 Primitive		$2.00 daily
Tent Spaces	Primitive	None	2.00 daily

SUPPORT FACILITIES:			
	Beach	Boat Launch	Boat Rental
	Boat Slip Rntl	Camp Equip Rntl	Gas
	Golf	Grills	Marina
	Picnic Area	Racquetball	Restrooms
	Showers	Sports Fields	Tennis Courts
	Trails	Water Sports Equipment Rental	
	Patio Room at Marina for parties, by reservation		

ACTIVITIES:			
	Boating	Fishing	Hunting (lic)
	Jet Skiing	Swimming	Water Skiing

RESTRICTIONS: Pets allowed. Call ahead to coordinate visit.

Onslow Beach Campsites and Recreation Area (NC14R1)
Camp Lejeune Marine Corps Base
Camp Lejeune, NC 28542-5001

Comm: 919-451-1113
ATVN: 484-1113
FTS: 676-1113

LOCATION: On base. Main gate is off NC-24 6 mi E of junction with US-17. Campsites are located approx 10 mi from gate on NC-172. Clearly marked. RM: p-73, J/19. NMC: Wilmington, 45 mi SW.

DESCRIPTION OF AREA: Located on an island between Intracoastal Waterway and Onslow Bay. Campsites are on beach or in wooded area. Many commercial fishing and beach areas are also available. ITT Office on base has information on rec activities and discount tickets. Full range of military facilities on base.

SEASON OF OPERATION: Year round.

ELIGIBILITY: Active/Retired.

RESERVATIONS: Accepted up to 30 days in adv. Address: Cabins and Cottages, Goettge Memorial Field House, Bldg 751, Special Services, Camp Lejeune, NC 28542-5001. Comm: (duty hrs) 919-451-5398; (after hrs-caretaker) 919-451-7473.

CAMP FACILITIES:	NO UNITS	HOOKUPS	FEE
Mobile Homes*	18		$6.00-19/summer;
Cabanas*	12		4.50-15/winter
Beach Houses*	2		
Camper Spaces (Area 1)	28	W/S/E (30A)	6.00 daily**
Camper Spaces (Area 2)	28	W/E (some 30A)	5.00 daily**
Tent Spaces (Area 3)	18	W/E	5.00 daily

*For use of AD on PCS orders only; fees apply to all three facilities.
**Rate applies for stays up to 7 days; daily rate increases for longer stays.

SUPPORT FACILITIES:			
	Bait/Tackle	Boat Launch	Bogey/Surf Boards
	Fishing Eq Rntl	Fishing Pier	Golf (on base)
	Grills	Ice	Marina (on base)

Onslow Beach Campsites & Rec Area, Cont'd

        Picnic Area   PX (small)   Restrooms
        Sewage Dump Sta   Showers   Snack Bar

Areas 1 and 3 have all the facilities listed above. Area 2 is located in a
wooded area and only has a restroom and showers.

ACTIVITIES: Deep-Sea Fishing Fishing   Swimming

RESTRICTIONS: Pets allowed on leash; must be under positive control.

Rogers Bay Family Campway (NC16R1)   Comm: 919-736-0000
Seymour Johnson Air Force Base, NC 27531-5225   ATVN: 488-1110

LOCATION: Off base. 6.5 mi N of Surf City on NC-210. RM: p-73, K/19. NMI: Camp
Lejeune, 15 mi N. NMC: Wilmington, 45 mi S.

DESCRIPTION OF AREA: Situated on SE shore of NC. Great area for water sports.
All sites are less than 50 yards from Atlantic Ocean in shaded area. Inland
Waterway on W side of campway. Full range of military fac at Camp Lejeune.

SEASON OF OPERATION: 1 March-30 November.

ELIGIBILITY: Active/Retired/DOD and NAF Civilians.

RESERVATIONS: Required, in person, with $20 dep: up to 60 days in adv for AD at
Seymour Johnson AFB; up to 30 days in adv for all others. Address: MWR Supply,
4 CSG/SSS, Seymour Johnson AFB, NC 27531-5225. Comm: 919-736-5263;
ATVN: 488-5263.

CAMP FACILITIES:	NO UNITS	HOOKUPS	FEE
Mobile Homes	6	W/S/E	$20-25 dly/150 wkly

SUPPORT FACILITIES: Beach (public)   Boat Launch   Chapel
                            Gas & LP   Laundry   Quick Shop
                            Restrooms   Sewage Dump Sta Showers
                            Teen Ctr (wknd)   Video Game Rm
                            There are several fishing piers in local area.

ACTIVITIES: Boating   Fishing   Swimming
                            Water Skiing

RESTRICTIONS: Pets allowed on leash; cannot remain in trailer unattended.
A cleaning deposit of $10 ($25 with pet) is required.

Seymour Johnson Fam-Camp (NC08R1)   Comm: 919-736-0000
Seymour Johnson Air Force Base, NC 27531-5004   ATVN: 488-1110

LOCATION: On base. Take US-70 to Seymour Johnson exit in Goldsboro. Take
Berkeley Blvd to base. RM: p-73, G/17. NMC: Raleigh, 50 mi NW.

DESCRIPTION OF AREA: Fam-Camp is surrounded by heavily forested areas and is
within walking distance of many of the military facilities available on base.

SEASON OF OPERATION: Year round.

ELIGIBILITY: Active/Retired.

Seymour Johnson Fam-Camp, Cont'd

RESERVATIONS: Accepted for TDY only. Address: Recreation Services, 4 CSG/SVH, Seymour Johnson AFB, NC 27531-5225. Comm: 919-736-6705; ATVN: 488-6705.

CAMPING FACILITIES:	NO UNITS	HOOKUPS	FEE
Camper Spaces	8 Hardstand	W/S/E	$6.00 daily

SUPPORT FACILITIES:			
	Chapel	Gas	Golf
	Grills	Laundry	Picnic Area
	Quick Shop	Racquetball	Rec Center
	Snack Bar	Sports Fields	Tennis Courts

ACTIVITIES:	Jogging	Rec Equip Avail

RESTRICTIONS: Pets allowed on leash only.

Smith Lake Army Travel Camp (NC12R1)
Fort Bragg, NC 28307-5000

Comm: 919-396-0011
ATVN: 236-0311

LOCATION: On post. From I-95 exit to NC-24 (Bragg Blvd). W to NC-210; N 4 mi to Smith Lake sign; L to camp. OR from US-401 (Fayetteville Bypass) exit to NC-210; N to Smith Lake. RM: p-72, H/13. NMC: Fayetteville, 15 mi SE.

DESCRIPTION OF AREA: JFK Special Warfare Museum and 82d Airborne Division Museum on post; Pinehurst Resort is nearby. Full range of mil fac on post.

SEASON OF OPERATION: Year round.

ELIGIBILITY: Active/Retired/Reserve on AD/DOD Civilians.

RESERVATIONS: No adv resv. Address: DPCA-CRD, Rec Branch, Outdoor Recreation, Smith Lake, Ft Bragg, NC 28307-5000. Comm: 919-396-5979.

CAMPING FACILITIES:	NO UNITS	HOOKUPS	FEE
Camper Spaces	13	W/S/E (110/30A)	$6.00 dly/30 wkly
Camper Spaces	11	W/E	5.00 dly/25 wkly

SUPPORT FACILITIES:			
	Beach	Boat Rental	Camp Equip Rntl
	Chapel	Gas	Golf
	Grills	Ice	Laundry
	Picnic Area	Restrooms	Sewage Dump Sta
	Showers		

ACTIVITIES:	Fishing (Oct-May/lic)	Swimming

RESTRICTIONS: Pets allowed on leash; must be kept under control at all times.

NORTH DAKOTA

Grand Forks Fam-Camp (ND01R3)
Grand Forks Air Force Base, ND 58205-5000

Comm: 701-747-3000
ATVN: 362-1110

LOCATION: On base. From I-29 take US-2 W for 14 mi to County Road B-3 (Emerado/Air Base); 1 mi to AFB. Check in at Billeting Office, Bldg 117. RM: p-71, D/15. NMC: Grand Forks, 20 mi SE.

Grand Forks Fam-Camp, Cont'd

DESCRIPTION OF AREA: Located in an open area. Wide variety of recreational activities available. 2-hour drive to Canada. Full range of mil fac on base.

SEASON OF OPERATION: 1 May-1 October.

ELIGIBILITY: Active/Retired/DOD Civilians.

RESERVATIONS: Accepted up to 30 days in adv. Address: Recreation Services, 321 SVS/SVH, Grand Forks Air Force Base, ND 58205-5000. Comm: 701-594-8431.

CAMPING FACILITIES:	NO UNITS	HOOKUPS	FEE
Camper Spaces	10 Hardstand	W/S/E	$5.00 daily

SUPPORT FACILITIES:			
	Boat Rental*	Camper Rental*	Camp Equip Rntl*
	Chapel	Fishing Eq Rntl	Gas
	Golf*	Grills	Picnic Area
	Restrooms	Showers	
	*on base		

ACTIVITIES:			
	Boating (nearby)	Fishing (lic)	Hiking
	Hunting (lic)		

RESTRICTIONS. Pets allowed on leash. 7-day limit.

OHIO

Wright-Patterson Fam-Camp (OHO3R2)

Wright-Patterson Air Force Base, OH 45433-5000

Comm: 513-257-1110
ATVN: 787-1110

LOCATION: On base. S of I-70, off Routes OH-4, OH-444; OR I-675 at Fairborn. Clearly marked. You must register at Outdoor Recreation Checkout, Bldg 95, Area C, before occupying Fam-Camp space. RM: p-76, SC/6. NMC: Dayton, 8 mi NE.

DESCRIPTION OF AREA: Home of world's largest and most complete military aviation museum and Wright Brothers Memorial. Full range of military fac on base.

SEASON OF OPERATION: Year round; no water in winter.

ELIGIBILITY: Active/Retired.

RESERVATIONS: No adv resv. AD on PCS are given priority. Address: Outdoor Recreation, 2750 ABW/SSRO, Bldg 95, Area C, Wright-Patterson AFB, OH 45433-5000. Comm: 513-257-4374; ATVN: 787-4374.

CAMPING FACILITIES:	NO UNITS	HOOKUPS	FEE
Camper Spaces	16-20	W/E	$5.00 daily
		E	3.00 daily
Tent Spaces	Unlimited	None	1.00 daily

SUPPORT FACILITIES:			
	Beach	Chapel	Gas
	Golf	Lakes (3)	Mini Marina
	Picnic Lodge/fee	Quick Shop	Racquet Sports
	Rec Center	Sewage Dump Sta	Snack Bar
	Sports Fields		

Wright-Patterson Fam-Camp, Cont'd

ACTIVITIES: Bicycling   Boating   Fishing/stocked
             Jogging   Kayaking   Rec Equip Avail
             Sailboarding

RESTRICTIONS: Pets allowed on leash. Fishing and hunting in the area near the campsites are not permitted except according to WPAFBR 126-2.

OKLAHOMA

Altus Fam-Camp (OKO6R3)
Altus Air Force Base, OK 73523-5000

Comm: 405-481-8100
ATVN: 866-1110

LOCATION: On base. Located off US-62 S of I-40 and W of I-44. From US-62 traveling W from Lawton, turn R at 1st traffic light in Altus and follow road to main gate NE of Falcon Rd. RM: p-78, J/12. NMC: Lawton, 56 mi E.

DESCRIPTION OF AREA: The Museum of the Western Prairie (history of SW Oklahoma) is located 5 min from base. Outdoor rec area at Lake Altus is 17 mi N on US-283. Full range of military facilities available on base.

SEASON OF OPERATION: Year round.

ELIGIBILITY: Active/Retired/DOD Civilians.

RESERVATIONS: Accepted. Address: Altus AFB Fam-Camp, 443 ABG/SSR, Altus AFB, OK 73523-5000. Comm: 405-481-6420, ATVN: 866-6420.

CAMPING FACILITIES:	NO UNITS	HOOKUPS	FEE
Camper Spaces	4	W/E	$3 dly/$5 key dep
	3	None	3 dly/$5 key dep

SUPPORT FACILITIES:			
	Chapel	Family Bowling	Gas
	Golf (9 holes)	Picnic Area	Racquet Sports
	Restrooms	Sewage Dump Sta	Showers
	Sports Fields		

ACTIVITIES:			
	Basketball	Jogging	Rec Equip Avail
	Soccer	Softball	Tennis

RESTRICTIONS: Pets allowed on leash. Signature required for action to be taken in the event of severe weather.

Lake Elmer Thomas Recreation Area (OKO3R3)
Fort Sill, OK 73503-5100

Comm: 405-351-8111
ATVN: 639-8111

LOCATION: On post. From I-44 at Lawton, take US-62/277 4 mi NW to post. Clearly marked. RM: p-79, J/14. NMC: Lawton, 11 mi SE.

DESCRIPTION OF AREA: Lake Elmer Thomas Rec Area is located in NW corner of Ft Sill 11 mi from main post. It is situated on approx 250 acres and shares the lake with the Wichita Mountains Wildlife Refuge featuring buffalo, elk and longhorn cattle in their natural habitat. Unfortunately, the dam has been deemed unsafe and the lake is being drained. Only sewer and electric hookups are available and campers should be as fully self-contained as possible. (For more info contact Outdoor Rec, Ft Sill.) Full range of military fac on post.

SEASON OF OPERATION: Year round.

ELIGIBILITY: Active/Retired.

RESERVATIONS: Accepted: Up to 30 days in adv for AD; up to 21 days in adv for Retired. Address: LETRA, US Army Field Artillery Center and Ft Sill, Ft Sill, OK 73503-5100. Comm: 405-351-2025; ATVN: 639-2025.

CAMPING FACILITIES:	NO UNITS	HOOKUPS	FEE
Camper Spaces	14 Hardstand	S/E (110/30A)	$6.00 daily
Camper Spaces, pull thru	7	S/E (110/30A)	6.00 daily
Tent Spaces	15	None	3.00 daily

SUPPORT FACILITIES:		
Bicycle Rental	Camp Equip Rntl	Grills
Nature Trails	Picnic Area	Restrooms
Sewage Dump Sta		

ACTIVITIES:		
Bicycling	Hiking	

RESTRICTIONS: Pets allowed on leash; must be attended at all times.

Murphy's Meadow (OKO7R3)

McAlester Army Ammunition Plant, OK 74501-5000

Comm: 918-421-2011
ATVN: 956-6011

LOCATION: On post. Off US-69 S of McAlester. RM: p-79, I/21. NMC: Tulsa, 90 mi N.

DESCRIPTION OF AREA: Located in SE Oklahoma on the shores of Brown Lake. Mostly rolling pasture land with timber-covered hills and creek bottoms. Great area for vacationing; many lakes offer fishing, boating and water sports. 30-min drive to Lake Eufaula, 3d largest artificial lake in the US. The small community of Savannah, approx 2 mi away, provides the essentials not available on post. Limited military fac on post are within walking distance of camp; full range of faciities available at Tinker AFB, 116 mi NW.

SEASON OF OPERATION: 15 January-1 October

ELIGIBILITY: Active/Retired/DOD Civilians.

RESERVATIONS: Recommended. Address: McAlester Army Ammunition Plant, ATTN: SMCMC-PTC, McAlester, OK 74501-5000. Comm: 918-421-2780/2673; ATVN: 956-2780.

CAMPING FACILITIES:	NO UNITS	HOOKUPS	FEE
Camper Spaces	17 Hardstand	W/E	$5.00 daily
Camper Spaces	17 Overflow	W/E	5.00 daily
Tent & Camper Spaces	Primitive	None	3.00 daily

SUPPORT FACILITIES:		
Auto Hobby Shop	Boat Launch	Boat Rental
Golf Driv Range	Grills	Health Clinic
Pavilions	Picnic Area	Playground
PX (small)	Restrooms*	Sewage Dump Sta
Showers*	Softball Field	Tennis Court
*Equipped for handicapped		

ACTIVITIES:		
Boating	Fishing (lic)	Rec Equip Avail

RESTRICTIONS: No pets allowed. No swimming. No water skiing. Nonresidents do not require a fishing license for overnight stay.

Tinker Fam-Camp (OKO8R3)
Tinker Air Force Base, OK 73145-5000

Comm: 405-734-1110
ATVN: 884-1110

LOCATION: On base. Off I-40 (Tinker Expressway) 10 mi E of Oklahoma City. Enter Gate 1 off Air Depot Blvd. Ask directions to Outdoor Recreation. RM: p-78, O/6. NMC: Oklahoma City, 10 mi W.

DESCRIPTION OF AREA: Located in the midst of Oklahoma City/Norman metropolitan area. Fam-Camp is situated in well-developed recreation area offering three fishing ponds. Full range of military facilities available on base.

SEASON OF OPERATION: Year round.

ELIGIBILITY: Active/Retired/DOD Civilians.

RESERVATIONS: No adv resv. Address: Outdoor Recreation, 2854 ABG/SSRR, Tinker AFB, OK 73145-5000. Comm: 405-734-2289; ATVN: 884-2289.

CAMPING FACILITIES:	NO UNITS	HOOKUPS	FEE
Camper Spaces	29	W/E	$6.00-7.00 daily
Tent Spaces	10	None	2.00 daily

SUPPORT FACILITIES:			
	Chapel	Gas	Golf
	Laundry	Picnic Areas	Playgrounds
	Restrooms	Sewage Dump Sta	Showers

ACTIVITIES: Fishing

RESTRICTIONS: No swimming or boating in ponds.

OREGON

-None-

PENNSYLVANIA

Letterkenny Army Travel Camp (PA1OR1)
Letterkenny Army Depot, PA 17201-4150

Comm: 717-267-8111
ATVN: 570-1110

LOCATION: On post. From I-81 take exit 8. W on PA-997 to gate 6. Clearly marked with signs for depot. Check in at Travel Camp (located along Pennsylvania Ave near gate 17) during duty hours; at Security Bldg after hours. RM: p-85, EU/1. NMC: Harrisburg, 40 mi NE.

DESCRIPTION OF AREA: Beautiful Cumberland Valley of Pennsylvania. Near historic Gettysburg and Antietam Battlefields and Caledonia State Park. Some mil fac on base within walking distance; full range avail at Carlisle Barracks, 30 mi N.

SEASON OF OPERATION: 1 April-31 October.

ELIGIBILITY: Active/Retired/DOD Civilians at Letterkenny.

RESERVATIONS: Accepted. Address: Letterkenny Army Depot, ATTN: SDSLE-BAR, Chambersburg, PA 17201-4150. Comm: 717-267-9494/8666; ATVN: 570-9494/8666.

CAMPING FACILITIES:	NO UNITS	HOOKUPS	FEE
Camper Spaces	9 Concrete	None*	$4.00-5.00 daily
Tent Spaces	Many	None*	4.00-5.00 daily

*Access to water and electricity at Rec Bldg.

SUPPORT FACILITIES:			
	Chapel	Fitness Trail	Game Room
	Golf	Grills	Laundry
	Picnic Area	Playground	Rec Bldg
	Rec Equip Rntl	Restrooms	Sewage Dump Sta
	Showers		

ACTIVITIES:			
	Boating	Fishing	Hunting (lic)
	Jogging	Swimming	

RESTRICTIONS: Pets allowed on leash.

RHODE ISLAND

-None-

SOUTH CAROLINA

Charleston Fam-Camp (SC12R1)
Charleston Air Force Base, SC 29404-5000

Comm: 803-554-0230
ATVN: 583-0111

LOCATION: On base. From I-26 exit E to West Aviation Ave; continue through 2d traffic light; R and follow road around end of runway to gate. RM: p-88, L/16. NMC: Charleston, 5 mi SE.

DESCRIPTION OF AREA: Situated near wooded picnic area in one of the country's most picturesque and historic seaport cities. Full range of mil fac on base.

SEASON OF OPERATION: Year round.

ELIGIBILITY: Active/Retired/DOD Civilians.

RESERVATIONS: No adv resv. Address: Recreation Services, 437 ABG/SSRR, Charleston AFB, SC 29404-5000. Comm: 803-554-2280; ATVN: 583-2280.

CAMPING FACILITIES:	NO UNITS	HOOKUPS	FEE
Camper Spaces	5 Hardstand	W/E	$5.00-7.00 daily
Camper Spaces	2 Hardstand	E	5.00-7.00 daily

SUPPORT FACILITIES:			
	Boat Rental	Chapel	Grills
	Picnic Area	Playground	Restrooms
	Sewage Dump Sta	Showers	Nature Trails

ACTIVITIES:			
	Fishing	Rec Equip Avail	Swimming

RESTRICTIONS: Pets allowed. Fam-Camp parking is not authorized for Space-A travelers. (Contact Aerial Port Squadron, Comm: 803-554-2280, about parking in a secured lot.)

Folly Beach Recreation Facility (SC15R1)
Coast Guard Group, Charleston, SC 29401-5000

Comm: 803-724-7600
FTS: 724-7600

LOCATION: Off base. On NE end of Folly Island. From US-17 S of Charleston take SC-171 S through James Island to L at first traffic light on Folly Beach. Road ends at Loran Station. RM: p-88, J/12. NMI: Charleston Naval Base, 14 mi NW. NMC: Charleston, 9 mi NW.

DESCRIPTION OF AREA: Folly Beach is a quiet vacation island with many summer homes dotting the beach front. Short drive to the historic and beautiful city of Charleston. Full range of military facilities avail at Charleston Naval Base.

SUPPORT FACILITIES: 15 March-15 December.

ELIGIBILITY: Active/Retired/Reserve.

RESERVATIONS: Req, by application only, with adv payment, at least 6 weeks in adv. Address: Commander, Coast Guard Group, 196 Tradd St, Charleston, SC 29401-5000, ATTN: Cottage Reservations. Comm: 803-724-7600; FTS: 724-7600.

LODGING: Two mobile homes, 2 bdrm, 2 bath, dbl bed & 2 bunk beds, slp 6 adults. Completely furnished, A/C, W/D, color TV.
FEE: $10.00-$20.00, depending on rank.

ACTIVITIES:

Crabbing	Fishing	Hiking
Picnicking	Surfing	Swimming

RESTRICTIONS: No pets allowed.

Lake Wateree Recreation Area and Fam-Camp (SCO5R1)
Shaw Air Force Base, SC 29152-5000

Comm: 803-668-8110
ATVN: 965-1110

LOCATION: Off base. Off SC-97 NW of Camden. Accessible from I-77 and I-20. RM: p-88, D/9-10. NMI: Ft Jackson, 25 mi S. NMC: Columbia, 25 mi S.

DESCRIPTION OF AREA: Situated in peaceful, quiet, 23-acre, wooded area bordering Lake Wateree approx 34 mi from Shaw AFB. Full range of military facilities available at Ft Jackson and Shaw AFB.

SEASON OF OPERATION: Year round.

ELIGIBILITY: Active/Retired/DOD Civilians.

RESERVATIONS: Required. Address: Recreation Service, Bldg 1411, 363 CSG/SSRR, Shaw Air Force Base, SC 29152-5000. Comm: 803-668-2205; ATVN: 965-2205.

CAMP FACILITIES:	NO UNITS	HOOKUPS	FEE
Cabins, 2 & 3 bdrm	4		$35-55 daily
Mobile Homes, 2 & 3 bdrm	14		20-25 daily
Camper Spaces	10	E	10.00 daily
Tent Spaces	10	E	10.00 daily

SUPPORT FACILITIES:		
Boat Launch	Boat Rental	Grills
Ice	Marina	Picnic Area
Playground	Restrooms	Sewage Dump Sta
Showers	Water Sports Equipment Rental	

Lake Wateree Rec Area & Fam-Camp, Cont'd

ACTIVITIES: Fishing (lic)   Water Skiing

RESTRICTIONS: Pets allowed on leash. No swimming.

Myrtle Beach AF Fam-Camp (SC13R1)

Myrtle Beach Air Force Base, SC 29579-5000

Comm: 803-238-7211
ATVN: 748-7211

LOCATION: On base. From I-95 exit E on US-501, R on US-17 (Business) to AFB. Clearly marked. RM: p-88, F/15. NMC: Myrtle Beach, 1 mi N.

DESCRIPTION OF AREA: Located in the heart of South Carolina's Atlantic Ocean beaches N of Charleston. Fam-Camp is situated near main gate; ocean is 1,000 yards away. Commercial fishing pier and other off-base rec facilities readily accessible. Full range of military facilities available on base.

SEASON OF OPERATION: Year round.

ELIGIBILITY: Active/Retired/DOD Civilians.

RESERVATIONS: Accepted up to 30 days in adv by mail with $10 dep. (Mobile homes require $30 dep.) Address: Recreation Services, 354 CSG/SSRO, Myrtle Beach AFB, SC 29579-5000. Comm: 803-238-7708; ATVN: 748-7708.

CAMPING FACILITIES:	NO UNITS	HOOKUPS	FEE
Mobile Homes	14	W/S/CTV/E	$19-30 daily
Camper Spaces	26 Hardstand	W/CTV/E (110)	7-9 daily
Tent Spaces	30 Improved	None	3-4 daily

SUPPORT FACILITIES:			
	Archery	Beach	Chapel
	Deep-Sea Fishing	Gas	Golf
	Laundry	Picnic Pav/fee	Racquetball
	Rec Center	Restrooms	Sewage Dump Sta
	Showers	Skeet/Trap Range	Sports Fields
	Swimming Pools	Tennis Courts	Trail

ACTIVITIES:	Boating	Fishing	Rec Equip Avail
	Swimming		

RESTRICTIONS: No pets allowed in mobile homes; allowed on leash in other areas.

Myrtle Beach Army Fam-Camp (SC14R1)

Fort Bragg, NC 28307-5000

Comm: 919-396-0011
ATVN: 236-0311

LOCATION: Off post. On Myrtle Beach AFB, SC. From I-95 W of Florence, SC, exit E on US-501; R on US-17 (Business) to Myrtle Beach AFB, SC. Clearly marked. Fam-Camp is near the main gate. RM: p-88, F/15. NMC: Myrtle Beach, SC, 1 mi N.

DESCRIPTION OF AREA: Co-located with Myrtle Beach AFB Fam-Camp in the heart of South Carolina's beaches N of Charleston. Ocean is 1,000 yards away. Commercial fishing pier and other off-base recreational facilities readily accessible. Full range of military facilities available on base.

SEASON OF OPERATION: Year round.

ELIGIBILITY: Active/Retired.

Myrtle Beach Army Fam-Camp, Cont'd

RESERVATIONS: Req with $30 deposit. Address: Morale Support Activities, Rec Issue Center, Bldg 2-S-4309, Ft Bragg, NC 28307-5000. Comm: 919-396-7520.

CAMP FACILITIES:	NO UNITS	HOOKUPS	FEES
Resort Travel Trailers	11	Self-contained	$30.00 daily

24', A/C; bring pots, pans, dishes, utensils, bed linens and towels.

SUPPORT FACILITIES:			
	Archery	Beach	Chapel
	Deep-Sea Fishing	Gas	Golf
	Laundry	Pavilion/fee	Picnic Area
	Rec Center	Restrooms	Sewage Dump Sta
	Showers	Skeet/Trap Range	Sports Fields
	Tennis Courts	Trail	

ACTIVITIES:	Fishing	Rec Equip Avail	Swimming

RESTRICTIONS: No pets allowed.

Short Stay (SCO2R1)
Charleston Naval Base, SC 29408-5000

Comm: 803-743-4111
ATVN: 563-4111
FTS: 679-4111

LOCATION: Off base. On Lake Moultrie. Take US-52 N from Charleston. Follow the signs. RM: p-88, H/12. NMI: Charleston NB, 35 mi S. NMC: Charleston, 30 mi S.

DESCRIPTION OF AREA: Situated on a 55-acre peninsula at southern tip of Lake Moultrie. Excellent freshwater fishing. Children's and family programs avail during the summer months. Trailers fully equipped except for cooking and eating utensils. Full range of military facilities available at Charleston NB.

SEASON OF OPERATION: Year round.

ELIGIBILITY: Active/Retired/DOD Civilians. Some limitations in summer months for DOD Civilians.

RESERVATIONS: Required. Address: ITT Office, Naval Base (Code 15), Charleston, SC 29408-5000. Comm: 803-743-5233; ATVN: 794-5233. For information call the rec area, Comm: 803-761-8353.

CAMP FACILITIES:	NO UNITS	HOOKUPS	FEE
Cabins, furn	6		$29-31 daily
Mobile Homes, 3 bdrm	Total		18-26 daily
Mobile Homes, 2 bdrm	of 43		15-17 daily
Camper Spaces	22 Hardstand	W/E (110/15A)	6.00-6.50 daily
Camper & Tent Spaces	80 Primitive	None	3.50-4.00 daily

SUPPORT FACILITIES:			
	Bait/Tackle	Beach	Boat Rental
	Conv Store	Game Room	Gas
	Fishing Piers	Grills	Ice
	Laundry	Marina	Picnic Area
	Playground	Restrooms	Sewage Dump Sta
	Showers	Snack Bar	TV Rental

ACTIVITIES:	Boat Tours	Fishing	Rec Equip Avail
	Swimming		

RESTRICTIONS: No pets allowed. Nominal admission charge during summer.

SOUTH CAROLINA
Weston Lake Recreation Area
and Travel Camp (SCO3R1)
Fort Jackson, SC 29207-5000

Comm: 803-751-7511
ATVN: 734-1110

LOCATION: On post. Exit from I-20 N of Fort; OR from US-76/378 S of Fort; OR from US-601 E of Fort. Ft Jackson is located 12 mi E of Columbia on SC-262 (Leesburg Rd). Travel camp is 8 mi E of main post on SC-262. RM: p-88, E/9. NMC: Columbia, 12 mi SW.

DESCRIPTION OF AREA: Located adjacent to 240-acre lake. Site offers wide range of outdoor activities. Museum and Ernie Pyle Media Center located on post. Columbia, the state capital, offers varied sightseeing, including zoo, Capitol and Coliseum. Full range of military facilities available on post.

SEASON OF OPERATION: Year round.

ELIGIBILITY: Active/Retired/DOD Civilians.

RESERVATIONS: No adv resv. Address: Outdoor Recreation Div, Bldg 3392, Ft Jackson, SC 29207-5000. Comm: 803-751-6013; ATVN: 734-6013.

CAMP FACILITIES:	NO UNITS	HOOKUPS	FEE
Cabins, 2 bdrm	4		$25.00 daily
Cabin, 3 bdrm, new	1		40.00 daily
Cabin, 4 bdrm	1		30.00 daily
Duplex, 1 bdrm	1		20.00 daily
Camper Spaces	6 Hardstand	W/S/E	8.00 daily
Camper Spaces	15 Hardstand	W/E	5.50 daily
Tent Spaces	10 Improved	W/E	4.00 daily

SUPPORT FACILITIES:			
	Archery	Beach	Boat Rental
	Gas	Golf	Marina
	Miniature Golf	Picnic Area	Sewage Dump Sta
	Skeet Range	Snack Bar (May-Aug)	
	Sports Fields	Trails	

ACTIVITIES:			
	Boating	Fishing	Hunting
	Jet Ski	Rec Equip Avail	Swimming (May-Sep)

RESTRICTIONS: No pets allowed. Boat rental and hunting require state and post permits. Nominal fee charged for use of recreation area.

SOUTH DAKOTA

Ellsworth AFB Fam-Camp (SDO2R3)
Ellsworth Air Force Base, SD 57706-5000

Comm: 605-385-1000
ATVN: 675-1110

LOCATION: On base. N of I-90, 10 mi NE of Rapid City. Check in at Fam-Camp, inside and R of school gate entrance. RM: p-89, F/4. NMC: Rapid City, 10 mi SW.

DESCRIPTION OF AREA: Located in the SW corner of SD. Black Hills National Forest, Mount Rushmore National Memorial and Badlands National Park are an easy drive away. Full range of military facilities available on base.

SEASON OF OPERATION: 1 May-15 October.

ELIGIBILITY: Active/Retired/DOD and NAF Civilians.

Ellsworth AFB Fam-Camp, Cont'd

RESERVATIONS: Accepted. Address: Ellsworth Fam-Camp, Bldg 88421, 44 CSG/SSRO, Ellsworth AFB, SD 57706-5000. Comm: 605-385-2996/2997; ATVN: 675-2996/2997.

CAMPING FACILITIES:	NO UNITS	HOOKUPS	FEE
Camper Spaces	14 Hardstand	W/E (110)	$8.00 daily
Tent Spaces	10 Open	None	5.00 daily

SUPPORT FACILITIES:			
	Chapel	Grills	Laundry
	Picnic Areas	Playgrounds	Rec Equip Rntl
	Restrooms	Sewage Dump Sta	Showers

ACTIVITIES:			
	Fishing (lic)	Hiking	Hunting (lic)
	Snow Skiing	Water Skiing	

RESTRICTIONS: Pets allowed on leash. 7-day limit. No open fires.

TENNESSEE

Arnold Fam-Camp (TNO3R2)
Arnold Air Force Station, TN 37389-5000

Comm: 615-454-3000
ATVN: 340-3000

LOCATION: On base. Take Arnold Engineering Development Center (AEDC) exit 117 from I-24; turn W, traveling toward Tullahoma about 5 mi until passing gate 2; L on Pump Station Rd to flashing caution light; R to top of hill and another flashing light; turn L. Hobby Shop is first Bldg on R; Fam-Camp is to the L on Woods Reservoir. RM: p-91, G/16. NMC: Chattanooga, 60 mi SE, and Nashville, 60 mi NW.

DESCRIPTION OF AREA: Terrain is flat to rolling hills. Area offers a variety of recreational and historical sites within 70-mi radius of the base. Tim's Ford State Park and Lake, and Old Stone Fort State Park are located within a 45-min drive. Jack Daniel's Distillery in Lynchburg and George Dickle Distillery in Tullahoma offer tours. Full range of military facilities available on base.

SEASON OF OPERATION: 1 April-1 October (depending on the weather).

ELIGIBILITY: Active/Retired/Civ Employees at Arnold AFS/AEDC Camper Club.

RESERVATIONS: Required with security dep within 72 hrs of phone resv (M-F). Address: Hobby Shop's-Fam Camp, 4960 ABS/SSR, Arnold AFB, TN 37389-5000. Comm: 615-454-6084; ATVN: 340-6084.

CAMPING FACILITIES:	NO UNITS	HOOKUPS	FEE
Camper Spaces	13 under 15'	W/E (110)	$4.00 daily
	4 15'-20'	W/E (110)	5.00 daily
	5 20'-25'	W/E (110)	5.00 daily

SUPPORT FACILITIES:			
	Beach	Boat Rental	Golf (9 holes)
	Hobby Shop	Marina	Picnic Areas
	Playground	Racquet Sports	Rec Equip Rntl
	Restrooms	Showers	Snack Bar
	Sewage Dump Sta	Swimming Pools	Trails

ACTIVITIES:			
	Boating	Fishing (lic)	Hunting (lic)
	Softball	Swimming	Water Skiing

RESTRICTIONS: Pets allowed on leash. No pets in rec center.

Navy Lake Recreation Area (TN04R2)
Memphis Naval Air Station
Millington, TN 38054-5000

Comm: 901-872-5111
ATVN: 966-5111

LOCATION: On base. From US-51 in Millington exit to Navy Road; E to main gate (first on R). RM: p-90, G/3. NMC: Memphis, 20 mi SW.

DESCRIPTION OF AREA: There are 2 lakes and 14 picnic areas with cabanas and barbecue facilities. The lakes are stocked with bass, bream, catfish and crappie. Full range of military facilities available on base.

SEASON OF OPERATION: Year round.

ELIGIBILITY: Active/Retired/DOD Civilians.

RESERVATIONS: No resv req. Address: Recreational Services, NAS Memphis, Millington, TN 38054-5000. Comm: 901-872-1573; ATVN: 966-5163.

CAMPING FACILITIES:	NO UNITS	HOOKUPS	FEE
Camper Spaces	12	None	$3.00 daily
Tent Spaces			3.00 daily

SUPPORT FACILITIES:			
	Boat Rental	Ice	Picnic Areas
	Playgrounds	Rec Equip Rntl	Rec/TV Room
	Restrooms	Sewage Dump Sta	Showers
	Snack Bar	Sports Fields	Stables
	Vending Machines		

ACTIVITIES:			
	Boating	Canoeing	Fishing
	Softball	Volleyball	

RESTRICTIONS: Pets allowed on leash.

TEXAS

Belton Lake Recreation Area (TX07R3)
Fort Hood, TX 76544-5000

Comm: 817-287/288-1110
ATVN: 737/738-2131

LOCATION: On post. 14 mi NE of main post area. From I-35 take Killeen/Ft Hood exit; W on US-190; R on Hood Rd; R on North Ave; L on Martin Dr; R on N Nolan Rd. Area marked. RM: p-94, EJ/7. NMC: Austin, 60 mi S.

DESCRIPTION OF AREA: A very large area located along Belton Lake. Recreational opportunities include hiking in nearby wooded areas and a wide variety of water sports. Belton Lake is known for black and white bass and crappie. Full range of military facilities available on post.

SEASON OF OPERATION: Year round. Beach: 15 April-15 October.

ELIGIBILITY: Active/Retired/DOD Civilians currently employed.

RESERVATIONS: Required with $25 deposit for cottages. Address: Community Recreation Div, AFZF-PA-CRD-OR-BLORA, Ft Hood, TX 76544-5056. Comm: 817-287-8303; ATVN: 737-8303.

Belton Lake Rec Area, Cont'd

CAMP FACILITIES:	NO UNITS	HOOKUPS	FEE
Cottages, 1 bdrm, slp 4; A/C, TV; furn, except utensils, towels, soap	10		$15-20 dly/winter 20-25 dly/summer
Camper Spaces	11 Hardstand	W/S/E	4/winter;6/sumr
Camper Spaces	53 Hardstand	W/E	4/winter;6/sumr
Tent Spaces	6 Primitive	W/E	4/winter;6/sumr
Camper & Tent Spaces	20 Primitive	None	1/tent;4/RV dly

SUPPORT FACILITIES:			
	Boat Launch	Boat Rental	Fishing Marina
	Chapel (on post)	Grills	Ice
	Laundry	Marina	Nature Trail
	Party Boat	Pavilions (resv)	Picnic Area
	Playground	Restrooms	Sewage Dump Sta
	Showers	Snack Bar	Sports Fields
	Water Slide	Water Sports	Equipment Rental

ACTIVITIES:			
	Fishing (lic)	Hunting* (lic)	Jet Skiing
	Rec Equip Avail	Swimming	Water Skiing

*Annual deer harvest: Oct-Nov, bow and shotgun; Nov-Dec, rifle (guided hunt). Wild turkey hunt: April. Dove and quail: Sep.

RESTRICTIONS: Pets must be on leash at all times; not allowed in cottages or in swimming area; owner must clean up after pets; owner will be assessed charges for any damage incurred by pets. No hunting in park. Swimming only at Sierra Beach while lifeguards are on duty. Nominal user fee for use of park.

Bliss Family Campgrounds (TX31R3)
Fort Bliss, TX 79916-6200

Comm: 915-568-2121
ATVN: 978-0831

LOCATION: On post. From E on I-10 take airport exit to Robert E Lee entrance of Ft Bliss; R at 1st traffic light on Jeb Stuart Rd, past Hahn Rd to Campgrounds. From W on I-10 take US-54 E to Forrest Rd exit and enter Ft Bliss; L at 5th traffic light on Jeb Stuart Rd to Campgrounds. RM: p-93, WX/4. NMC: El Paso, adjacent.

DESCRIPTION OF AREA: In west Texas near Rio Grande River. Carlsbad Caverns National Park, easy drive W. White Sands National Monument, 2-hr drive N. Ciudad Juarez, Mexico's largest border city, is a short distance across Rio Grande River. 4 museums on post. Full range of military facilities on post.

SEASON OF OPERATION: Year round.

ELIGIBILITY: Active/Retired/DOD Civilians at Fort Bliss.

RESERVATIONS: No adv resv. Address: Fort Bliss Family Campground, Outdoor Recreation Equipment Center, Bldg 645N, Fort Bliss, TX 79916-5135. Comm: 915-568-4693; ATVN: 978-4693.

CAMPING FACILITIES:	NO UNITS	HOOKUPS	FEE
Camper Spaces	40 Gravel	W/E (110)	$7.00 daily
Camper & Tent Spaces	50	None	2.00 daily

SUPPORT FACILITIES:			
	Chapel	Gas	Golf
	Grills	Laundry	Miniature Golf
	Pavilion	Picnic Area	Playground
	Restrooms	Sewage Dump Sta	Showers
	Sports Fields		

Bliss Family Campgrounds, Cont'd

ACTIVITIES: Horseshoes   Rec Equip Avail Swimming

RESTRICTIONS: Pets allowed on leash only; owner must clean up after pets. Check-out time is 1300 hrs. 14-day limit; may be extended if space is available on scheduled date of departure. No open fires.

Canyon Lake Army Recreation Area (TX29R3)
Fort Sam Houston, TX 78234-5000   **Comm: 512-221-1211**
               ATVN: 471-1110

LOCATION: Off post. From I-35 N of San Antonio near New Braunfels, take FM-306 W for approx 15 mi to Jacobs Creek Park. Sign on R side on Jacobs Creek Park Rd. RM: p-95, EV/16. NMI: Ft Sam Houston, 50 mi S. NMC: San Antonio, 50 mi S.

DESCRIPTION OF AREA: Located in terrain that is characteristically hilly and rocky, with cedar and oak trees. Recreation area has 300 feet of sandy beach and a .25-acre marina. Full range of military facilities at Ft Sam Houston.

SEASON OF OPERATION: Year round.

ELIGIBILITY: Active/Retired/DOD Civilians at Ft Sam Houston.

RESERVATIONS: Required: in person only for patrons in San Antonio area; by phone for others; up to 28 days in adv for AD at Ft Sam Houston; up to 7 days in adv for all others. Address: Leisure Sales and Service, Bldg 2797, Outdoor Recreation Branch, Ft Sam Houston, TX 78234-5000. Comm: 512-221-3703/2333; ATVN: 471-3703/2333.

CAMP FACILITIES:	<u>NO</u> UNITS	HOOKUPS	<u>FEE</u>
Mobile Homes, 3 bdrm furn, exc towels, soap	32		$13-20 daily*
Camper Spaces	32 Hardstand	W/E (110/30A)	4.00 daily
Tent Spaces	Open	None	2.00 daily

*Includes 2 persons; $1 each add person.

SUPPORT FACILITIES:		
Boat Launch	Boat Rental	Fishing Tackle
Grills	Marina	Picnic Area
Playground	PX (small)	Restrooms
Sewage Dump Sta	Showers	TV Room

ACTIVITIES:		
Boating	Fishing	Hiking
Swimming	Water Skiing	

RESTRICTIONS: Pets allowed on leash. Open fires in designated areas only. Nominal entrance fee to rec area.

Carswell Fam-Camp (TX30R3)
Carswell Air Force Base, TX 76127-5000   **Comm: 817-782-5000**
               ATVN: 739-1110

LOCATION: On base. From I-30 take Carswell AFB/Horne St exit (TX-183). Follow signs to main gate. Fam-Camp located on Roaring Springs Rd by main gate. Register at Billeting Office, Bldg 3140. RM: p-96, D/2. NMC: Fort Worth, 7 mi E.

DESCRIPTION OF AREA. Located on installation in Dallas-Ft Worth metropolitan area just NW of downtown Ft Worth. Situated in residential area of installation, adjacent to golf course. Eagle Mountain Lake and Lake Worth recreation complex adjacent to installation. Full range of military facilities on base.

Carswell Fam Camp, Cont'd

SEASON OF OPERATION: Year round.

ELIGIBILITY: Active/Retired/DOD Civilians.

RESERVATIONS: No adv resv. Address: Billeting Office, Bldg 3140, Carswell AFB, TX 76127-5000. Comm: 817-782-5274; ATVN: 739-5274.

CAMPING FACILITIES:	NO UNITS	HOOKUPS	FEE
Camper Spaces self-contained	10 Gravel	W/S/E (220)	$5.00 daily

SUPPORT FACILITIES:	Chapel	Golf	Marina

ACTIVITIES:	Fishing (lic)	Water Sports

RESTRICTIONS: Pets allowed on leash. 7-day limit.

Circle B Recreation Area (TXO1R3)
Bergstrom Air Force Base, TX 78743-5000

Comm: 512-479-4100
ATVN: 685-1110

LOCATION: Off base. From I-35 take TX-71 W to TX FM-2322 to Pace Bend County Park. RM: p-94, EL/6. NMI: Bergstrom AFB, 40 mi SE. NMC: Austin, 38 mi SE.

DESCRIPTION OF AREA: The recreation area is in the heart of the beautiful hill country on Lake Travis within Travis County's Pace Bend Park. Patrons wishing to utilize only the Circle B area will not be charged an entrance fee. Patrons who wish to swim must use Pace Bend Park. Lake Travis is a flood control lake subject to severe fluctuations in water level. Areas which had been safe for skiing, diving or boating may on your next visit prove to be extremely hazardous to health, life and sporting property. Full range of military facilities available at Bergstrom AFB.

SEASON OF OPERATION: Year round.

ELIGIBILITY: Active/Retired/DOD Civilians at Bergstrom AFB.

RESERVATIONS: Required for mobile homes only. Address: 67 CSG/SSRR, Bergstrom AFB, TX 78743-5000. Comm: 512-369-2838; ATVN: 685-2838. Rec area address: Circle B Rec Area, Rt 1, Box 30, Spicewood, TX 78669-5000. Comm: 512-264-1752.

CAMPING FACILITIES:	NO UNITS	HOOKUPS	FEE
Mobile Homes, 2 bdrm; furn, except towels	8		$15-20 daily
Camper Spaces	12	W/E	5.00 daily
Camper Spaces	24	None	2.00 daily

SUPPORT FACILITIES:	Boat Launch/fee	Boat Rental	Marina
	Pavilions	Picnic Areas	Playgrounds
	Restrooms	Quick Shop	Sewage Dump Sta
	Showers		

ACTIVITIES:	Boating	Fishing	Hiking
	Water Skiing		

RESTRICTIONS: Pets allowed on leash no more than 10'. At no time will pets be allowed in trailers. No firearms. No swimming/wading at the recreation area. No fireworks.

Elliott Lake Recreation Area (TX15R3)
Red River Army Depot, TX 75507-5000

Comm: 214-334-2141
ATVN: 829-2141

LOCATION: On post. Red River is W of Texarkana S of I-30 on US-82. Take Red River Army Depot exit. RM: p-94, ED/14. NMC: Texarkana, 18 mi E.

DESCRIPTION OF AREA: Located in a wooded area on 183-acre Elliott Lake in NE corner of state. Excellent for overnight camping, vacationing, sightseeing and trips into scenic Arkansas mountains. Recreation area is a 210-acre reserve. Wide range of military facilities available on post.

SEASON OF OPERATION: Year round.

ELIGIBILITY: Active/Retired/Reserve/DOD Civilians.

RESERVATIONS: Required. Address: Community Recreation Branch, Bldg S-05, Red River Army Depot, ATTN: SDSRR-AN, Texarkana, TX 75507-5000. Comm: 214-334-3506/2694; ATVN: 829-3506.

CAMP FACILITIES:	NO UNITS	HOOKUPS	FEE
Cabins	10		$17.00 daily
Camper Spaces	16	W/E	5.00 daily
Shelters	5	Cots/Toilets	5.00 dly+15 dep
Tent Spaces	20	None	1.00 daily

SUPPORT FACILITIES:			
	Beach	Boat Launch	Boat Rental
	Canoes	Laundry	Marina
	Picnic Areas	Playground	Rec Equip Rntl
	Restrooms	Sewage Dump Sta	Showers

ACTIVITIES:			
	Archery	Boating	Fishing (lic)
	Hiking	Hunting (lic)	Swimming

RESTRICTIONS: No pets allowed in cabins. Recreation permit required for civilians and unaccompanied dependents.

Flying K Recreation Ranch (TX11R3)
Kelly Air Force Base, TX 78241-5000

Comm: 512-925-1110
ATVN: 945-1110

LOCATION: Off base. Approximately 100 mi N of San Antonio on Lake Lyndon B Johnson. From US-281 in Marble Falls go W on TX FM-1431 for 3.3 mi; L on Wirtz Dam Rd; follow signs for 2.5 mi. RM: p-94, EL/5. NMI: Bergstrom AFB, 60 mi SE. NMC: Austin, 60 mi SE.

DESCRIPTION OF AREA: Located in Texas hill country, Lake Lyndon B Johnson is one of the three lakes in Texas where the annual Black Bass Fishing Contest is held. The area, described as a region of scenic beauty, has an average temperature of 66 degrees. Full range of military facilities at Bergstrom AFB.

SEASON OF OPERATION: Year round.

ELIGIBILITY: Active/Retired/DOD Civilians at Kelly AFB.

RESERVATIONS: Required, 21 days in adv, beginning Th at 0800, in person, and 1300, by phone. Address: MWR Office, Kelly AFB, TX 78241-5000. Comm: 512-925-4585; ATVN: 945-4585. Rec area address: Flying K Ranch, PO Box 155, Marble Falls, TX 78654. Comm: 512-693-4433.

Flying K Rec Ranch, Cont'd

CAMP FACILITIES:	NO UNITS		FEE
Mobile Homes, 2 bdrm	21		$16-26 daily

furn except for bath and kitchen linens and soap.

SUPPORT FACILITIES:	Boat Launch	Boat Rental	Fishing Pier
	Ice	Marina	Picnic Area
	Restrooms	Swimming Area	

ACTIVITIES:	Boating	Fishing (lic)	Swimming

RESTRICTIONS: Pets allowed on leash no more than 10', kept at unit only, and walked outside ranch grounds. 7-day limit.

Goodfellow Recreation Camp (TX32R3)
Goodfellow Air Force Base, TX 76908-5000

Comm: 915-657-3217
ATVN: 477-3217

LOCATION: Off base. From US-87, take Knickerbocker Rd S to Lake Nasworthy. RM: p-93, WO/16. NMI: Goodfellow AFB, 10 mi NE. NMC: San Angelo, 10 mi N.

DESCRIPTION OF AREA: Located on Lake Nasworthy in flat, open terrain with some trees and covered picnic areas. Full range of military fac on base.

SEASON OF OPERATION: Year round; Wednesday-Monday. (See "Restrictions.")

ELIGIBILITY: Active/Retired/DOD Civilians.

RESERVATIONS: Accepted. Address: Recreation Services, 3480 ABGP/SSRO, Goodfellow AFB, TX 76908-5000. Comm: 915-944-1012; ATVN: 477-3217 (ask operator to ring 944-1012).

CAMPING FACILITIES:	NO UNITS	HOOKUPS	FEE
Camper Spaces	8	E	$4.00 daily
Camper Spaces	Unlimited	None	4.00 daily
Tent Spaces	Unlimited	None	2.00 daily

SUPPORT FACILITIES:	Boat Launch	Boat Rental	Fishing Pier
	Gas	Marina	Pavilions
	Picnic Area	Racquet Courts	Rec Equip Rental
	Restrooms	Sewage Dump Sta	Snack Bar
	Sports Fields		

ACTIVITIES:	Fishing	Sailing	Water Skiing

RESTRICTIONS: Pets allowed on leash; owner must clean up after pets. Campers already in the camping area on Monday will not be required to leave. No open fires. Nominal daily entrance fee.

Kelly Fam-Camp (TX33R3)
Kelly Air Force Base, TX 78241-5000

Comm: 512-925-1110
ATVN: 945-1110

LOCATION: On base. From US-90 go S on Cupples Rd for 2 mi (past the Kelly AFB main gate and over the overpass); L at the East Kelly AFB entrance. The Fam-Camp is just inside the gate to the right. Check in at Fam-Camp, Bldg 3503. RM: p-95, EX/13. NMC: San Antonio, 3 mi NE.

TEXAS

Kelly Fam-Camp, Cont'd

DESCRIPTION OF AREA: Located in the San Antonio metropolitan area which offers many sightseeing opportunities, e.g., the Alamo, Mission Concepcion (the oldest church in Texas), Institute of Texan Cultures, zoological gardens and aquarium and Fiesta Week in April. Fam-Camp is surrounded by pecan trees. Full range of military facilities available on base.

SEASON OF OPERATION: Year round.

ELIGIBILITY: Active/Retired.

RESERVATIONS: No adv resv. Address: MWR Office, 2851 ABG/SSRO, Kelly AFB, TX 78241-5000. Comm: 512-925-5725.

CAMPING FACILITIES:	NO UNITS	HOOKUPS	FEE
Camper Spaces	32	W/S/E	$8.00 daily
Tent Spaces	Many	None	3.00 daily

SUPPORT FACILITIES:			
	Laundry	Picnic Area	Playground
	Restrooms	Sewage Dump Sta	Showers

ACTIVITIES:		
	Rec Equip Avail	Sightseeing

RESTRICTIONS: 1 pet per family allowed. 15-day limit.

Lake Amistad Recreation Area (TX34R3)

Laughlin Air Force Base, TX 78843-5000

nm: 512-298-3511
ATVN: 732-1110

LOCATION: Off base. From US-90 N of Del Rio, take Amistad Dam Rd to Rec Area. RM: p-93, WU/15. NMI: Laughlin AFB, 22.5 mi SE. NMC: Del Rio, 10 mi SE.

DESCRIPTION OF AREA: Situated near Amistad Dam which serves as passageway to and from Mexico. Ideal fresh water recreation area and outstanding fishing. Good base for day trips into Mexico. Convenient to Cuidad Acuna, Mexico. Full range of military facilities available at Laughlin AFB.

SEASON OF OPERATION: Year round.

ELIGIBILITY: Active/Retired/DOD and NAF Civilians.

RESERVATIONS: Required. Address: Lake Amistad AF Military Rec Area, Laughlin Air Force Base, TX 78843-5000. Comm: 512-298-5224; ATVN: 732-5224. (Rec Area) Comm: 512-775-5971; ATVN: 732-5971.

CAMPING FACILITIES:	NO UNITS	HOOKUPS	FEE
Camper, 20', slp 4	2	W/E	$10.00 dly/50 wkly
Cabanas	5	W/E	4.00 daily
Camper Spaces	2	W/E	3.00 daily
Camper & Tent Spaces	5	W	2.50 daily

SUPPORT FACILITIES:			
	Marina	Picnic Areas	Quick Shop
	Rec Equip Rntl	Restrooms	Sewage Dump Sta

ACTIVITIES:			
	Boating	Fishing	Hunting (lic)
	Sailing	Water Skiing	

RESTRICTIONS: Pets allowed on leash.

Lake Medina Recreation Camp (TX38R3)
Lackland Air Force Base, TX 78236-5000

Comm: 512-671-1110
ATVN: 473-1110

LOCATION: Off base. From I-410 on NW side of San Antonio, take Loop 1604 N to TX FM-471 (Grissom Rd); W to TX FM-1283. Turn L at Hill Top Cafe; follow sign to camp near the dam. RM: p-95, EO/4. NMI: Lackland AFB, 30 mi SE. NMC: San Antonio, 30 mi SE.

DESCRIPTION OF AREA: Wooded area on beautiful, large, fresh-water Lake Medina. Boat certification is required for use of the large boats. For certification boaters must view a 1-hour film followed by a written test at the camp. Full range of military facilities at Lackland AFB.

SEASON OF OPERATION: Year round; closed Tuesday and Wednesday.

ELIGIBILITY: Active/Retired/DOD Civilians.

RESERVATIONS: Accepted. Address: Lake Medina Recreation Camp, Lackland AFB, TX 78238-5000. Comm: 512-671-4267; ATVN: 473-4267.

CAMPING FACILITIES:	NO UNITS	HOOKUPS	FEE
Campers, 22'	6	W/E (110)	$15.00 daily
RV Spaces	9 Gravel	W/E (110)	5-8 daily
Tent Spaces	6 Pads	None	None
Tent Spaces	10 Primitive	None	None

SUPPORT FACILITIES:			
	Beach	Boat Launch	Boat Rental
	Fishing Tackle	Grills	Marina
	Pavilions	Picnic Area	Rec Center

ACTIVITIES:			
	Fishing	Swimming	Water Skiing

RESTRICTIONS: No pets allowed.

Lake Texoma Recreational Annex (TX16R3)
Sheppard Air Force Base, TX 76311-5000

Comm: 817-851-2511
ATVN: 736-1001

LOCATION: Off base. From US-82 E of Gainesville, take US-337 North. Rec area is located on Texas side of Lake Texoma. RM: p-94, EC/8. NMI: Dallas Naval Air Station, 95 mi S. NMC: Dallas, 95 mi S.

DESCRIPTION OF AREA: Located approx 120 mi E of base at Wichita Falls, near the Texas-Oklahoma line on one of the largest, most popular inland lakes in the area. Some of the best fishing is available as well as a variety of other water sports. Full range of military facilities avail at Dallas Naval Air Station.

SEASON OF OPERATION: Year round.

ELIGIBILITY: Active/Retired/DOD Civilians.

RESERVATIONS: Required. Address: MWR Div, Bldg 832, Sheppard AFB, TX 76311-5000. Comm: 817-851-2876; ATVN: 736-2876.

CAMP FACILITIES:	NO UNITS	HOOKUPS	FEE
Cabins, sleep 4-6	44		$20.00 daily
Camper Spaces	14	W/S/E	5.00 daily
Tent Spaces	Many	None	2.00 daily

TEXAS

Lake Texoma Rec Annex, Cont'd

SUPPORT FACILITIES:

Bait	Boat Launch	Boat Rental
"Crappie" House	Gas	Grocery Store
A/C, heat	Pavilions	Picnic Area
Playgrounds	Rec Equip Rntl	Rec Room/TV
Restrooms	Sewage Dump Sta	Showers

ACTIVITIES:

Fishing	Hiking	Swimming
Water Skiing		

RESTRICTIONS: Pets allowed.

Laughlin Fam-Camp (TX13R3)
Laughlin Air Force Base, TX 78843-5000

Comm: 512-298-3511
ATVN: 732-1110

LOCATION: On base. Off US-90 E of Del Rio. Clearly marked. Report to Rec Ctr, Bldg 235, just past gas station. RM: p-93, WU/15 and p-95, EX/12. NMC: San Antonio, 150 mi E.

DESCRIPTION OF AREA: Fam-camp is situated near Texas-Mexico border opposite Ciudad Acuna and also near Presa de la Amistad Reservoir and recreation area. Full range of military facilities available on base.

SEASON OF OPERATION: Year round.

ELIGIBILITY: Active/Retired/DOD Civilians.

RESERVATIONS: No adv resv. Address: Recreation Services, 47 ABG/SSRR, Laughlin AFB, TX 78843-5000. Comm: 512-298-5224/5474; ATVN: 732-5224/5474.

CAMPING FACILITIES:	NO UNITS	HOOKUPS	FEE
Camper Spaces	5	W/S/E	$6.00 daily
Camper Spaces	5	W/S	4.00 daily
Tent Spaces	15	None	2.50 daily

SUPPORT FACILITIES:

Grills	Grocery Store	Picnic Area
Playgrounds	Restrooms	Sewage Dump Sta

ACTIVITIES: Recreation Equipment Available

RESTRICTIONS: Pets allowed on leash.

Randolph Off-Base Recreation Area (TX35R3)
Randolph Air Force Base, TX 78150-5000

Comm: 512-652-1110
ATVN: 487-1110

LOCATION: Off base. From I-35 N of San Antonio on N side of New Braunfels, FM-306 W to Canyon Lake Dam; R approx 2.5 mi to Jacobs Creek Rd; L to Rec Area. RM: p-95, EN/6. NMI: Randolph AFB, 43 mi SE. NMC: San Antonio, 50 mi S.

DESCRIPTION OF AREA: Located on NE end of Canyon Reservoir. Terrain is characteristically hilly and rocky with scatterings of cedar, live oak and Spanish oak trees. Campground located around cove; majestic view of 8,240-acre lake and its 80-mi shoreline. Temperatures in summer make air conditioning desirable for enclosed trailers and recreational vehicles. Heat is needed only occasionally in winter. Variety of water-oriented activities. Full range of military facilities available at Randolph AFB.

SEASON OF OPERATION: Year round; closed Monday and Tuesday.

Randolph Off-Base Rec Area, Cont'd

ELIGIBILITY: AF Active/AF Retired/DOD Civilians at Randolph AFB.
All others: space available.

RESERVATIONS: Accepted; contact Rec Center Ticket and Tours Office M-F; Comm: 512-652-4125. Rec area address: Randolph Off-Base Rec Area, HC 4 Box 201, Canyon Lake, TX 78133-3501. Comm: 512-964-3804.

CAMPING FACILITIES:	NO UNITS	HOOKUPS	FEE
Pop-up Campers (Resv Req)	12	W/E	$12.00 daily
Camper Spaces	10 Hardstand	W/E	4.00 daily
Tent Spaces	45 Improved	None	3.00 daily

Camping shelters are under construction.

SUPPORT FACILITIES:
Boat Launch	Boat Rental	Fishing Pier
Gas/boats only	Grills	Marina
Picnic Areas	Playground	Rec Equip Rntl
Restrooms	Sailboat/minifish	Snacks
Sewage Dump Station (nearby)		Sports Fields

Sailing and scuba classes are offered seasonally.

ACTIVITIES:
Fishing	Sailing	Scuba Diving
Water Skiing	Windsurfing	

RESTRICTIONS: Pets allowed on leash. Entry fee ($2) to rec area.

Shields Park NAS Recreation Area (TX36R3)

Corpus Christi Naval Air Station, TX 78419-5000

Comm: 512-939-2811
ATVN: 861-1110

LOCATION: On base. From Corpus Christi take TX-358 E to Padre Island. Follow sign to NAS. Ask gate sentry for directions to marina and camping area. RM: p-95, ET/8. NMC: Corpus Christi, 8 mi W.

DESCRIPTION OF AREA: Padre Island Natl Seashore stretches 110 mi from Corpus Christi to Brownsville. Beautiful bay and gulf offering many water sports and recreational opportunities. Corpus Christi offers a symphony, historical homes and a museum. Full range of military facilities available on base.

SEASON OF OPERATION: Year round; beach: 1 April-1 October.

ELIGIBILITY: Active/Retired/Reserve.

RESERVATIONS: No adv resv. Address: Recreation Division, Bldg 1738, Naval Air Station, Corpus Christi, TX 78419-5000. Comm: 512-937-5071.

CAMPING FACILITIES:	NO UNITS	HOOKUPS	FEE
Camper Spaces	24 Hardstand	W/E (110)	$5.00 daily
Camper Spaces	4	W	3.00 daily
Tent Spaces	1	None	3.00 daily

SUPPORT FACILITIES:
Beach	Boat Launch	Boat Rental
Camp Equip Rntl	Chapel	Fishing Piers,
Gas	Golf	lighted
Laundry	Marina	Mini Mart
Pavilion	Picnic Area	Racquet Sports
Restrooms	Sewage Dump Sta	Skeet/Trap Range
Sports Fields	Trailer Rental	

ACTIVITIES: Fishing   Rec Equip Avail Sailing
                       Shelling   Swimming

RESTRICTIONS: Pets allowed on leash.

Shoreline Recreation Area (TX04R3)
Carswell Air Force Base, TX 76127-5000

Comm: 817-782-5000
ATVN: 739-1110

LOCATION: On base. From I-30, take Carswell/Horne St exit (TX-183); follow
signs to main gate. Located on Meandering Rd at N end of base. RM: p-96, D/2.
NMC: Ft Worth, 7 mi E.

DESCRIPTION OF AREA: Located in Ft Worth which offers much in the way of entertainment, including "Six Flags." The beautiful city of Dallas is nearby and
also has many things to do. Full range of military facilities on base.

SEASON OF OPERATION: Year round.

ELIGIBILITY: Active/Retired/DOD Civilians.

RESERVATIONS: Accepted. Address: Recreation Services, Carswell AFB, Fort
Worth, TX 76127-5000. Comm: 817-782-7972; ATVN: 739-7972.

CAMPING FACILITIES:	NO UNITS	HOOKUPS	FEE
Camper Spaces	10 Gravel	W/E (30A)	$10.00 daily

SUPPORT FACILITIES: Boat Rental   Canoe Rental   Grills
                       Marina   Pavilion   Picnic Areas
                       Playground   Rec Equip Rental Restrooms
                       Sewage Dump Sta   Snack Bar   Tours

ACTIVITIES: Boating   Canoeing   Fishing
                       Sightseeing   Tennis   Water Skiing

RESTRICTIONS: No pets allowed.

West Fort Hood Travel Camp (TX08R3)
Fort Hood, TX 76544-5056

Comm: 817-288-1110
ATVN: 738-1110

LOCATION: On post. Four mi W of main post area. From I-35 take Killeen/Fort
Hood exit; W on US-190; L on West Fort Hood turn off. Travel Camp is .25 mi
on your right. Area marked. RM: p-94, EJ/7. NMC: Austin, 60 mi S.

DESCRIPTION OF AREA: Ft Hood, the largest military reservation in the world, is
located in ranching and recreation country in central Texas. A 30-min drive to
Lake Belton and Lake Stillhouse which are famous for recreation, black and
white bass, and catfish. Full range of military facilities available on post.

SEASON OF OPERATION: Year round.

ELIGIBILITY: Active/Retired/DOD Civilians.

RESERVATIONS: Not req except for groups with 20 to 60 units. Address:
Community Recreation Division, AFZF-PA-CRD-OR-WFHTC, Ft Hood, TX 76544-5056.
Comm: 817-288-9926; ATVN: 738-9926.

TEXAS

West Fort Hood Travel Camp, Cont'd

CAMPING FACILITIES:	NO UNITS	HOOKUPS	FEE
Camper Spaces	64	W/S/E (110/220)	$7.00 dly/200 mo
Tent Spaces	20	W/E	2.00 daily
RV Storage	200	Padlock	8.00 monthly

SUPPORT FACILITIES:			
	Chapel	Conv Store	Game Room
	Gas	Golf	Grills
	Laundry	Moto-cross	Picnic Area
	Playground	Restrooms	Sewage Dump Sta/fee
	Showers	Trails	

ACTIVITIES:			
	Fishing (lic)	Hunting* (lic)	Jogging
	Rec Equip Avail	Swimming	Water Skiing

*Annual deer harvest: Oct-Nov, bow and shotgun; Nov-Dec, rifle (guided hunt). Wild turkey hunt: April. Dove and quail: Sep.

RESTRICTIONS: Pets allowed on leash. Vehicles over 36' are not permitted.

UTAH

Carter Creek Recreation Area (UTO1R4)
Hill Air Force Base, UT 84056-5000

Comm: 801-777-7221
ATVN: 458-1110

LOCATION: Off base. From I-80 near Evanston, WY, take WY/UT-150 SE 34 mi to Bear River Gas Station; E on Millcreek Ranger Station Rd for 4 mi. RM: p-97, C/8. NMI: Hill AFB, 105 mi W. NMC: Salt Lake City, 105 mi SW.

DESCRIPTION OF AREA: The surroundings of Carter Creek are typical of the Uinta Mountains with lodgepole pines and quaking aspen, a perfect combination of sight and sound. Rustic campsite in mountains reaching heights of 13,500 feet. Fishing lakes and ponds nearby. Full range of military facilities at Hill AFB.

SEASON OF OPERATION: 1 July-31 October.

ELIGIBILITY: Active/Retired/DOD Civilians.

RESERVATIONS: Required. Address: Ticket and Tour Office, 2849 ABG/SS, Hill Air Force Base, UT 84056-5000. Comm: 801-777-2892; ATVN: 458-2892.

CAMP FACILITIES:	NO UNITS	HOOKUPS	FEE
Cabins, 2 rm, slp 5	6		$15.00 daily
Camper Spaces	4 Gravel	W/E (110)	5.00 daily
Tent Spaces	Wilderness	None	2.00 daily

SUPPORT FACILITIES:			
	Grills	Laundry	Picnic Area
	Playground	Restrooms	Showers
	Trails		

ACTIVITIES:			
	Fishing (lic)	Hiking	Horseshoes
	Hunting (lic)	Volleyball	

RESTRICTIONS: Pets allowed on leash. No shooting in or near camp.

Hill Fam-Camp (UTO7R4)
Hill Air Force Base, UT 84056-5000

Comm: 801-777-7221
ATVN: 458-1110

LOCATION: On base. Between Ogden and Salt Lake City. I-15 to exit 336; E on UT-193 2 mi to South Gate of base. RM: p-97, C/6. NMC: Ogden, 10 mi N.

DESCRIPTION OF AREA: Located near mountains at edge of urban area. Fam-Camp provides immediate proximity to recreation areas and points of interest around Great Salt Lake. Pineview Reservoir for boating and swimming, 25 mi E. Museum and aerospace park on base. Full range of military facilities avail on base.

SEASON OF OPERATION: 1 April-31 October.

ELIGIBILITY: Active/Retired.

RESERVATIONS: Confirmed resv only for AD on PCS or TDY orders; others will be put on a waiting list. Address: Outdoor Recreation, 2849 ABG/SVH, Hill AFB, UT 84056-5000. Comm: 801-777-2601/1844; ATVN: 458-2601/1844.

CAMPING FACILITIES:	NO UNITS	HOOKUPS	FEE
Camper Spaces	10 Hardstand	W/S/E (110/220)	$10.00 daily
Camper Spaces	14 Overflow	W/S/E	10.00 daily

SUPPORT FACILITIES:			
	Boat Rental	Chapel	Gas
	Golf	Grills	Laundry
	Picnic Area	Restrooms	Sewage Dump Sta
	Sports Equip Rntl		

ACTIVITIES:		
	Jogging	Recreation Equipment Available

RESTRICTIONS: Pets allowed on leash only; must be walked out of camping pad area. 10-day limit. No tent camping.

Hillhaus Lodge (UTO3R4)
Hill Air Force Base, UT 84056-5000

Comm: 801-777-7221
ATVN: 458-1110

LOCATION: Off base. I-15 to Ogden's 12th St exit; E to Ogden Canyon; pass Pineview Reservoir Dam. Proceed to Snow Basin turn-off (UT-226); S 6.2 mi to Hillhaus sign. RM: p-97, C/6. NMI: Hill AFB, 30 mi SW. NMC: Ogden, 20 mi E.

DESCRIPTION OF AREA: Located high in the mountains of Wasatch National Forest. Small lodge is less than a mile from Snow Basin, a major ski resort. Full range of military facilities available at Hill Air Force Base.

ELIGIBILITY: Active/Retired/DOD Civilians.

INFORMATION: The Lodge is currently in a period of transition. The following numbers may be called for current info. Comm: 801-777-2892; ATVN: 458-2892.

OVERNIGHT FACILITIES: Small lodge with lounge and fireplace; food service provided by staff. Contains sleeping areas below:

    One Family Room with 4 beds
    One Suite with double bed and 2 single beds
    Two Sleeping Lofts (dormitory type)

SUPPORT FACILITIES:			
	Grills	Ice	Picnic Area
	Restrooms	Showers	Snack Bar

Hillhaus Lodge, Cont'd

ACTIVITIES: Hiking   Horseshoes   Skiing (fee)

RESTRICTIONS: No pets allowed.

Oquirrh Hills Travel Camp (UTO6R4)

Tooele Army Depot
Tooele, UT 84074-5008

Comm: 801-833-0110
ATVN: 790-1110

LOCATION: On post. From I-80 take UT-36 S approx 15 mi to main entrance. RM: p-97, E/5. NMC: Salt Lake City, 35 mi NE.

DESCRIPTION OF AREA: View of largest open pit copper mine from top of Settlement Canyon. Enjoy sightseeing of canyons, mountains and desert. Wide range of military fac on post; full range avail at Dugway Proving Ground, 40 mi SW.

SEASON OF OPERATION: 1 May-30 October.

ELIGIBILITY: Active/Retired/DOD Civilians.

RESERVATIONS: Accepted 5 to 30 days in adv. Address: Community Family Activities, Bldg 1002, Tooele Army Depot, Tooele, UT 84074-5001. Comm: 801-833-3129; ATVN: 790-3129.

CAMPING FACILITIES:	NO UNITS	HOOKUPS	FEE
Camper Spaces	14 Hardstand	W/E (110)	$4.00 dly/25 wkly
Tent Spaces	8 Open Area	None	2.00 daily

SUPPORT FACILITIES:			
	Archery	Boat Rental	Bowling Alley
	Camp Equip Rntl	Camper Rental	Chapel
	Golf Driv Range	Laundry	Playground
	PX (small)	Racquetball	Restrooms
	Sewage Dump Sta	Showers	Skeet/Trap Range
	Sports Eq Rntl	Sports Fields	Stables
	Swimming Pool (summer)		Tennis Courts

ACTIVITIES: Rec Equip Avail Snow Skiing (1 hour away)

RESTRICTIONS: Pets allowed on leash.

VERMONT

-None-

Thank you for showing this book to a friend!

VIRGINIA

A. P. Hill Recreation Facilities (VA39R1)
Fort A. P. Hill, Bowling Green, VA 22427-5000

Comm: 804-633-5041
ATVN: 934-8110

LOCATION: On post. From N, exit I-95 at Bowling Green/Fort A P Hill, US-17 (bypass); E to VA-2; S to Bowling Green; take US-301 NE to main gate. From S, exit I-95 to VA-207; N to US-301 and main gate. 3 mi E of Bowling Green. RM: p-99, K/20. NMC: Fredericksburg, 14 mi NW.

DESCRIPTION OF AREA: Several lakes and ponds with excellent fishing. Some military facilities on post. Full range of mil fac at Quantico, 45 mi NW.

SEASON OF OPERATION: Year round.

ELIGIBILITY: Active/Retired/DOD Civilians.

RESERVATIONS: Required for lodging. Address: Commander US Army Garrison, ATTN: Morale Support Activities Division, Fort A P Hill, Bowling Green, VA 22427-5000. Comm: 804-633-8219; ATVN: 934-8219.

LODGING:

	FEE
The Lodge, overlooking a lake, has 9 bdrm units; max 18 occupants in mixed group, 20 in same group; DR, kit and lobby. 2 NIGHTS' STAY REQUIRED DURING WEEKENDS.	Min of $100 dly, includes up to 6 pers; ea add pers, $10; canvas cots after all beds are used, $5.
3 Log Cabins, on Bullocks Pond, 3 bdrm, LR, DR and kit. Sleep 6.	$10-13 each person daily Max per fam: $40 daily

All units are fully furnished, including linens and kitchen utensils.

CAMPING FACILITIES:	NO UNITS	HOOKUPS	FEE
Camper spaces	48 Hardstand	W/S/E	$5.00 daily

SUPPORT FACILITIES:		
Boat Rental	Camp Equip Rntl	Camper Rental
Rec Center	Rec Equip Rntl	Skeet Range
Swimming Pool		

ACTIVITIES:		
Bicycling	Fishing	Hunting

RESTRICTIONS: No pets allowed.

Bethel Park Recreation Area (VA22R1)
Langley Air Force Base, VA 23665-5000

Comm: 804-764-9990
ATVN: 432-1110

LOCATION: Off base. From I-64 take VA-134 N approx 4.5 mi to entrance to Bethel Manor Housing area. Stay on entry road (First Avenue) to "T" intersection; L on Big Bethel Road. Entrance to rec area is approx 1/4 mi on R. RM: p-98, A/2. NMI: Langley AFB, 7 mi SE. NMC: Newport News, 10 mi S.

DESCRIPTION OF AREA: Situated along Big Bethel Reservoir in beautiful VA tidewater area offering activities such as boating, fishing and water sports. The rec area provides fac for squadron-sponsored and family picnic activities and can accommodate approx 2,000 patrons. This is a recreation area; no camping facilities are available. Full range of military facilities available on base.

SEASON OF OPERATION: 1 April-31 October.

Bethel Park Rec Area, Cont'd

ELIGIBILITY: Active/Retired/DOD Civilians at Langley AFB.

RESERVATIONS: Required for large groups. Address: Outdoor Rec Office, 1 CSG/SSRO, Langley AFB, VA 23665-5534. Comm: 804-764-4616; ATVN: 432-4616.

SUPPORT FACILITIES:			
	Boat Launch	Boat Rental	Chapel
	Fishing Pier	Fishing Tackle	Gas
	Golf (on base)	Grills	Marina
	Picnic Area	Playground	PX Annex
	Rec Equip Rntl	Restrooms	Snack Bar
	Sports Fields	Tennis Courts	

ACTIVITIES:			
	Badminton	Boating	Fishing (lic)
	Horseshoes	Volleyball	

RESTRICTIONS: Pets allowed on leash. Off limits from sunset to sunrise. Swimming is not allowed in the reservoir.

Cameron Station Trailer Park (VA23R1)
Cameron Station, Alexandria, VA 22304-5050

Comm: 202-545-6700
ATVN: 227-0101

LOCATION: On post. From I-395 take VA-236 (Duke St) exit E. 2 mi to entrance to Cameron Station on R. RM: p-42; J/5. NMC: Washington DC, 5 mi N.

DESCRIPTION OF AREA: Located a short drive from Washington DC and Old Towne Alexandria. Lovely lake with water fowl. Wide range of mil fac on post.

SEASON OF OPERATION: 1 May-1 October.

ELIGIBILITY: Active/Retired.

RESERVATIONS: Accepted. Address: Cameron Station Outdoor Recreation, 5010 Duke St, Alexandria, VA 22304-5050. Comm: 202-274-7199.

CAMPING FACILITIES:	NO UNITS	HOOKUPS	FEE
Camper Spaces	12	None	$3.00 daily
self-contained only			

SUPPORT FACILITIES:			
	Camp Equip Rntl	Gas	Grills
	Picnic Area	Playground	Shoppette
	Snack Bar	Sports Fields	

ACTIVITIES: Recreation Equipment Available

RESTRICTIONS: Pets allowed on leash.

Cheatham Annex Recreation Cabins and RV Park (VA31R1)
Cheatham Annex Naval Supply Center
Williamsburg, VA 23187-5000

Comm: 804-887-7224
ATVN: 953-7224

LOCATION: On base. From I-64 near Williamsburg, take exit 57B; E on VA-199 to main gate. RM: p-99, B/19. NMC: Newport News, 8 mi S.

DESCRIPTION OF AREA: Located in historical triangle of Jamestown, Colonial Williamsburg and Yorktown. Convenient to Busch Gardens, Pottery Factory, and College of William and Mary. Limited military facilities on base. Full range of facilities available at Yorktown Naval Weapons Station, 7 mi S.

Cheatham Annex Rec Cabins & RV Park, Cont'd
SEASON OF OPERATION: Year round.

ELIGIBILITY: Active/Retired.

RESERVATIONS: Req up to 90 days in adv. Address: Special Services, Cheatham Annex, Williamsburg, VA 23187-8792. Comm: 804-887-7224, ATVN: 953-7224.

FACILITIES AT RECREATION CABINS located along Cheatham Lake:	**FEE**
5 Cabins, sleep 6-8	$26-45 dly/156-264 wkly
6 Cabins, sleep 4-6	Depending on the cabin

Each unit is furnished with kitchen utensils, dishes, linens, color TV, refrigerator and a boat on Cheatham Lake with motor, battery, battery charger, paddles and cushions. All cabins have A/C and central heat, woodburning stove or fireplace.

FACILITIES AT RV PARK overlooking York River and Kings Creek:	**FEE**
10 Camper Spaces with full hookups (110/220)	$ 8 dly/48 wkly
Play-Mor Campers, 12' & 16' ($2 add for A/C)	10-12 dly
Off-base deposit required	

SUPPORT FACILITIES:			
	Boat Rental	Camp Equip Rntl	Fishing Pier
	Golf (9 holes)	Grills	Laundry
	Nature Trails	Picnic Area	Playground
	Restrooms	Sewage Dump Sta	Showers

ACTIVITIES:			
	Bicycling	Boating	Crabbing
	Fishing	Rec Equip Avail	Swimming

RESTRICTIONS: No pets allowed.

"The Colonies" Travel Park (VA32R1)

Fort Monroe, VA 23651-6144

Comm: 804-727-2111
ATVN: 680-2111

LOCATION: On post. From I-64 at Hampton, take exit 69. Follow historic sign markers to Fortress Monroe. RM: p-98, B/3. NMC: Hampton, adjacent to post.

DESCRIPTION OF AREA: Quiet, serene campsite named after the Thirteen Colonies. Each site has a state sign showing the state bird, flower, tree, and date it joined the Union. The post is located at the hub of many historical and recreational areas, e.g., Williamsburg, Jamestown, Yorktown, Busch Gardens, Virginia Beach, etc. Full range of military facilities available on post.

SEASON OF OPERATION: Year round.

ELIGIBILITY: Active/Retired/Reserve on AD/DOD Civilians at Fort Monroe.

RESERVATIONS: Recommended up to 30 days in adv with deposit. Address: Outdoor Recreation Office, Bldg 165, Ft Monroe, VA 23651-6144. Comm: 804-727-2384; ATVN: 680-2384.

CAMPING FACILITIES:	NO UNITS	HOOKUPS	FEE
Camper Spaces, up to 35'	13 Hardstand	W/S/E (110/220)	$6.00-10.00 daily

SUPPORT FACILITIES:			
	Archery	Beach/fee	Bicycle Rental
	Boat Rental	Camp Equip Rntl	Camper Rental
	Chapel	Gas	Grills
	Laundry*	Picnic Area	Playground

"The Colonies" Travel Park, Cont'd

Port-a-Potties	Racquetball	Rec Equip Rntl
Restrooms*	Sewage Dump Sta	Showers*
Swimming Pool(sumr)		Tennis Courts
*nearby		

ACTIVITIES:

Bicycling	Boat Tours	Crabbing
Fishing	Hunting (lic),	Jogging
Windsurfing	organized only	

RESTRICTIONS: Pets allowed on leash no longer than 6 feet; proof of rabies vaccination required; owner must clean up after pet. 14-day limit in a 30-day period. No open fires. No firearms. No metal detectors or digging permitted.

Freedom Star Recreation Area (VA34R1)
Fort Lee, VA 23801-5000

Comm: 804-734-1011
ATVN: 687-0111

LOCATION: On post. Exit I-95 at Ft Lee/Hopewell; take VA-36 E to main gate. Camp located off "A" Ave & 38th St. RM: p-99, N/20. NMC: Petersburg, 4 mi W.

DESCRIPTION OF AREA: Located at hub of one of Virginia's most historic areas. Convenient to Richmond, Colonial Williamsburg, Jamestown, other colonial and Civil War sites. Norfolk and Atlantic Ocean beach areas within day's travel. Army's Quartermaster Museum and full range of military facilities on post.

SEASON OF OPERATION: March-November.

ELIGIBILITY: Active/Retired/DOD Civilians on TDY Orders.

RESERVATIONS: Accepted. Address: Freedom Star Recreation Area, Bldg 15014, Fort Lee, VA 23801-5000. Comm: 804-734-2882; ATVN: 687-5038.

CAMPING FACILITIES:	NO UNITS	HOOKUPS	FEE
Camper Spaces	7	W/E(110/220/30A)	$10.00 daily
Camper Spaces	6	None	6.00 daily
Tent Spaces	7	None	6.00 daily

SUPPORT FACILITIES:

Chapel	Gas	Laundry
Picnic Area	Playground	Restrooms
Sewage Dump Sta	Showers	Sports Fields

ACTIVITIES:

Fishing (lic)	Rec Equip Avail	Softball
Volleyball		

RESTRICTIONS: Pets allowed on leash. 14-day limit.

Lunga Reservoir (VA35R1)
Marine Corps Combat Development Command
Quantico, VA 22134-5000

Comm: 703-640-2121
ATVN: 278-2121

LOCATION: On base. From I-95 take exit 49 (MCCDC Quantico). Take MCB-4 W approx 7 mi to Lunga Reservoir office (1 mi past FBI Academy). RM: p-99, I/19. NMC: Washington, DC, 30 mi N.

DESCRIPTION OF AREA: Campgrounds situated along the reservoir in a wooded park. Area is within driving distance of Fredericksburg, Manassas, Mount Vernon and Washington, DC. Full range of mil fac on base approx 13 mi from campgrounds.

SEASON OF OPERATION: 15 April-15 October.

Lunga Reservoir, Cont'd

ELIGIBILITY: Active/Retired.

RESERVATIONS: No adv resv. Address: Lunga Reservoir, c/o Special Services, PO Box 186, Marine Corps Combat Development Command, Quantico, VA 22134-0186. Comm: 703-640-5270.

CAMPING FACILITIES:	NO UNITS	HOOKUPS	FEE
Camper Spaces	4 Hardstand	W/S/E	$9.00 daily
Camper Spaces	7 Hardstand	S/E	7.00 daily
Camper Spaces	2 Hardstand	W/E	7.00 daily
Camper Spaces	5 Hardstand	E	7.00 daily
Tent Spaces	5 Wilderness	None	5.00 daily

SUPPORT FACILITIES:		
Boat Launch/fee	Boat Rental	Chapel (on base)
Gas	Golf (on base)	Grills
Marina/Potomac	Pavilions/fee	Picnic Area
Playground	Port-a-Potties	Sewage Dump Sta
Stables (on base)		

ACTIVITIES:		
Boating Eq Avail	Fishing (lic)	Hunting (lic)

RESTRICTIONS: Pets allowed on leash. No swimming in the reservoir.

Pickett Travel Camp (VA33R1)
Fort Pickett, Blackstone, VA 23824-5000

Comm: 804-292-8621
ATVN: 438-8621

LOCATION: On post. From US-460 W of Petersburg, take Ft Pickett exit and follow the signs to Ft Pickett. RM: p-99, O/18. NMC: Petersburg, 40 mi NE.

DESCRIPTION OF AREA: 9 lakes and ponds avail within installation boundaries. Travel camp is in wooded area adjacent to main post. Petersburg and Richmond have many museums, dinner theaters and historical sights. Wide range of military facilities available on post.

SEASON OF OPERATION: Year round.

ELIGIBILITY: Active/Retired.

RESERVATIONS: Required. Address: Commander, US Army Garrison, ATTN: AFZA-FP-EH, Fort Pickett, Blackstone, VA 23824-5000. Comm: 804-292-8309/8320; ATVN: 438-8309/8320.

CAMPING FACILITIES:	NO UNITS	HOOKUPS	FEE
Pegram Camper Spaces	27 Hardstand	W/S/E	$3.00 daily
Tent Spaces	8	None	2.00 daily

SUPPORT FACILITIES:		
Bicycle Rental	Boat Rental	Camp Equip Rntl
Chapel	Gas	Laundry
Restrooms	Sewage Dump Sta	Showers
Sports Fields	Tennis Courts	

ACTIVITIES:		
Boating	Fishing (lic)	Hunting (lic)
Rec Equip Avail		

RESTRICTIONS: Pets allowed on leash. Boating permits required ($10 annually).

Stewart Campground (VAO4R1)

Naval Security Group Activity Northwest
Chesapeake, VA 23322-5000

Comm: 804-421-8262
ATVN: 564-1336-EX-260

LOCATION: On base. 3 mi W of VA-168 at NC/VA border, between Moyock, NC, and Hickory, VA. Check in at Rec Services, Bldg 269 (duty hours), or Quarterdeck (after hours). RM: p-99, P/24. NMC: Norfolk, VA, 35 mi N.

DESCRIPTION OF AREA: Located 25 mi N of Outer Banks, NC. Region noted as vacationer's and sportsman's paradise. Campgrounds are in a wooded area secluded from installation operations area. 6 mi from Northwest River Park (NWRP), a boating and fishing area. Limited military facilities on base; full range available at Norfolk Naval Station, 30 mi N.

SEASON OF OPERATION: April-October. (Nov-Mar: self-contained camping only; water and comfort stations closed.)

ELIGIBILITY: Active/Retired/DOD Civilians.

RESERVATIONS: Recommended. Address: Recreation Services, MOU #1 Box 697, NSGA Northwest, Chesapeake, VA 23322-5000. Comm: 804-421-8262; ATVN: 564-1336-EX-262.

CAMPING FACILITIES:	NO UNITS	HOOKUPS	FEE
Campers	13	W/E	$7-12 daily
Camper Spaces	18	E (110/30A)	5.00 daily

SUPPORT FACILITIES:	Grills	Picnic Area	Playground
	Screened Pav	Showers	Softball Field
	Tent Rental		

ACTIVITIES:	Fishing (lic)	Hunting (lic)	Rec Equip Avail
	Softball		

RESTRICTIONS: Pets allowed on leash. No open fires on ground. No all-terrain vehicles.

Story Travel Camp (VAO5R1)

Fort Story, VA 23459-5000

Comm: 804-422-7111
ATVN: 438-7111

LOCATION: On post. From S exit of Chesapeake Bay Bridge Tunnel (US-13), take US-60 (Atlantic Ave) E to Fort Story. From I-64 take US-60 E. From VA-44 (Norfolk-VA Beach Expressway) exit US-58; L turn to N on Atlantic Ave (US-60) to 89th St to Ft Story. RM: p-98, D/6. NMC: Virginia Beach, 3 mi S.

DESCRIPTION OF AREA: Ft Story, a sub-installation of Ft Eustis, is the site of the first stop of the English settlers in the USA. The Cross at Cape Henry is located here. The Old Cape Henry Lighthouse is the first lighthouse built by the Federal Government. The statue of Admiral Francois Joseph Paul de Grasse presented to the Virginia Beach Bicentennial Commission in 1976 is also located here. Full range of military facilities available on post.

SEASON OF OPERATION: Campground: April-October; Mobile Homes: Year round.
Beach: Memorial Day-Labor Day.

ELIGIBILITY: Active/Retired/DOD Civilians at Ft Story and Ft Eustis.

RESERVATIONS: Required. Address: Outdoor Recreation, ATTN: Travel Camp, Ft Story, VA 23459-5034. Comm: 804-422-7601; ATVN: 438-7601.

CAMP FACILITIES:

	NO UNITS	HOOKUPS	FEE
Mobile Homes	11		$25.00 daily*
Camper Spaces	27 Hardstand	W/E	12.00 daily

*Includes sponsor and spouse. $5 for each additional person over 6 years old.

SUPPORT FACILITIES:

Beach	Chapel	Gas
Picnic Area	Restrooms	Sewage Dump Sta
Showers	Sports Fields	Tennis Courts

ACTIVITIES: Rec Equip Avail Swimming

RESTRICTIONS: Pets allowed on leash; dogs in mobile homes must be under 20 pounds; for more details call "Reservations" numbers above.

Yorktown CG Campground (VA37R1)

Yorktown CG Reserve Training Center, VA 23690-9761

Comm: 804-898-3500
FTS: 827-3500

LOCATION: On base. I-64 to exit 60B; E on Ft Eustis Blvd; L on US-17, R at Cook Rd (VA-704); R at VA-238. RM: p-99, N/23. NMC: Newport News, 15 mi SE.

DESCRIPTION OF AREA: Situated in wooded area along Chesapeake Bay. Historic and recreational areas of Yorktown, Jamestown, Williamsburg, Busch Gardens and Water Country USA nearby. Limited military facilities on base; full range of facilities at Yorktown Naval Weapons Station.

SEASON OF OPERATION: Year round; water and electricity: May-October.

ELIGIBILITY: Active/Retired/Reserve on AD.

RESERVATIONS: Required for camper spaces, by mail at least 1 week in adv, with $5 deposit. Address: USCG RESTRACEN, Special Services Branch, Yorktown, VA 23690-9761. Comm: 804-898-2127; FTS: 827-2127.

CAMPING FACILITIES:

	NO UNITS	HOOKUPS	FEE
Camper Spaces	10 Gravel	W/E	$6.00 daily
Tent Spaces	5	None	3.00 daily

SUPPORT FACILITIES:

Bicycle Rental	Boat Rental	Camp Equip Rntl
Chapel	Fishing Gear	Fitness Trail
Gas	Grills	Gymnasium
Ice	Laundry	Picnic Area
Rec Equip Avail	Restrooms	Sewage Dump Sta
Showers	Snack Bar	Sports Fields

ACTIVITIES:

Boating	Fishing (lic)	Racquetball
Softball	Swimming	Tennis

RESTRICTIONS: Pets allowed on leash; owner must clean up after pets. Prior to pitching tent, check in with Gym Watch, Bldg 53, for approval of location. 2-week limit. No vehicles permitted in tent areas. No open fires. Trash cans and bags are provided for daily clean-up, which is the responsibility of campers.

Yorktown Naval Weapons Station
Campsite (VA36R1)
Yorktown, VA 23691-5000

Comm: 804-887-4000
ATVN: 953-4000

LOCATION: On base. Between Williamsburg and Yorktown, VA on I-64. Take Lee Hall exit. Follow VA-143 .5 mi to installation gate. RM: p-99, C/19. NMC: Newport News, 20 SE.

DESCRIPTION OF AREA: This is a small rest area but convenient to a wealth of historical and recreational points of interest. Near Chesapeake Bay and Atlantic Ocean. Full range of military facilities available on base.

SEASON OF OPERATION: April-October.

ELIGIBILITY: Active/Retired.

RESERVATIONS: Required. Address: Special Services, Naval Weapons Station, Yorktown, VA 23691-5000. Comm: 804-887-4601/4741; ATVN: 953-4601/4741.

CAMPING FACILITIES:	NO UNITS	HOOKUPS	FEE
Camper Spaces	10	W/S/E	$6.00 daily

SUPPORT FACILITIES:	Fishing Pier Playground Showers	Laundry Restrooms	Picnic Areas Sewage Dump Sta
ACTIVITIES:	Bowling Swimming	Fishing Tennis	Softball

RESTRICTIONS: No pets allowed.

WASHINGTON

Clear Lake Resort (WAO1R4)
Fairchild Air Force Base, WA 99011-5000

Comm: 509-247-1212
ATVN: 352-1110

LOCATION: Off base. From I-90 take exit 264 N on Salnave Rd; R on Clear Lake Rd .5 mi to area. RM: p-101, G/23. NMI: Fairchild AFB, 13 mi N. NMC: Spokane, 12 mi NE.

DESCRIPTION OF AREA: Located on Clear Lake in a state where natural wildlife is a challenge and recreational adventure for the naturalist, photographer, artist, birdwatcher, fisherman or camper. Area offers many outdoor activities. Full range of military facilities available on base.

SEASON OF OPERATION: 15 Apr-30 Sep. Th-M: 0700-2100; W: 1000-1800.

ELIGIBILITY: Active/Retired/DOD Civilians.

RESERVATIONS: Accepted up to 30 days in adv with deposit. Address: Clear Lake Resort, 92 CSG/SSROL, Fairchild AFB, WA 99011-5000. Comm: 509-299-5129; ATVN: 352-2333.

Clear Lake Resort, Cont'd

CAMP FACILITIES:	NO UNITS	HOOKUPS	FEE
Cabins, kitchen, shower	Total		$15.00 dly/75 wkly
kitchen	of 3		10.00 dly/50 wkly
Mobile Homes, A/C, slp 4	6		10.00 dly/55 wkly
Camper Spaces	10 Hardstand	W/E (110/30A)	6.00 daily
Tent Spaces	28	Some with water	2.00 daily

SUPPORT FACILITIES:			
	Beach	Boat Rental	Camp Equip Rntl
	Fishing Pier	Gas	Laundry
	Picnic Area	Playground	Sewage Dump Sta
	Showers	Snack Bar	Tackle Shop

ACTIVITIES:	Fishing	Rec Equip Avail	Swimming

RESTRICTIONS: Pets allowed on leash.

Cliffside RV Park (WA12R4)
Whidbey Island Naval Air Station, WA 98278-5000

Comm: 206-257-2211
ATVN: 820-0111

LOCATION: On base. Off WA-20, 4 mi NW of Oak Harbor. RM: p-100, D/10. NMC: Seattle, 60 mi SE.

DESCRIPTION OF AREA Beautiful scenic area with marina offering many water sports. Full range of military facilities on base.

SEASON OF OPERATION: 15 April-1 November.

ELIGIBILITY: Active/Retired.

RESERVATIONS: Required with payment in full. Address: Recreational Services Office, Bldg 117, Naval Air Station, Whidbey Island, Oak Harbor, WA 98278-2100. Comm: 206-257-2432/2434; ATVN: 820-2432.

CAMP FACILITIES:	NO UNITS	HOOKUPS	FEE
Camper Spaces	18	W/E	$4.50 daily
Camper Spaces, 40'	2	W/E	4.50 daily
Tent Spaces	4	None	2.50 daily

SUPPORT FACILITIES:			
	Boat Launch	Boat Rental	Marina
	Picnic Area	Rec Equip Rntl	Sewage Dump Sta
	Showers		

ACTIVITIES:	Boating	Fishing	Water Sports

RESTRICTIONS: House pets allowed. 2-week limit during July and August.

Holiday Park Fam-Camp (WA03R4)
McChord Air Force Base, WA 98438-5000

Comm: 206-984-1910
ATVN: 976-1110

LOCATION: On base. From I-5 S of Tacoma, take exit 125 E. Follow signs to McChord AFB. RM: p-100, I/10. NMC: Tacoma, 8 mi N.

DESCRIPTION OF AREA: Located in western area of state at base of Puget Sound. Fam-Camp offers base for prime sightseeing and recreational opportunities on the numerous waterways and lakes in the Puget Sound area and nearby national parks: Mt Ranier, Olympic and North Cascades. Camp area is surrounded by giant firs and pines. Full range of military facilities available on base.

Holiday Park Fam-Camp, Cont'd

SEASON OF OPERATION: Year round.

ELIGIBILITY: Active/Retired/DOD Civilians.

RESERVATIONS: No adv resv. Address: Recreational Services, McChord AFB, WA 98438-5000. Comm: 206-984-3281; ATVN: 976-3281.

CAMPING FACILITIES:	NO UNITS	HOOKUPS	FEE
Camper Spaces	18	W/S/E	$7.50 dly/45.50 wkly
Tent Spaces	Many	None	Call For Rates

SUPPORT FACILITIES:	Boat Rental	Picnic Area	Playground
	Rec Equip Rntl	Restrooms	Sewage Dump Sta
	Showers		

ACTIVITIES:	Boating	Fishing	Hiking

RESTRICTIONS: Pets allowed; <u>must</u> have certificate and tag for current rabies vaccination. 2-week limit.

Jim Creek Campground (WA07R4)
Whidbey Island Naval Air Station, WA 98278-5000

Comm: 206-257-2211
ATVN: 820-0111

LOCATION: Off base. From I-5, take exit 208; E on WA-530 for approx 12 mi, thru Arlington, crossing river, passing grocery on L; R at next exit approx 8 mi to Radio Station/Jim Creek Campground. RM: p-100, E/12. NMI: NAS Whidbey Island, 60 mi W. NMC: Seattle, 60 mi SW.

DESCRIPTION OF AREA: Jim Creek is a beautiful area located in the foothills of the Cascade Mountain range. The Twin Lakes are heavily stocked with trout. Full range of military facilities available at NAS Whidbey Island.

SEASON OF OPERATION: 22 April-1 October (subject to change due to weather).

ELIGIBILITY: Active/Retired/DOD Civilians.

RESERVATIONS: Required. Address: Recreational Services Office, Bldg 117, NAS Whidbey Island, Oak Harbor, WA 98278-2100. Comm: 206-257-2432/2434; ATVN: 820-2432.

CAMPING FACILITIES:	NO UNITS	HOOKUPS	FEE
Campers, sleep 4	4		$8.00 daily
Camper & Tent Spaces	23	None	1.75 daily

SUPPORT FACILITIES:	Boat Launch	Boat Rental	Gym/Showers
	Picnic Area	Playground	Rec Equip Rntl
	Restrooms	Sewage Dump Sta	Softball Field
	Tennis Courts		

ACTIVITIES:	Boating	Fishing (lic)	Hiking
	Hunting		

RESTRICTIONS: No pets, no cameras, no motorcycles or off-road vehicles, and no swimming allowed. Level of radio frequency is considered a potential hazard to people employing electronic life aid/support systems. Smoking and open fires only in designated areas. Check-out time: 1100 hrs.

Lewis Travel Camp (WA13R4)
Fort Lewis, WA 98433-5000

Comm: 206-967-1110
ATVN: 357-1110

LOCATION: On post. From I-5 take exit 120. Follow signs to N Fort Lewis. Take first R after guard shack. RM: p-100, I/10. NMC: Tacoma, 15 mi N.

DESCRIPTION OF AREA: Located at southern end of Puget Sound in unique, snow-topped Olympia Mountain region. Tranquil, wooded site along American Lake. **In addition, there are 120 rustic camper and tent spaces available at Chambers Lake, Lewis Lake and Nisqually River.** Full range of military fac on post.

SEASON OF OPERATION: Year round.

ELIGIBILITY: Active/Retired/Reserve/National Guard/DOD and NAF Civilians.

RESERVATIONS: Advised. Address: Ft Lewis Travel Camp, Community Recreation Division, Outdoor Rec Bldg 2409, Ft Lewis, WA 98433-5000. Comm: 206-967-7744; ATVN: 357-7744.

CAMP FACILITIES:	NO UNITS	HOOKUPS	FEE
Mobile Homes			Call
Camper Spaces	24 Hardstand	W/E	For
Camper Spaces	1 Overflow	None	Current
Tent Spaces	5 Wilderness	None	Rates

SUPPORT FACILITIES:			
	Beach	Boat Rental	Camp Equip Rntl
	Chapel	Dirt Bike Trail	Game Room/TV
	Gas	Golf	Laundry
	Marina	Picnic Areas	Playground
	Restrooms	Sewage Dump Sta	Showers
	Snack Bar	Sports Equip Rntl	

ACTIVITIES:	Fishing	Hunting	Snow Skiing

RESTRICTIONS: Pets allowed on leash; owner must clean up after pets.

Westport Recreation Park (WA14R4)
Grays Harbor USCG Station, Westport, WA 98595-0568

Comm: 206-268-0121
FTS: 420-9307

LOCATION: On base. At Grays Harbor Light. US-12 to Aberdeen; SW on WA-105 to Westport. Take 1st exit into Westport; approx 3 mi to R turn, following signs to US Coast Guard. Check in with OD at Coast Guard Station. RM: p-100, J/6. NMI: Ft Lewis, 85 mi E. NMC: Olympia, 50 mi E.

DESCRIPTION OF AREA: The salmon capital of the world with 18 mi of sandy beach and excellent clam digging. Great salmon fishing from charter boats. Full range of military facilities available at Ft Lewis.

SEASON OF OPERATION: 1 March-31 October.

ELIGIBILITY: Active/Retired/Reserve/DOT Civilians.

RESERVATIONS: Req, in writing, with payment (check payable to: Thirteenth Coast Guard District Morale Fund); as early as possible but no later than 2 wks in adv. Address: Commanding Officer, USCG Station Grays Harbor, Westport, WA 98595-0568. Comm: 206-268-0121; FTS: 420-9307.

Westport Rec Park, Cont'd

CAMPING FACILITIES:	NO UNITS	HOOKUPS	FEE
Camper Spaces	6	W/E	$4.00 daily
Tent Spaces	6	None	2.50 daily

SUPPORT FACILITIES:	Beach	Grills	Grocery (nearby)
	Laundry (nearby)	Marina (nearby)	Nature Trails
	Picnic Area	Playground	Restrooms
	Sewage Dump Sta	Showers	

ACTIVITIES:	Baseball	Fishing	Hiking
	Surfing	Surf Fishing	Swimming

RESTRICTIONS: Pets allowed on leash no longer than 6'; owner must clean up after pets. 7-day limit, to include only 1 weekend. No motorcycles.

WEST VIRGINIA

-None-

WISCONSIN

Rawley Point Light Recreation Cottage (WIO4R2)
Coast Guard Group, Milwaukee, WI 53207-1997

Comm: 414-291-1886
FTS: 362-1886

LOCATION: Off base. From I-43 near Two Rivers take exit 79; N on WI-42 into the city. R on 17th St; cross drawbridge; R on East St. Check in at CG Sta. RM: p-103, N/15. NMI: Two Rivers CG Sta, 4 mi S. NMC: Manitowoc, 10 mi S.

DESCRIPTION OF AREA: This recreational facility is a historical 115-year-old lighthouse. A ship that sank near the Point carried a cargo of gold that has never been found. The cottage is situated within 2800-acre Point Beach State Park. The twin cities of Two Rivers/Manitowoc are rich in festivals, fishing derbies and maritime events. Charter boats provide offshore fishing for lake trout and salmon. Limited military facilities at Twin Rivers CG Station; full range available at Ft McCoy, 175 mi W.

SEASON OF OPERATION: Year round.

ELIGIBILITY: Active/Retired/Reserve/DOT Civilians.

RESERVATIONS: Required, by telephone: up to 60 days in adv for AD CG; up to 40 days in adv for all other AD, Retired and DOT civilians; up to 15 days in adv for Reserve. Adv payment required 7 days prior to check-in. Address: Commander, USCG Group, 2420 S Lincoln Memorial Dr, Milwaukee, WI 53207-1997. Comm: 414-291-1886; FTS: 362-1886.

LODGING: The cottage contains 2 apts, each has 2 bdrms and sleeps 8 adults. PB, kit, MW, TV, W/D; furn, except linens (queen, full and twin). FEE: $15.00 daily.

SUPPORT FACILITIES:	Beach	Bicycles	Grills
	Picnic Tables		

Nearby park and commercial facilities offer:

Camping	Chapel	Golf
Grocery	Laundry	Marina
Rec Center	Tours	Trails

ACTIVITIES:

Fishing	Hiking	Hunting
Rec Equip Avail	Swimming	Snow Skiing

RESTRICTIONS: Pets allowed on leash; add fee of $5 daily. 2-week limit.

Sherwood Point Cottage (WIO3R2)
Coast Guard Group, Milwaukee, WI 53207-1997

Comm: 414-291-1886
FTS: 362-1886

LOCATION: Off base. From Sturgeon Bay, take WI-57 S to County 'S'; turn R on
Duluth St; L on Elm St to County 'M'; R to Potawatomi St Pk; turn L at tavern
(on L). This is access road to CG light. Approx 8 mi from Elm and County 'M'.
RM: p-102, L/16. NMI: Fort McCoy, 190 mi SW. NMC: Green Bay, 45 mi SW.

DESCRIPTION OF AREA: Situated on western shores of Lake Michigan. Beautiful
cottage overlooking bay and wooded area. Near winter ski area. Wide range of
military facilities available at Ft McCoy.

SEASON OF OPERATION: Year round.

ELIGIBILITY: Active/Retired/Reserve/DOT Civilians.

RESERVATIONS: Required, by telephone only: up to 60 days in adv for AD CG; up
to 40 days in adv for other AD and Retired; up to 15 days is adv for Reserve.
Full payment required no later than 7 days prior to check-in. Address: Commander, USCG Group, 2420 S Lincoln Memorial Dr, Milwaukee, WI 53207-1997.
Comm: 414-291-1886; FTS: 362-1886.

LODGING: 1 cottage, 2 bdrm, sleeps 8 adults; furnished, except bed
linens, blankets, towels and toilet items; community kitchen,
MW, color TV.
FEE: $15.00 daily.

SUPPORT FACILITIES:

Fishing Pier	Picnic Area

ACTIVITIES:

Bicycling	Boating	Fishing
Hiking	Hunting	

RESTRICTIONS: Pets allowed; add fee of $5 daily. 2-week limit (weekly basis
preferred.)

Squaw Lake Recreation Area (WIO1R2)
Fort McCoy, WI 54656-5000

Comm: 608-388-2222
ATVN: 280-1110

LOCATION: On post. Exit I-90 at Sparta to WI-21; 8 mi NE to main gate. Well
marked. Rec Area off W Headquarters Rd, 1 mi E of Post Headquarters. RM: p-103,
O/7. NMC: LaCrosse, 35 mi W.

DESCRIPTION OF AREA: Beautiful wooded area bounded by Squaw Lake and LaCrosse
River. 13 ponds and small lakes on post are ideal for fishing and boating.
Wide range of military facilities available on post.

SEASON OF OPERATION: 15 April-1 December.

Squaw Lake Rec Area, Cont'd

ELIGIBILITY: Active/Retired/Reserve/NG/DOD and NAF Civilians.

RESERVATIONS: Accepted. Address: Community Recreation Div, ATTN: Squaw Lake Campground, Ft McCoy, Sparta, WI 54656-5000. Comm: 608-388-3517/3360; ATVN: 280-3517/3360.

CAMPING FACILITIES:	NO UNITS	HOOKUPS	FEE
Duplex, 1 bdrm	2		Call
Campers	6	E (110)	For
Camper Spaces	105	E (110)	Current
Tent & Camper Spaces	12	None	Rates

SUPPORT FACILITIES:			
	Archery	Bicycle Rntl	Boat Rental
	Hiking Trail	Laundry (nearby)	Miniature Golf
	Picnic Area	Playground	Restrooms
	Sewage Dump Sta	Showers	Snack Bar

ACTIVITIES:			
	Bicycling	Boating	Fishing (lic)
	Hunting (lic)	Swimming	Volleyball
	Winter Sports		

RESTRICTIONS: Pets allowed on leash.

WYOMING

Warren Fam-Camp (WYO2R3)
Francis E. Warren Air Force Base, WY 82005-5000

Comm: 307-775-1110
ATVN: 481-1110

LOCATION: On base. Off I-25, 2 mi N of I-80. Clearly marked. RM: p-104, J/1. NMC: Cheyenne, adjacent.

DESCRIPTION OF AREA: Located in open, rolling country in SE corner of state. Laramie and Medicine Bow National Forest are short distances W. Full range of military facilities available on base.

SEASON OF OPERATION: May-September.
October-April (off-season): Electric only.

ELIGIBILITY: Active/Retired/DOD Civilians.

RESERVATIONS: Required. Address: Recreation Services, 90 CSG/SVH, Francis E. Warren AFB, WY 82005-5000. Comm: 307-775-3077; ATVN: 481-3077.

CAMPING FACILITIES:	NO UNITS	HOOKUPS	FEE
Camper Spaces	24	W/E	$8.50 dly; $2 dly*
		E	5.00 dly; $2 dly*
Tent Spaces	10	None	4.00 dly; $1 dly*
	*Off-season rates		

SUPPORT FACILITIES:			
	Laundry	Picnic Area	Playground
	Rec Equip Rntl	Restrooms	Sewage Dump Sta
	Showers		

ACTIVITIES:			
	Fishing	Hiking	Hunting

RESTRICTIONS: Pets allowed.

OUTSIDE CONTINENTAL UNITED STATES (OCONUS)

ALASKA

Birch Lake Recreation Area (AK01R5)
Eielson Air Force Base, AK 99702-5000

Comm: 907-377-1110
ATVN: 317-377-1110

LOCATION: Off base. On SW side of Richardson Highway (AK-2) at mile post 305, 38 mi S of AFB. Turn at Rec Area sign; 1 mi to entrance. Check in at Boat Shop. RM: p-6, E/6. NMI: Eielson AFB, 38 mi N. NMC: Fairbanks, 64 mi N.

DESCRIPTION OF AREA: Located on Birch Lake. Birch Lake covers 804 acres, is spring fed, and is stocked with rainbow trout and silver salmon. Harding Lake Rec Area approx 10 mi N; Mt McKinley Natl Park, 130 mi SW. Rec area provides rustic base for enjoying state's unlimited outdoor rec resources. Spectacular mountain scenery, unsurpassed fishing and hunting in general area. Full range of military facilities available at Eielson AFB.

SUPPORT FACILITIES: Memorial Day-Labor Day.

ELIGIBILITY: Active/Retired/DOD Civilians.

RESERVATIONS: Recommended. Address: 343 MSSQ/SSRO, Birch Lake Rec Area, Eielson AFB, AK 99702-5000. Comm: 907-488-6161; ATVN: 317-377-4214.

CAMP FACILITIES:	NO UNITS	HOOKUPS	FEE
Cabins, Deluxe	2	E	$18.00 daily
Cabins, Family	16	E	15.00 daily
Cabins, Two-man	4	E	5.00 daily
Camper Spaces	40	E	5.00 daily
Tent Spaces	Many	None	2.00 daily

SUPPORT FACILITIES:			
	Beach	Boat Launch	Boat Rental
	Country Store	Lodge	Playground
	Restrooms	Showers	

ACTIVITIES:			
	Fishing (lic)	Hiking	Water Skiing

RESTRICTIONS: Pets allowed on leash. No linens or utensils provided. No laundry facilities or dump station.

Black Spruce Army Travel Camp (AK16R5)
Fort Richardson, AK 99505-5100

Comm: 907-864-0121
ATVN: 317-864-0121

LOCATION: On post. Main gate is on Glenn Highway, 5 mi S of Eagle River. Camp is located off Loop Road. Patrons may go directly to camp and report to Recreation Center, Bldg 636, the next day. RM: p-6, B/12. NMC: Anchorage, 8 mi SW.

DESCRIPTION OF AREA: Campground opened in Jul 87. Beautiful mountain scenery. Lakes and rivers provide excellent fishing. Varied sightseeing and outdoor recreational opportunities. Full range of military facilities available on post.

Black Spruce Army Travel Camp, Cont'd

SEASON OF OPERATION: May-September.

ELIGIBILITY: Active/Retired/DOD and NAF Civilians.

RESERVATIONS: Accepted for incoming PCS only. Address: Outdoor Rec Div, PO Box 5-367, Ft Richardson, AK 99505-5100. Comm: 907-864-3217; ATVN: 317-864-3217.

CAMPING FACILITIES:	NO UNITS	HOOKUPS	FEE
Camper Spaces	23	W/E (110/220)	$7.50-10 daily

There are also 7 Camper Spaces available at **Upper Otter Lake Campground.**

SUPPORT FACILITIES:	Archery	Golf	Grills
	Laundry	Racquetball	Rec Equip Rntl
	Sewage Dump Sta	Showers	Tennis Courts

ACTIVITIES	Fishing	Hunting*	Snow Skiing

*Hunters must check with Fish & Wildlife as there are many regulations.

RESTRICTIONS: Pets allowed on leash. 14-day limit. A break of 7 days is required between stays.

Eielson Fam-Camp (AKO2R5)
Eielson Air Force Base, AK 99702-5000

Comm: 907-377-1110
ATVN: 317-377-1110

LOCATION: On base. On Richardson Highway (AK-2). Clearly marked. RM: p-6, E/6. NMC: Fairbanks, 26 mi NW.

DESCRIPTION OF AREA: Located in interior of Alaska. Provides base for enjoying state's unlimited outdoor recreation resources. Spectacular mountain scenery; unsurpassed fishing and hunting in general area. McKinley Natl Park approx 130 mi SW. Full range of military facilities available on base.

SEASON OF OPERATION: 1 May-30 September.

ELIGIBILITY: Active/Retired/DOD Civilians.

RESERVATIONS: Resv preferred. Address: Eielson Fam-Camp, 343 MSSQ/SSRO, Eielson AFB, AK 99702-5000. Comm: 907-377-4214; ATVN: 317-377-4214.

CAMPING FACILITIES:	NO UNITS	HOOKUPS	FEE
Camper Spaces	24 Hardstand	W/S/E	$5.00 daily

SUPPORT FACILITIES:	Chapel	Gas	Grills
	Laundry	Picnic Area	Sewage Dump Sta

ACTIVITIES:	Boating	Fishing	Hiking

RESTRICTIONS: Pets allowed on leash. 14-day limit.

Elmendorf Fam-Camp (AK12R5)
Elmendorf Air Force Base, AK 99506-5000

Comm: 907-552-1110
ATVN: 317-552-1110

LOCATION: On base. From AK-1 enter installation at hospital gate. Follow signs. Fam-Camp is adjacent to hospital. RM: p-6, A/11. NMC: Anchorage, adjacent.

ALASKA
Elmendorf Fam-Camp, Cont'd

DESCRIPTION OF AREA: Located in Anchorage at head of Cook Inlet on state's southern coast. Camp is low-timbered area surrounded by mountains; provides good base for enjoying spectacular and varied sightseeing and outdoor recreation opportunities. Full range of military facilities available on base.

SEASON OF OPERATION: May-October.

ELIGIBILITY: Active/Retired/DOD Civilians.

RESERVATIONS: No adv resv. Address: Recreation Services, 21 CSG/SSR, Elmendorf AFB, AK 99506-5000. Comm: 907-552-2468; ATVN: 317-552-2468.

CAMPING FACILITIES:	NO UNITS	HOOKUPS	FEE
Camper Spaces	39 Hardstand	W/S/E	$8.00 daily
Tent Spaces	Open	None	Call For Rates

SUPPORT FACILITIES:			
	Boat Rental	Camp Equip Rntl	Golf
	Laundry	Picnic Area	Playground
	Rec Equip Rntl	Restrooms	Sewage Dump Sta
	Showers	Ski Lodge	

ACTIVITIES:			
	Fishing	Hiking	Ice Skating

RESTRICTIONS: Pets allowed. Boating safety course required prior to renting a boat.

Glass Park (AK14R5)
Fort Wainwright, AK 99703-5320

Comm: 907-353-7000
ATVN: 317-353-7000

LOCATION: On post. On eastern side of Fairbanks. Take AK-2 E to main gate. Glass Park is 500 yds inside main gate. RM: p-6, E/12. NMC: Fairbanks, 3 mi W.

DESCRIPTION OF AREA: Alaska's lakes and rivers abound with many species of fish, and forests teem with many kinds of wildlife. Snow skiing is a popular recreational activity. Full range of military facilities on post.

SEASON OF OPERATION: Year round.

ELIGIBILITY: Active/Retired/DOD Civilians.

RESERVATIONS: Accepted 30 days in adv for large groups only. Address: Commander, FWA, ATTN: Boat Shop, Ft Wainwright, AK 99703-5320. Comm: 907-353-6350; ATVN: 317-353-6350/6349.

CAMPING FACILITIES:	NO UNITS	HOOKUPS	FEE
Camper Spaces	12	E (110) (Ltd #)	$5.00 daily

SUPPORT FACILITIES:			
	Arts&Crafts Ctr	Boat Rental	Camper Rental
	Chapel	Gas	Golf (9 holes)
	Grills	Marina (N Post)	Pavilions
	Picnic Area	Rec Center	Rec Equip Rntl
	Restrooms	Shoppette	

ACTIVITIES:			
	Boating	Fishing	Hunting
	Snow Skiing (DH & XC)		

RESTRICTIONS: Pets allowed on leash. Sewage dump station available at gas station on post.

Ravenwood Ski Lodge (AK13R5)
Eielson Air Force Base, AK 99702-5000

Comm: 907-377-1110
ATVN: 317-377-1110

LOCATION: On base. On Richardson Highway (AK-2). Clearly marked. RM: p-6, E/6. NMC: Fairbanks, 26 mi NW.

DESCRIPTION OF AREA: Located 4 mi SE of main base. Spectacular mountain scenery. Full range of military facilities available on base.

SEASON OF OPERATION: Depends on snowfall (normally November-March).

ELIGIBILITY: Active/Retired/DOD Civilians.

RESERVATIONS: No adv resv. Address: 343 MSSQ/SSRO, Ravenwood Ski Lodge, Eielson AFB, AK 99702-5000. Comm: 907-377-1328.

SUPPORT FACILITIES:	Ski Equip Rental	Ski Lift	Ski Lodge
	Ski Trails	Snack Bar	

ACTIVITIES: Snow Skiing

RESTRICTIONS: No pets allowed. Closed Monday and Tuesday.

Seward AF Recreation Area (AKO5R5)
Elmendorf Air Force Base, AK 99506-5000

Comm: 907-552-1110
ATVN: 317-552-1110

LOCATION: Off base. Located near Seward off AK-1 on AK-9. Follow signs. RM: p-6, G/6. NMI: Elmendorf AFB, 130 mi N. NMC: Anchorage, 130 mi N.

DESCRIPTION OF AREA: Located on peninsula in the Gulf of Alaska along state's rugged southern seacoast. Heavily wooded; surrounded by mountains. Near Caines Head Recreation Area. Resurrection Bay has excellent fishing: halibut, salmon, cod, flounder. Abundant wildlife includes: porpoise, whale, puffin, sea otter, and much more. The rec area is being renovated and there may be some inconveniences due to construction. Full range of military fac at Elmendorf AFB.

SEASON OF OPERATION: Last week in May through first week in September.

ELIGIBILITY: Active/Retired/DOD Civilians.

RESERVATIONS: Required. Resv are accepted starting the beginning of May. Call for specific information. Address: Recreation Services, 21 CSG/SSR, Elmendorf AFB, AK 99506-5000. Comm: 907-224-5425; ATVN: 317-552-5425; during the hours 0600-2330, local time, 7 days a week.

CAMP FACILITIES:	NO UNITS	HOOKUPS	FEE *
Mobile Homes, 3 bdrm	10		$40.00 dly/4 pers**
Motel Units, 2 bdrm	10		15.00 dly/2 pers**
Camper Spaces	30 Hardstand	E	8.00 daily
Camper Spaces	33 Hardstand	None	4.00 daily
Tent Spaces	12 Improved	None	4.00 daily
	*20% discount for AD E1-E4		*$5 each add person.

SUPPORT FACILITIES:	Bicycle Path	Boat Launch	Boat Rental
	Deep-Sea Fishing	Dining Fac	Fish House/Freezer
	Fishing Tackle	Food Vending	Ice
	Laundry	Marina	Nature Trail
	Off-Road Veh	Picnic Area	Playground
	PX	Rec Room	Restrooms
	Sewage Dump Sta	Showers	Tours

Seward AF Rec Area, Cont'd

ACTIVITIES:　　　　　　Fishing　　　　　Hiking　　　　　Hunting

RESTRICTIONS: Pets allowed on leash. The quantity of recreational equipment avail for rental is insufficient for the number of patrons who use the area.

Seward Army Recreation Camp (AKO6R5)
Fort Richardson, AK 99505-5100

Comm: 907-864-0121
ATVN: 317-864-0121

LOCATION: Off post. Located near Seward off AK-1 on AK-9. RM: p-6, G/6. NMI: Fort Richardson, 133 mi N. NMC: Anchorage, 110 mi N.

DESCRIPTION OF AREA: Located on Resurrection Bay near Seward. Pine trees throughout picturesque 12-acre site surrounded by mountains on three sides. Superb fishing for salmon, halibut, snapper, ling cod, sea bass and flounder. Nearby streams and lakes also offer outstanding fishing. Area is a photographer's dream. Travelers in late July to mid-August see active salmon spawning areas on drive to Seward. Full range of military facilities at Ft Richardson.

SEASON OF OPERATION: Memorial Day through Labor Day.

ELIGIBILITY: Active/Retired/Reserve/DOD, NAF and Contract Civilians.

RESERVATIONS: Required, in person only, in Bldg 636 (Rec Center). Resv are accepted starting in May. Call for specific information between the hours of 0900-1800, local time, Monday-Saturday. Priority is given to AD in Alaska. Address: ITT Office, PO Box 5-367, Ft Richardson, AK 99505-5100. Comm: 907-862-3217; ATVN: 317-862-3217.

CAMP FACILITIES:	NO	UNITS	HOOKUPS	FEE
Cabins, sleep up to 4	25			$25.00-30 daily
Campers, pop-up	3		None	7.50 daily
Camper Spaces	45	Gravel	W/E (110)	7.50 daily
Tent Spaces	7	Open	None	5.00 daily

SUPPORT FACILITIES:　Boat Rental*　　Deep Sea Rods　Dining Fac
　　　　　　　　　　　　Grills　　　　　Picnic Area　　Playground
　　　　　　　　　　　　PX Annex　　　　Rec Center　　　Restrooms
　　　　　　　　　　　　Sewage Dump Sta　Showers　　　　Vending Machines
　　　　　　　　　*Boat rental/boat fishing (fee), by drawing.

ACTIVITIES:　　　　　Basketball　　　Fishing (lic)　Hiking
　　　　　　　　　　　　Hunting (lic)　Volleyball　　　Tour Boat/fee

RESTRICTIONS: Pets allowed on leash no longer than 6'; will not be left in cabins unattended; are not allowed on boats; owner must clean up after pets. No open fires are permitted. Charcoal grills may be used. NO cooking in cabins. Patrons must provide own bedding, towels and soap.

GUAM

Guam USA and Marianas Islands
Consolidated Recreation (GUO4R8)
FPO San Francisco 96630-5000

Comm: 646-5278/9
ATVN: 349-5210/11/12

LOCATION: Consolidated Recreation is comprised of 3 recreation districts. **District I** is Naval Sta; **District II** is located between Agana and Tamuning, Guam, on Naval Air Station; and **District III** is located between Tamuning and Dededo, Guam, on the back road to Andersen AFB. There is only one main road on Guam. Marine Drive goes completely around the island which is 37 miles long.

DESCRIPTION OF AREA: Guam has a tropical climate and warm humid weather. Attractions vary considerably including secluded beaches, cooling waterfalls, historic villages, caves and mountains. Many are accessible only by hiking. Hikers and swimmers should be aware of the unusual terrain, jagged limestone, slippery red mud, hidden gullies, changing weather, tide and surf conditions. It is recommended that tourists do not hike or swim alone, but in groups of three or more. Full range of military facilities avail at NS, NAS and AFB.

SEASON OF OPERATION: Year round.

ELIGIBILITY: Active/Retired/NG/Reserve/DOD Civilians.

RESERVATIONS: Not required. Address: COMNAVMARIANAS Guam, Consolidated Recreation, Box 11, FPO San Francisco 96630-5000. ATVN: 349-5210/11/12.

CAMPING FACILITIES: Camping is allowed on all beaches on Guam with no hook-ups and no fees.

SUPPORT FACILITIES:

Archery (III)	Beaches	Boat Rental*
Cabanas	Chapels	Gas
Golf (III)	Gun Ranges (I)	Laundry
Marinas* (I)	Picnic Areas	Racquet Sports
Rec Equip Rental	Sports Fields	Vending Machines

*Civilian marinas at Proteus Point, Agana and Merizo. Boat rental at Agana and Merizo.

ACTIVITIES:

Bicycling	Fishing	Hiking
Hunting (III)	Scuba Diving	Swimming

RESTRICTIONS: Pets allowed.

HAWAII

Barbers Point Recreation Area (HIO1R6)
Barbers Point Naval Air Station, HI 96862-5000

Comm: 808-684-6266
ATVN: 430-0111

LOCATION: On base. I-H1 W to Barbers Point exit. Bear L at sign; go through main gate. Reservations Office is in Fitness Center, Bldg 19. RM: p-7, I/2. NMC: Pearl City, 10 mi NE.

DESCRIPTION OF AREA: A small but nice facility located on SW coast of Oahu, 13 mi from Pearl Harbor and 29 mi from Honolulu. Enlisted cottages are on Nimitz Beach; Officer cottages and campsites are on White Plains Beach. Beaches excellent for surfing. Nearby attractions include: Castle Park, Ala Moana Park, Waianae Beach parks, Pearl Harbor Park and Ice Palace (skating). Full range of military facilities available on base.

SEASON OF OPERATION: Year round.

ELIGIBILITY: Active/Retired/Reserve/DOD Civilians.

RESERVATIONS: Required with payment. No phone resv accepted for cottages. Resv for campsites must be completed at least 5 working days in adv of use. Address: Recreation Services Dept, Reservations Office, Barbers Point Naval Air Station, HI 96862-5050. Comm: 808-682-2019.

CAMP FACILITIES:	NO UNITS	HOOKUPS	FEE
Cottages, 2 bdrm, furn	14 Enlisted		$20.00 daily
	6 Officer		25.00 daily
	2 VIP (O6+)		30.00 daily
Camper & Tent Spaces	14	W	5.00 daily

SUPPORT FACILITIES:			
	Beach	Bicycle Rental	Cabanas
	Chapel	Gas	Golf
	Grills	Laundry	Mini Mart
	Picnic Area	Playground	Racquetball
	Rec Center	Restrooms	Showers
	Snack Bar	Sports Fields	Tennis Courts

ACTIVITIES:			
	Fishing (lic)	Rec Equip Avail	Scuba Diving
	Snorkeling	Surfing	Swimming

RESTRICTIONS: No pets allowed. No open fires. Cottages may not be used as a party facility. No glass bottles at beaches. Alcohol: beer only.

Bellows Recreation Area (HIO2R6)
Bellows Air Force Station, HI 96795-1010

Comm: 808-259-8841
ATVN: 259-8841

LOCATION: On base. From Honolulu take I-H1 E to HI-72 to AFS. Clearly marked. RM: p-7, H/7. NMC: Kailua, 9 mi NW.

DESCRIPTION OF AREA: A seaside recreational facility located on eastern shore of the Island of Oahu, 22 mi from downtown Honolulu. Beautiful beach. Some mil fac on base. Full range avail at Kaneohe Marine Corps Air Station, 10 mi NW.

SEASON OF OPERATION: Year round.

ELIGIBILITY: Active/Retired/DOD Civilians employed in Hawaii.

Bellows Rec Area, Cont'd

RESERVATIONS: Required with $25 dep. Resv may be made 30-90 days in adv, the max time depending on branch of service, status, and place of duty of sponsor. Address: Bellows Reservation Office, PO Box 1010, Waimanalo, HI 96795-1010. Comm: 808-259-8841.

CAMPING FACILITIES:	<u>NO</u> <u>UNITS</u>	<u>HOOKUPS</u>	<u>FEE</u>
Camper & Tent Spaces	38	None	$2.50 daily

BEACH COTTAGES: 101 single and duplex cottages, furn, PB, kitchenette. All are equipped with TV, linens, towels, pots, pans, utensils and dishes. Extra cots and cribs available for $1 per day.

	<u>FEE</u>
Studio	$20.00 daily
Backrow	25.00 daily
Oceanview	30.00 daily

SUPPORT FACILITIES:		
Bath Houses	Beach	Beach Club
Boat Rental	Camp Equip Rntl	Gas
Golf Driv Range	Grocery Store	Laundry
Library	Nature Trails	Picnic Area
PX	Rec Equip Rental	Tennis Courts

ACTIVITIES:		
Fishing	Snorkeling	Swimming

RESTRICTIONS: No pets allowed. 14-day limit; resv for Friday or Saturday night must include both nights. Hiking is prohibited on Bellows AFS. Dependents and guests are not permitted to remain overnight without the sponsor present. Rental cars are <u>not</u> available on-station. City bus service is available; however, off-island visitors are advised to obtain rental cars for mobility.

Hale Koa Hotel AFRC (HIO8R6)
2055 Kalia Road
Honolulu, HI 96815-1998

Comm: 808-955-0555 (24 hrs dly)
800-367-6027 (0800-1600 dly
HI time, except holidays)

LOCATION: At 2055 Kalia Rd, Waikiki Beach, Honolulu. The installation (Ft De Russy) is on Waikiki Beach, between Ala Moana Blvd, Kalakaua Ave and Saratoga Rd, approx 9 mi E of Honolulu International Airport. RM: p-7, L/11. NMC: Honolulu, in the city.

DESCRIPTION OF AREA: This morale-boosting, all ranks hotel, has 14 stories with 420 guest rooms with view of Pacific Ocean and/or Koolau Mountains. All rooms are identical in size; most have private lanai, room-controlled A/C, message lights and color TV. Coin-operated washers and dryers available. Some rooms specially fitted for handicapped veterans. Hotel has swimming pool, landscaped gardens, and offers indoor and outdoor sports activities on the most beautiful golden sand beach in Waikiki. Also avail: cocktail lounges, snack bar, Post Exchange, Show Room, meeting rooms, conference facilities, fine dining in the Hale Koa Room, sauna and locker rooms, coffee house, barber and beauty shops, rental cars, and discount tour and travel desk. With its magnificent dining, cocktail and entertainment rooms, the Hale Koa is one of the island's most complete resorts. In addition, ocean and pool swimming, snorkeling, tennis, volleyball, sailboats, racquetball and paddle tennis are avail at your door. One of the world's largest shopping centers is nearby. Dress is resortwear and aloha attire at all times.

SEASON OF OPERATION: Year round.

ELIGIBILITY: Active/Retired/DOD Civilians on TDY.

Hale Koa Hotel AFRC, Cont'd

RESERVATIONS: Required with deposit; may be made up to 365 days in adv for a maximum stay of 30 days. Address: Hale Koa Hotel, 2055 Kalia Road, Honolulu, HI 96815-1998. Ask for free information packet.

1986-1987 DOUBLE RATES (FOR 2 PERSONS) ARE QUOTED BELOW

CATEGORIES (Active & Retired)*	I	II	III
Standard	$29 daily	$38 daily	$50 daily
Superior	35 daily	44 daily	60 daily
Partial Ocean View	40 daily	53 daily	70 daily
Ocean View	45 daily	58 daily	75 daily

A limited number of ocean front rooms (with queen bed only) are available upon request at additional cost.

Rates are based on room location (generally the higher floors and view reflect the higher rates). RATES ARE SUBJECT TO CHANGE ON OR BEFORE 1 OCTOBER 1988. Deduct $2 for single occupancy. Add $7 for each additional occupant. MOST rooms are furnished with two double beds, for a maximum occupancy of 4 persons. With Family Plan, children under 12 are free in parents' room if no additional beds are required. Rollaway beds are available at $7 daily for use ONLY in rooms with one queen bed. Cribs are available at $3 daily.

*I: E-1 to E-5; II: E-6 to E-9, WO-1 to CW-3, O-1 to O-3; all TDY, TLA, DAV (must have DD 1173) and widows; III: CW-4, O-4 to O-10, foreign, others. Active and Retired (DD Form 2, Ret - gray or blue) and family members (DD 1173), all services, all ranks, family and guests meeting eligibility requirements.

The Luau at the Hale Koa is every Thursday evening on the beach. Adults, $21.95; children under 12, $12.95. ID cardholders can sponsor guests.

RESTRICTIONS: No pets allowed.

Hickam Harbor Recreation Area
(HIO7R6)
Hickam Air Force Base, HI 96853-5000

Comm: 808-422-0531
ATVN: 430-0111

LOCATION: On base. S coast of Oahu, next to Pearl Harbor. Follow I-H1 signs to Pearl Harbor/Hickam AFB; take Hickam exit thru main gate; follow signs to Hickam Harbor/Beach. RM: p-7, H/4. NMC: Honolulu, 6 mi E.

DESCRIPTION OF AREA: Many outdoor recreational activities such as fishing (surf and big game), sightseeing, hiking and backpacking, body and bogey board surfing are possible year round. This is a recreation area; no camping facilities are available. Full range of military facilities on base.

SEASON OF OPERATION: Year round.

ELIGIBILITY: Active/Retired/DOD Civilians.

RESERVATIONS: Required for charter boats and some other rentals. Address: Recreation Services, 15ABW/SSRO, Hickam AFB, HI 96853-5000. Comm: 808-449-5215; ATVN: 430-5215.

SUPPORT FACILITIES:	Boat Launch	Boat Rental	Cabanas/fee
	Chapel	Laundry	Marina
	Picnic Areas/fee	Racquet Sports	Rec Equip Rental
	Restrooms	Showers	Snack Bars

Hickam Harbor Rec Area, Cont'd

ACTIVITIES:	Boating	Fishing	Golf (on base)
	Racquetball	Squash	Swimming

RESTRICTIONS: No pets allowed. Alcohol is prohibited in wet-sand/beach area.

Kaneohe Bay Beach Cottages
and Campsites (HIO6R6)
Kaneohe Bay Marine Corps Air Station, HI 96863-5010

Comm: 808-257-2747
ATVN: 430-0111

LOCATION: On base. At the end of I-H3 on windward side of Oahu. Clearly marked off Mokapu Blvd and Kaneohe Bay Dr. RM: p-7, G/6. NMC: Honolulu, 14 mi SW.

DESCRIPTION OF AREA: Located in a secluded area overlooking beautiful Kaneohe Bay. Cottages are across the airstrip along the coastline, near Pyramid Rock. Campsites are near the northern area of the base in a sheltered cove with an excellent view. Full range of military facilities available on base.

SEASON OF OPERATION: Year round.

ELIGIBILITY: Active/Retired/DOD Civilians.

RESERVATIONS: Required. Up to 60 days in adv for cottages; address: TLF, Bldg 3038, MCAS Kaneohe Bay, HI 96863-5000; Comm: 808-254-2806; ATVN: 430-3513. Campsites, address: Special Services, Bldg 219, MCAS Kaneohe Bay, HI 96863-5000; Comm: 808-257-2808; ATVN: 430-2808.

CAMP FACILITIES:	NO UNITS	HOOKUPS	FEE
Cottages, 2 bdrm, furn	12		$22.00 daily
Camper Spaces	4 Primitive	None	None

SUPPORT FACILITIES:	Beach	Chapel	Gas
	Golf	Grills	Marina
	Picnic Area	Playground	Rec Equip Rntl
	Restrooms	Short Stop	Showers
	Skeet Range	Snack Bar	Sports Fields
	Swimming Pool	Tennis Courts	

ACTIVITIES:	Boating	Fishing	Swimming

RESTRICTIONS: No pets allowed.

KMC Volcanoes Recreation Area (HIO4R6)
Kilauea Military Camp, HI 96718-5000

Comm: 808-521-7801
ATVN: None

LOCATION: On post. Off HI-11, in Volcanoes National Park, SW of Hilo on Island of Hawaii. Honolulu is 216 air miles NW. RM: p-7, H/11. NMC: Hilo, 32 mi NE.

DESCRIPTION OF AREA: This Joint Armed Forces Rec Center is situated on Kilauea Volcano at an elevation of 4000 feet. A 65-degree day is warm and morning temps in the 50's are common. Limited military facilities available on base.

SEASON OF OPERATION: Year round.

ELIGIBILITY: Active/Retired/Reserve/NG/DOD Civilians.

RESERVATIONS: Required. Address: KMC Reservations, Kilauea Military Camp, Hawaii Volcanoes National Park, HI 96718-5000. Comm: 808-521-7801.

HAWAII

KMC Volcanoes Rec Area, Cont'd

LODGING: 53 units (cabins/apartments) with cable TV and refrigerators in all units. Fee includes up to two occupants per unit and use of scheduled bus for an unlimited number of guests to and from Hilo airport.
   FEE: $14.00-21.00 daily. $2 ea add pers; $7 add per day w/kit.

SUPPORT FACILITIES:

Cafeteria	Chapel	Dispensary
Fitness Center	Gas	General Store
Gift Shop	Golf	Laundry
Multi-Purpose Ct	Post Office	Rec Center
Tennis Courts		

ACTIVITIES:

Bicycling	Bowling	Hiking
Rec Equip Avail	Tours	

RESTRICTIONS: No pets allowed. Use of dispensary limited to emergency care.

WARNING: Venting gas surrounds the area as a result of volcanic acid. The sulfur fumes could be noxious or hazardous to people with heart or lung disorders.

Waianae Army Recreation Center (HIO5R6)

Army Support Command Fort Shafter, HI 96858-5000

Comm: 808-471-7411
ATVN: 430-0111

LOCATION: Off post. On west coast of Oahu. Take I-H1 W to HI-93 (Farrington Hwy); N to Waianae. RM: p-7, G/1. NMI: Schofield Barracks, 20 mi NE. NMC: Honolulu, 35 mi SE.

DESCRIPTION OF AREA: Located along beach of Pokai Bay in once-quiet fishing and plantation village. It is one of the favorite swimming and fishing spots on Oahu. The beach facility is regarded as one of the finest on the island. Full range of military fac available at Schofield Barracks.

SEASON OF OPERATION: Year round.

ELIGIBILITY: Active/Retired/Reserve/DOD Civilians.

RESERVATIONS: Required: up to 30 days in adv for AD Army; up to 20 days in adv for other AD and Retired; up to 10 days in adv for Reserve on AD and Civilians. Address: Waianae Army Recreation Center, 85-010 Army Street, Waianae, HI 96792-5000. Comm: 808-696-2494.

CAMP FACILITIES:

	NO UNITS	HOOKUPS	FEE
Camper Spaces	3	None	$ 2.00 daily
Cabins	33		13-23 daily

Accommodations range from 6-bed lodges and single-room studios to 2-bdrm fam apt. All except studios have kit with dishes and utensils. All have linens. Fees are based on rank and type of accommodation.

SUPPORT FACILITIES:

Boat Rental	Club (all ranks)	First Aid Sta
Laundry	Picnic Area	PX
Restrooms	Showers	Snack Bar
TV Room	Water Sports Equipment Rental	

ACTIVITIES:

Deep-Sea Fishing	Scuba Diving	Surf Fishing
Surfing	Snorkeling	Swimming
Windsurfing		

Outdoor sports facilities, 5-minute walk from camp.

RESTRICTIONS: No pets allowed. 14-day limit.

FOREIGN COUNTRIES

CANADA

North East Arm Camp (CNO1R1)
Argentia USN Facility, FPO New York 09597-5000

Comm: 709-227-8555
ATVN: 622-1690

LOCATION: Off base. Argentia is reached by car or by ferry from N Sydney, Nova Scotia. The nearest airport is at St. John's. The camp is located at ocean terminus of the Argentia access to Trans-Canadian Highway (TCH-1). RM: p-117, G/24. NMI: Argentia USN Facility, 7 mi E. NMC: St John's, 75 mi NE.

DESCRIPTION OF AREA: Wild, beautiful country with abundant fishing and hunting. The naval facility is now a small command with most support facilities avail.

SEASON OF OPERATION: Recreation Lodge: Year round
9 Cabins: April-January
4 Cabins: January-April

ELIGIBILITY: Active/Retired/DOD Civilians.

RESERVATIONS: Required at least 30 days in adv. Address: Recreational Services Director, PO Box 12, US Naval Facility, Argentia, FPO New York, NY 09597-5000. Comm: 709-227-2017; ATVN: 622-2017.

LODGING: 9 Cabins: 7 slp up to 8 pers; 2 slp up to 4 pers. One-room with bath/shower, fireplace, cooking utensils, dishes, bunk beds. No bedding.
    <u>FEE:</u> $20.00 daily for any one-night stay
        15.00 daily, F-Su, for more than one night
        10.00 daily, M-Th, for more than one night

SUPPORT FACILITIES:	BBQ Pits	Boat Launch	Boat Rental
	Camper Rental	Canoe Rental	Picnic Area
	Playground	Rec Lodge	Sailboats
ACTIVITIES:	Fishing	Hiking	Swimming

RESTRICTIONS: 7-day limit per month. Pets, except Alaskan Huskies, allowed on leashes; must have International Health Certificate no more than 1 week old; must have Import Certificate from Province of Newfoundland.

GERMANY

Bad Kreuznach Army Travel Camp (GE56R7)
Bad Kreuznach MILCOM
APO New York 09252-0027

Comm: 49-0671-609-1110
ATVN: 490-1110
ETS: 490-XXXX

LOCATION: Off post. Approx 60 mi SW of Frankfurt. Camping area is located 2.8 mi SW of Rose Barracks near Hackenheim on the Kuhberg Recreation Complex. Turn R at the Jugendherberge and L at Rheingrafenstein. HE: map 40, A/1. NMI: Bad Kreuznach Community, 2 mi N. NMC: Bad Kreuznach, 3 mi N.

Bad Kreuznach Army Tvl Camp, Cont'd

DESCRIPTION OF AREA: Germany's oldest radium spa is located in scenic Nahe Valley. Beautiful parks and forest areas to visit as well as Rhein River (castles and wine country). The camp is located in rustic setting with grassy fields and beautiful, forested area. Full range of mil fac at Bad Kreuznach Community.

SEASON OF OPERATION: Year round.

ELIGIBILITY: Active/Retired/DOD Civilians.

RESERVATIONS: Required. Address: MSA, Outdoor Recreation Director, ATTN: Army Travel Camp, APO New York 09252-0027. Comm: 49-0671-609-6498/6496; ATVN: 490-6498. Fees paid in full at time of registration.

CAMPING FACILITIES:	NO UNITS	HOOKUPS	FEE
Camper Spaces	26 Hardstand	E	$6.00 dly/36 wkly
Camper Spaces	15	None	4.00 dly/24 wkly
Tent Spaces	35 Primitive	None	2.50 dly/15 wkly

SUPPORT FACILITIES:			
	Dishwashing Area	Fitness Trail	Gas
	Grills	Grocery Store	Laundry
	Mini-Golf	Picnic Areas	Playground
	Rec Center	Rec Equip Rntl	Restrooms
	Sewage Dump Sta	Showers/hot	Snack Bar
	Sports Fields		

ACTIVITIES:			
	Backpacking	Bicycling	Castle Hikes
	Fishing (lic)	Horseshoe Tourn	Hunting (lic)
	Jogging	Volksmarching	Winter Sports

RESTRICTIONS: Pets on leash allowed.

Baumholder Rolling Hills Travel Camp (GE55R7)

Baumholder Community Recreation Area
APO New York 09034-0033

Comm: 49-06783-6+8333
ATVN: 485-6575
ETS: 485-XXXX

LOCATION: Off post. Camp is in the Baumholder Community Rec Area. Follow the signs from the Baumholder American High School to the camp. HE: map 39, G/1. NMI: Ramstein AB, 25 mi. NMC: Kaiserslautern, 35 mi SE.

DESCRIPTION OF AREA: The gem city of Idar-Oberstein, famous for its precious stone industry and diamond factory, is nearby. Two castles in the area as well as Palatinate Forest, Mosel River, and vineyards. **Bosen Lake, 19 mi from post, offers swimming, fishing and windsurfing.** Most support facilities in the recreation area.

SEASON OF OPERATION: Year round.

ELIGIBILITY: Active/Retired/DOD Civilians.

RESERVATIONS: Accepted. Address: CRD, Outdoor Rec, Baumholder MILCOM, APO New York 09034-0033. Fac #, Comm: 49-06783-6+7182; ETS: 485-7182.

CAMPING FACILITIES:	NO UNITS	HOOKUPS	FEE
Camper Spaces	30	E (220)	$ 8.00 daily
Camper & Tent Spaces	10	None	5.00 daily
Camping for groups of 20+	Primitive	None	20.00 daily/group

Baumholder Rolling Hills Tvl Camp, Cont'd

SUPPORT FACILITIES:	Chapel	Foodland Store	Golf (9 holes)
	Grills	Nature Trails	Picnic Areas
	Playgrounds	Rec Equip Rental	Restrooms
	Rod & Gun Club	Showers	Swimming Pool
	Tennis Courts		

ACTIVITIES:	Rafting	Rock Climbing	Sightseeing
	Snow Ski(DH&XC)	Windsurfing	

RESTRICTIONS: Pets on leash allowed. Elec/water turned off Nov-Apr.

Berchtesgaden Armed Forces Recreation Center (GE07R7)
APO New York, NY 09029-5000

Comm: 49-08652-58-3270
ATVN: 441-1110 Ask for
BGN 5613

LOCATION: Exit Munich-Salzburg Autobahn E-11 at Bad Reichenhall, S on national road 20, 11 mi to Berchtesgaden. HE: map 94, D/4. NMC: Munich, 100 mi NW.

DESCRIPTION OF AREA: Nestled in the heart of the Bavarian Alps just 8 mi from the Austrian border, Berchtesgaden is an 800-year-old storybook village with church spires framed by scenic mountains rising to nearly 9,000 feet. Breathtaking scenery and a wide variety of sports and tour opportunities await the visitor to this popular year-round vacation spot. Limited military facilities at AFRC; full range of facilities at McGraw Kaserne in Munich.

SEASON OF OPERATION: Year round.

ELIGIBILITY: Active/Retired/DOD Civilians stationed in USEUCOM.

RESERVATIONS: Accepted up to 90 days in adv with deposit. Address: Accommodations Office, AFRC, APO New York, NY 09053-5000. Comm: 49-08821-750575; ETS: 440-2575; Telex: 592417 AFRC BD.

CAMPING FACILITIES: There are no military camping facilities at Berchtesgaden. Both Chiemsee and Garmisch have complete travel camps.

SUPPORT FACILITIES:	Activity Center	Chapel	Game Room
	Golf (9 holes)	Grills	Laundry
	Picnic Area	Playground	Restaurants
	Sports Fields	Tennis Courts	Trails

ACTIVITIES:	Bicycling	Children's Prog	Hiking
	Hunting	Kayaking	Rec Equip Avail
	Snow Skiing	Tours	White-water Rafting

HOTEL ROOM RATES

Standard Category Hotels Alpine Inn, McNair		Superior Category Hotels Evergreen, Hof, Walker, Skytop	
Without Private Bath	E1-E5 / Others	**Without Private Bath**	All Grades
Single Occupancy	$ 9.00/14.00	Single Occupancy	$18.00
Double Occupancy	11.00/18.00	Double Occupancy	23.00
With Private Bath		**With Private Bath**	
Single Occupancy	$16.00/21.00	Single Occupancy	$26.00
Double Occupancy	20.00/28.00	Double Occupancy	34.00

GERMANY
Berchtesgaden AFRC, Cont'd

Suites are available at $50.00 per night (All Grades).

Children under 16 staying in sponsor's room (in existing beds) free. Cots are available at $6 per night. Cribs are free. In rooms with more than two beds installed, the use of additional beds by adults will be at the rate of $6 per person per night. Prices are subject to change without notice. Prices normally change as each new fiscal year begins on 1 Oct. The above prices are effective 3 Jan 88. VISA and Mastercard accepted.

RESTRICTIONS: No pets allowed.

Camp Dahn Travel Camp (GE47R7)

Pirmasens Military Community
APO New York 09189-5000

Comm: 49-06331-86-1110
ATVN: 495-1110 Ask for PMS
ETS: 495-1110

LOCATION: Off post. On the triangle of GE-10 from Zweibrucken and GE-270 from Kaiserslautern. The camp is 3 mi off GE-427 near Dahn. HE: map 39, G/2. NMI: Pirmasens Community, 10 mi NW. NMC: Pirmasens, 15 mi NW.

DESCRIPTION OF AREA: Situated in a primitive wooded area with some improvements Camp Dahn is conveniently located for a wide variety of sightseeing and recreational activities. There are hundreds of miles of trails through nature areas and through romantic villages, a health resort, or castle ruins. 30-min drive to Saarbacherhammer Lake for sailing and windsurfing. Full range of miliitary facilities available at Pirmasens Community.

SEASON OF OPERATION: 16 May-14 September: daily
                        1 Apr-15 May and 15 Sep-1 Nov: Friday-Sunday only.

ELIGIBILITY: Active/Retired/DOD Civilians.

RESERVATIONS: No adv resv for family camping; group resv (20 or more) accepted up to 1 year in adv with deposit. Address: USMCA-P, Outdoor Recreation, APO New York 01989-5000. Comm: 49-06331-86-6483; ETS: 495-6483. (Travel Camp) Comm: 49-06391-5670.

CAMPING FACILITIES:	NO UNITS	HOOKUPS	FEE *
Camper Spaces	24 Hardstand	W/S/E (220)	$5.00 daily
Tent Spaces	Primitive	None	2.00 daily
		E (220)	1.00 daily add

*Includes up to 5 persons; additional adults, $1.

SUPPORT FACILITIES:			
	Fitness Trail	Grills	Kitchen Fac
	Laundry	Multi-Purpose Ct	Picnic Area
	Playground	Restrooms	Sewage Dump Sta
	Showers	Snack Bar	

ACTIVITIES:			
	Horseshoes	Rec Equip Avail	Volleyball

RESTRICTIONS: Pets allowed. Groups larger than 20 require written request to USMCA-P Outdoor Recreation, APO 09189. There is a nominal fee ($1) for day use.

Chiemsee Armed Forces Recreation Center (GEO8R7)
APO New York 09029-5000

Comm: 49-08051-7264
ETS: 441-2630
ATVN: 440-1110 Ask
for Chiemsee Lake Hotel

LOCATION: Located directly off Munich-Salzburg Autobahn E-11 SE of Munich. Busses use Feldwies exit; automobiles continue for 800 meters and exit when you see the sign for AFRC Chiemsee. HE: map 94, B/3. NMC: Munich, 50 mi NW.

DESCRIPTION OF AREA: Situated along the shores of Chiemsee Lake, Germany's largest lake. Enjoy a variety of watersports or take advantage of the nearby Chiemgauer Alps which offer scenic panoramas and opportunities for hiking and hang gliding. Limited military fac at AFRC; full range available in Munich.

SEASON OF OPERATION: Year round.

ELIGIBILITY: Active/Retired/DOD Civilians stationed in USEUCOM.

RESERVATIONS: Accepted up to 90 days in adv with deposit. Address: Accommodations Office, AFRC, APO New York 09053-5000. Comm: 49-08821-750575; ETS: 440-2575; Telex: 592417 AFRC BD.

SUPPORT FACILITIES:

Activity Center	Beach	Boat Launch
Boat Rental	Conv Store	Fitness Center
Game Room	Laundry	Library
Picnic Area	Playground	Restaurant
Snack Bar	Sports Fields	Tennis Courts

ACTIVITIES:

Archery	Bicycling	Catamarans
Fishing	Hang Gliding	Hunting
Jogging	Mini-Golf	Paddle Boats
Rec Equip Avail	Sailing	Snow Skiing
Swimming	Tours	Water Skiing
Windsurfing		

HOTEL ROOM RATES

Standard Category Hotels		Superior Category Hotels	
Park Hotel		**Lake Hotel**	
Without Private Bath	**E1-E5 / Others**	**Without Private Bath**	**All Grades**
Single Occupancy	$ 9.00/14.00	Single Occupancy	$18.00
Double Occupancy	11.00/18.00	Double Occupancy	23.00
With Private Bath		**With Private Bath**	
Single Occupancy	$16.00/21.00	Single Occupancy	$26.00
Double Occupancy	20.00/28.00	Double Occupancy	34.00

Suites are available at $50.00 per night (All Grades).

Children under 16 staying in sponsor's room (in existing beds) free. Cots are available at $6 per night. Cribs are free. In rooms with more than two beds installed, the use of additional beds will be at the rate of $6 per person per night. Prices are subject to change without notice. Prices normally change as each new fiscal year begins on 1 October. The above prices are effective 3 Jan 88.

RESTRICTIONS: No pets allowed.

GERMANY
Chiemsee AFRC Campground
(GE57R7)
Armed Forces Recreation Center
APO New York 09029-5000

Comm: 49-08051-8733
ATVN: 440-1110 Ask
for Chiemsee Lake Hotel
ETS: 441-2719

LOCATION: Located directly off Munich-Salzburg Autobahn E-11 SE of Munich.
Exit 800 meters beyond Feldwies exit when you see the sign for AFRC Chiemsee.
HE: map 94, B/3. NMC: Munich, 50 mi NW.

DESCRIPTION OF AREA: Situated along shores of Chiemsee Lake, Germany's largest
inland lake. King Ludwig's Herrenchiemsee Castle is located on an island in
middle of lake. Berchtesgaden and Hitler's Eagles Nest are nearby. Additions
scheduled for summer of 1989 include: overflow areas, multi-purpose court,
pavilion, group camping facility and landscaping. Limited military facilities
at AFRC; full range of facilities available in Munich.

SEASON OF OPERATION: Year round.

ELIGIBILITY: Active/Retired/DOD Civilians stationed in USEUCOM.

RESERVATIONS: Accepted up to 90 days in adv with deposit. Address: Chiemsee
AFRC Campground, APO New York 09029-5000. Comm: 49-08051-8733; ETS: 441-2719.
Special rates for groups.

CAMPING FACILITIES:	NO UNITS	HOOKUPS	FEE *
Camper, slp 4			$20.00 daily
Camper & Tent Spaces	Total	W/S/E (220)	8.00 daily
	of 72	W/S	7.00 daily
Tent Spaces	120	None	Call For Rates

*Includes up to 4 persons; additional adults, $1.50.

SUPPORT FACILITIES:			
	Boat Rental	Camp Equip Rntl	Conv Store
	Game Room	Ice	Laundry
	Picnic Area	Playground	Restrooms
	Showers/hot	Snack Bar	TV Room/Video

ACTIVITIES:			
	Bicycling	Fishing	Hang Gliding
	Rec Equip Avail	Sailing	Snow Skiing
	Swimming	Water Skiing	Windsurfing

RESTRICTIONS: Pets allowed on leash; must be kept quiet.

Garmisch Armed Forces
Recreation Center (GE10R7)
APO New York 09053-5000

Comm: 49-08821-750575
Mil: 253-5575
ATVN: 440-1110 Ask for
Garmisch 575

LOCATION: Take Autobahn E-6 S from Munich to Garmisch. From Austria take
national roads numbered 2 or 187. HE: map 92, F/3. NMC: Munich, 60 mi N.

DESCRIPTION OF AREA: Located at foot of Zugspitze, Germany's highest mountain.
Unforgettable Alpine scenery and wide variety of sports activities are available at AFRC vacation area. Garmisch is one of the most popular Alpine resorts
in Germany. AFRC Garmisch offers four hotels and modern travel camp with accommodations for more than 1,300 guests. Full range of military facilities at
AFRC.

SEASON OF OPERATION: Year round.

Garmisch Armed Fcs Rec Ctr, Cont'd

ELIGIBILITY: Active/Retired/DOD Civilians stationed in USEUCOM.

RESERVATIONS: Accepted up to 90 days in adv with deposit. Address: Accommodations Office, AFRC Garmisch, APO New York 09053-5000. Comm: 49-08821-750575; ETS: 440-2575; Telex: 592417 AFRC BD.

SUPPORT FACILITIES:

Activity Center	Bank	Chapel
Commissary	Conv Store	Fitness Center
Game Room	Golf (9 holes)	Laundry
Library	Medical Clinic	Picnic Area
Playground	PX	Racquetball
Restaurants	Ski Lodge*	Sports Fields
Tennis Courts		

*__Hausberg Lodge__, nestled in the beautiful Bavarian Alps, features a huge restaurant, kitchen and classrooms. It provides a reception area for AFRC skiers, with ski equip/storage points, ski repair shop, and locker rooms connected to a central heating/ventilation system to dry equipment. It also offers ski equip rental, the AFRC Ski School, and lift tickets for all ski areas in Garmisch.

ACTIVITIES:

Bicycling	Children's Prog	Fishing
Hiking	Hunting	Ice Skating
Jogging	Kayaking	Rec Equip Avail
Swimming	Tours	White-water Rafting

HOTEL ROOM RATES

Standard Category Hotels	Superior Category Hotels
Abrams	Von Steuben, Haus Flora, Patton

Without Private Bath	E1-E5 / Others	Without Private Bath	All Grades
Single Occupancy	$ 9.00/14.00	Single Occupancy	$18.00
Double Occupancy	11.00/18.00	Double Occupancy	23.00
With Private Bath		**With Private Bath**	
Single Occupancy	$16.00/21.00	Single Occupancy	$26.00
Double Occupancy	20.00/28.00	Double Occupancy	34.00

Suites are available at $50.00 per night (All Grades).

Children under 16 staying in sponsor's room (in existing beds) free. Cots are available at $6 per night. Cribs are free. In rooms with more than two beds installed, the use of additional beds will be at the rate of $6 per person per night. Prices are subject to change without notice. Prices normally change as each new fiscal year begins on 1 October. The above prices are effective 3 Jan 88. VISA and Mastercard accepted.

RESTRICTIONS: No pets allowed.

Garmisch AFRC Campground (GE58R7)

Armed Forces Recreation Center
APO New York 09053-5000

Comm: 49-08821-750848
ETS: 440-2848
ATVN: 440-1110 Ask for
    Garmisch 848

LOCATION: Take Autobahn E-6 from Munich to Garmisch. From Austria take national roads numbered 2 or 187. The camp is adjacent to Breitenau Housing Area. HE: map 92, F/3. NMC: Munich, 60 mi N.

Garmisch AFRC Campground, Cont'd

DESCRIPTION OF AREA: Located at the foot of Zugspitze, Germany's tallest mountain. Oberammergau, famous for wood carving and for its Passion Play, is 13 mi away. Garmisch is one of the most popular Alpine resorts in Germany. Wide variety of sports available at AFRC. Full range of military facilities avail.

SEASON OF OPERATION: Year round.

ELIGIBILITY: Active/Retired/DOD Civilians stationed in USEUCOM.

RESERVATIONS: Accepted up to 90 days in adv with deposit. Address: Garmisch AFRC Campground, APO New York 09053-5000. Comm: 49-08821-750848; ETS: 440-2634/2725.

CAMPING FACILITIES:	NO UNITS	HOOKUPS	FEE
Camper, slp 4			$20.00 daily
Camper Spaces, gravel	85	W/S/E (220)	10.00 dly/4 pers*
Tent Spaces	Open Grass Area	W	3.00 dly/2 pers*
	*Additional adults, $1.50. Monthly fee, $150.00.		

SUPPORT FACILITIES:			
	Conv Store	Dishwashing Fac	Laundry
	Restaurant	Restrooms	Showers/hot

ACTIVITIES:			
	Bicycling	Fishing	Hiking
	Rec Equip Avail	Snow Skiing	Tours

RESTRICTIONS: Pets allowed on leash; must be kept quiet.

Rhein Main Travel Camp (GEO9R7)
APO New York 09057-5000

Comm: 49-0611-699-1110
ATVN: 330-1110

LOCATION: On base. From Autobahn E-5 take the Zeppelinheim/Rhein Main AB exit. The travel camp is across the Autobahn from the AB main gate. HE: map 40, B/1. NMC: Frankfurt, 10 mi N.

DESCRIPTION OF AREA: Cosmopolitan Frankfurt has a zoo, fairgrounds and convention center. Wiesbaden, with spas and gambling casinos, is nearby. There are also many vineyards and castles in the area. Campground is a well-preserved and maintained site. Full range of military facilities on base.

SEASON OF OPERATION: Year round.

ELIGIBILITY: Active/Retired/DOD Civilians.

RESERVATIONS: Required. Address: 435 CSG/SSR, ATTN: Campground, Rhein Main AB, APO New York 09057-5000. Comm: 49-069-699-7444; ATVN: 330-7444.

CAMPING FACILITIES:	NO UNITS	HOOKUPS	FEE
Camper Spaces	35 Hardstand	W/S	$4.00 daily
Tent Spaces	35	None	4.00 daily

SUPPORT FACILITIES:			
	Archery	Chapel	Gas
	Firearms Range	Picnic Areas	Racquet Courts
	Rec Equip Rntl	Restaurant	Restrooms
	Showers	Sports Fields	

ACTIVITIES:		
	Bicycling	Jogging

RESTRICTIONS: Pets allowed. No hunting.

GREECE

Iraklion Campground (GRO3R9)
Iraklion Air Station
APO New York 09291-5000

Comm: 30-81-761-281/2/3
ATVN: 668-1110

LOCATION: Off base. On the Greek island of Crete. From Iraklion Airport, turn R at main entrance; pass the Greek military base; turn L; go straight for 20 min to Gournes Air Station on L. HE: map 85, B/3. NMC: Iraklion, 8 mi W.

DESCRIPTION OF AREA: On the beach at Iraklion AS. Undeveloped. Full range of military facilities available on base.

SEASON OF OPERATION: Year round (best time: May-Oct).

ELIGIBILITY: Active/Retired/DOD Civilians.

RESERVATIONS: No adv resv. Campers must check in with security police.

CAMPING FACILITIES:	NO UNITS	HOOKUPS	FEE
Camper Spaces	10.	None	Call For Rates

SUPPORT FACILITIES:			
	Boat Rental	Rec Equip Rntl	Restrooms
	Showers		

ACTIVITIES:		
	Boating	Swimming

RESTRICTIONS: Pets allowed.

ITALY

Admiral Carney Park (ITO3R7)
Naples Naval Support Activity
FPO New York 09521-1000

Comm: 39-081-867-4158
ATVN: 625-1110-EX-4158

LOCATION: Off Base. On the west coast of Italy in Admiral Carney Park. HE: map 51, E/6. NMI: Naval Support Activity, Naples, 6 mi NE. NMC: Naples, 7 mi NE.

DESCRIPTION OF AREA: Active port city of Naples. Roman cities of Herculanum and Pompeii and the active volcano Vesuvius nearby. Beautiful island of Capri is 22 miles by boat or helicopter. The park has large grassy fields and paved roads. Full range of military facilities available at NSA Naples.

SEASON OF OPERATION: Year round.

ELIGIBILITY: Active/Retired/DOD Civilians assigned overseas.

RESERVATIONS: Required. Address: Recreational Services, Box 13, NAVSUPPACT, FPO New York 09521-1000. Comm: 39-081-867-1579; ATVN: 625-4163. Deposit req for 1st day; check payable to "Custodian, Composite Rec Fund"; include your address and ATVN number (if available) for confirmation.

CAMPING FACILITIES:	NO UNITS	HOOKUPS	FEE
Cabins, furnished	12		$25.00 daily
Camper Spaces	3 Hardstand	S/W/E (220)	6.00 daily
Tent Spaces	25 Grassy Area		3.00 daily

ITALY

Admiral Carney Park, Cont'd

SUPPORT FACILITIES:

Chapel (NSA)	Camp Equip Rntl	Conv Store
Golf/NATO Base	Grills	Laundry (NSA)
Picnic Area	Playground	Restrooms (flush)
Showers (hot)	Snack Bar	Sports Fields
Swim Pool/olymp	Tennis Courts	

ACTIVITIES:

Baseball	Basketball	Football
Soccer	Softball	Volleyball

RESTRICTIONS: No pets allowed.

Aviano Fam-Camp (ITO9R7)

Aviano Air Base
APO New York 09293-5000

Comm: 39-0434-65-1141
ATVN: 632-1110

LOCATION: On base. In NE Italy near Austrian border. Exit A-28 at Pordenone;
N on IT-159 8 mi to Aviano AB. HE: map 93, C/4. NMC: Pordenone, 8 mi S.

DESCRIPTION OF AREA: Located at the base of the Alps in beautiful surroundings.
Great beaches on Adriatic Coast, 50 mi S; snow skiing resorts, 50 mi N. Venice
is an hour away. There are many historical sights to see. Full range of military facilities available on base.

SEASON OF OPERATION: May-October.

ELIGIBILITY: Active/Retired/DOD Civilians assigned overseas.

RESERVATIONS: Required. Address: MWR Equipment Rental, 40 CSS/SSRO, Aviano Air
Base, APO New York 09293-5000. ATVN: 632-2633.

CAMPING FACILITIES:

	NO UNITS	HOOKUPS	FEE
Camper Spaces	8 Hardstand	E (110/220)	$3.00 daily
		None	2.00 daily

SUPPORT FACILITIES:

Chapel	Golf (9 holes)	Laundry
Picnic Areas	Rec Center	Rec Equip Rntl
Restrooms	Showers	Snack Bar

ACTIVITIES:

Hiking	Sightseeing	Snow Skiing

RESTRICTIONS: Must show ID card at gate.

Camp Darby Campgrounds and Sea Pines Lodge (ITO2R7)

Eighth Support Group, Leghorn
APO New York 09019-5000

Comm: 39-0586-94-7111
ATVN: 633-7225

LOCATION: On post. Located midway between Livorno and Pisa. From Autostrada E-1
take Pisa S exit. Turn L and continue to end of road; L onto Via Aurelia; R on
Cantiere Navale; follow Camp Darby signs. HE: map 50, A/3. NMC: Pisa, 6 mi N.

DESCRIPTION OF AREA: Famous Leaning Tower of Pisa is 6 mi away; the walled city
of Lucca, 20 mi; Florence, 75 mi. The site is just a few kilometers from the
American Beach on the Tyrrhenian Sea where safe swimming is available at no
charge. Many support facilities available on post.

SEASON OF OPERATION: Sea Pines Lodge: Year round.
Campgrounds: Easter Vacation-30 September.

Camp Darby Campgrounds & Sea Pines Lodge, Cont'd

ELIGIBILITY: Active/Retired/NATO Forces/DOD Civilians assigned overseas.

SEA PINES LODGE: A 24-room American-style motel. Each room has its own entrance, windows on 2 walls, priv bath, refr and TV, and sleeps 4. Also available are a comm kit, social room with TV/video, and the Camp Darby Telephone Office.

FEE: $20.00 daily for 1 pers; add charge for each add pers
5.00 daily for cot; $3 daily for crib

Reservations: Required up to 60 days in adv. Payment is upon arrival and in US dollars only. Address: Sea Pines Lodge, 8th Support Group, APO New York 09019-5000. Comm: 39-586-94-7225; ATVN: 633-7225.

CAMPING FACILITIES:	NO UNITS	HOOKUPS	FEE
Travel Trailers			$17.00 daily
Camper Spaces	125	Many with W/E (220)	7-10 daily

Reservations: Required up to 60 days in adv. Payment is upon arrival and in US dollars only. Address: Camp Darby Campgrounds, 8th Support Group, APO New York 09019-5000. Comm: 39-586-94-7775; ATVN: 633-7775.

SUPPORT FACILITIES:			
	Camp Equip Rntl	Chapel	Gas
	Grills	Laundry	Picnic Area
	Playground	Racquet Courts	Rec Center
	Rec Equip Rntl	Restrooms	Sewage Dump Sta
	Showers/hot	Snack Bars	Trailer Rental

ACTIVITIES:			
	Boating	Scuba Diving	Swimming
	Wind Surfing		

RESTRICTIONS: Pets allowed, $3.50 daily; $50 damage deposit; must have valid health certificate and vaccination record. 12-day limit. Limited off-season service at campground. No hunting.

Lake Marola Outdoor Recreation Area
(IT15R7)
Caserma Ederle, Vicenza, Italy
APO New York 09221-5000

Comm: 39-444-51-7111
ATVN: 634-1110/7301

LOCATION: Off post. Take Vicenza-EST exit off Venice/Milan Autostrada A-4. Turn R after toll booth to light; R on SS-11 to Via G B Marconi; L approx 1 mi to lake on R. HE: map 91, H/6. NMI: Caserma Ederle, 3 mi E. NMC: Vicenza, 3 mi E.

DESCRIPTION OF AREA: Located in a secluded area on the shores of Lake Marola. Excellent fishing; lake is stocked monthly (except Jul and Aug) with trout. Full range of military facilities available at Caserma Ederle.

SEASON OF OPERATION: Year round.

ELIGIBILITY: Active/Retired/DOD Civilians employed overseas.

RESERVATIONS: Recommended. Address: CRD, Outdoor Recreation Br, Hq 22d ASG/USMCAV, APO New York 09221-5000. Comm: 39-444-51-7861; ATVN: 634-7861.

CAMPING FACILITIES:	NO UNITS	HOOKUPS	FEE
Tent Spaces	20 Improved	None	$5.00 daily

ITALY
Lake Marola Outdoor Rec Area, Cont'd

SUPPORT FACILITIES:

Archery	Boat Rental	Camp Equip Rntl
Nature Trail	Pavilion/fee	Picnic Area
Playground	Rec Equip Rntl	Restrooms
Showers (cold)	Snack Bar	

ACTIVITIES:

Fishing Derby	Horseshoes	Softball
Volleyball		

RESTRICTIONS: Pets allowed on leash. No swimming. Fishing permits (fee) avail. Pavilion has 220V electrical outlets; transformers are not avail at the fac.

Vicenza Travel Camp (ITO8R7)
Caserma Ederle, Vicenza, Italy
APO New York 09221-5000

Comm: 39-444-51-7111
ATVN: 634-1110/7301

LOCATION: On post. Take Vicenza E exit from Venice/Milan Autostrada A-4. Follow signs to Caserma Carlo Ederle. Camp is at SE corner of post. HE: map 91, H/6. NMC: Vicenza, adj.

DESCRIPTION OF AREA: Great sightseeing opportunities: Venice, the canal city; Lido and Jesolo beaches on the Adriatic; and Romeo and Juliet's city, Verona. Full range of military facilities available on post.

SEASON OF OPERATION: Year round.

ELIGIBILITY: Active/Retired/DOD Civilians assigned overseas.

RESERVATIONS: No adv resv. Address: CRD, Outdoor Recreation, HQ 22d ASG/USMCAV, APO New York 09221-5000. Comm: 39-444-51-7861; ATVN: 634-7861.

CAMPING FACILITIES:

	NO UNITS	HOOKUPS	FEE
Camping Spaces	7 Hardstand	W/E (110/220)	$10.00 daily
Tent Spaces	8 Open Grass	None	5.00 daily

SUPPORT FACILITIES:

Chapel	Conv Store	Grills
Laundry (post)	Picnic Area	Rec Equip Rntl
Restrooms	Showers (hot)	Snack Bar

ACTIVITIES:

Snow Skiing nearby	Swimming (May-Sep)

RESTRICTIONS: Pets allowed on leash. No open fires. Noise control after 2300.

JAPAN

New Sanno U. S. Forces Center (JAO1R8)
APO San Francisco 96503-0110

Comm: 81-03-440-7871
ATVN: 229-7121

LOCATION: At 4-12-20 Minami Azabu, Minato-ku, Tokyo 106, a 5-minute walk from nearest subway station, Hiroo. NMI: Tokyo Administrative Facility, 10 mi.

DESCRIPTION: Located in quiet residential area not far from downtown Tokyo, the New Sanno opened in 1983 and offers its guests the finest accomodations and food service at affordable rates. Each of 149 guest rooms features quality furnishings and private bath or shower, as well as the comfort of central heating and air conditioning. Two suites are traditional Japanese-style for guests who want to enjoy the full flavor of the Orient.

New Sanno U.S. Forces Ctr, Cont'd

The facility includes a Japanese-style steak house and two other restaurants, one featuring fine Continental dining and the other featuring family-style dining. A lounge and a 24-hour snack bar are also available. Entertainment and special events are scheduled in the ballroom, which seats up to 300 guests. Party and conference facilities are available.

Guests can enjoy swimming in season in the outdoor pool, working out in the exercise room, playing in the video game room, or shopping in concessions, the Navy Exchange or the Stars & Stripes bookstore. There are also an APO, military banking facility, packing and wrapping service, barber shop, beauty salon, flower shop and many other American-style conveniences, including laundry and dry cleaning.

Personnel at the Information and Tours Desk (Comm: 03-440-7871-EX-7200/1; ATVN: 229-7200/1) can make all the necessary arrangements for touring local attractions or getting tickets for theater, concerts or sports events. They can also book airline or steamship reservations.

If you are arriving at Tokyo's Narita International Airport, an economical airport express bus is available into the city and to New Sanno's front door. There is also bus service available from Yokota Air Base (schedule available at MAC terminal).

The New Sanno is a joint services, all-grades, all-ranks facility managed by the US Navy as executive agent.

SEASON OF OPERATION: Year round.

ELIGIBILITY: Active/Retired/US Embassy Tokyo/UN Command/DOD Civilians stationed in Japan or on official DOD orders to Tokyo, or EML orders to Japan.

RESERVATIONS: Recommended at least 45 days in adv with deposit of 1 night's charge per room reserved, which may be charged to Visa, MasterCard, American Express or Diners Club by giving card number and expiration date. Refunds only if cancellation is at least 3 days before scheduled arrival. Address: The New Sanno, APO San Francisco 96503-0110. Comm: 81-3-440-7871; ATVN: 229-7121; Telex: 2427125 SANTEL J.

ROOM RATES FOR THE NEW SANNO U.S. FORCES CENTER

ROOM TYPE	NO.	I*	II*	III*	IV*
SINGLE (Qu bd)	43	$20	$26	$32	$44
DOUBLE (Qu + sgl bd)	78	28	34	40	55
KING SUITE (Kg + sofabed)	17	40	44	48	64
TWIN SUITE (Twns + sofabed)	4	40	44	48	64
FAMILY SUITE (Qu + bunk rm)	2	40	50	60	74
JAPANESE SUITE	2	60	60	60	80

*I: E1-E5; II: E6-O3, WO1-WO4; III: O4-O10; IV: Retired/Non-DOD.
I, II & III include comparable DOD Civilian grades. DAVs, URW and Orphans (all with DD1173) at II.

RESTRICTIONS: No pets allowed.

Okuma Recreation Center (JAO9R8)
Kadena Air Base, APO San Francisco 96239-5000

Comm: 81-098-041-5164
ATVN: 634-4322

LOCATION: Off base. On Okinawa, take Hwy 58 N from Kadena AB approx 50 mi. Turn L just before Hentona. NMI: Kadena AB, 50 mi S. NMC: Naha, JA, 62 mi S.

JAPAN
Okuma Rec Ctr, Cont'd

DESCRIPTION OF AREA: This 120-acre recreational complex is a beautiful, quiet getaway on a peninsula with snow-white beaches on both the Pacific Ocean and East China Sea. Picturesque drive takes you through pineapple fields and acres of sugar cane. Full range of military facilities available at Kadena AB.

SEASON OF OPERATION: Year round. 1 November-15 May: Wednesday-Sunday only.

ELIGIBILITY: Active/Retired/DOD Civilians assigned overseas.

RESERVATIONS: Required up to 30 days in adv. Write: Leisure Resource Center, Schilling Rec Center, 18th CSG/SSRR, APO San Francisco 96239-5000. Comm: 81-098-041-5164; ATVN: 634-4322.

CAMP FACILITIES:	NO UNITS	FEE
7 Cabanas	30 rooms/2 dbl beds/shared bath	$15.00 daily
	10 rooms/2 dbl beds/PB	20.00 daily
	12 rooms/1 dbl, 1 sgl bed/PB	20.00 daily
	9 suites/2 rms/4 dbl beds/PB	25.00 daily
	VIP suite	25.00 daily
Campsite #1	Families only, South Beach	5.00 per tent daily
Campsite #2	Singles only, West Beach #2	maximum of 7 persons
Campsite #3	Scenic area, West Beach #1	per tent

SUPPORT FACILITIES:

Beach	Bicycle Rental	BX (small)
Chapel	Conv Store	Dispensary
Golf	Laundry	Nature Trail
Picnic Area	Rec Center	Restrooms
Showers	Tennis Courts	Theater
Water Sports Equipment Rental		

ACTIVITIES:

Bicycling	Croquet	Fishing
Rec Equip Avail	Restaurant	Sailing
Scuba Diving	Skin Diving	Snorkeling
Swimming	Tours	Water Skiing
Windsurfing		

Glass bottom boat tours and water instructional classes are available.

RESTRICTIONS: No pets allowed. In order to rent sailboat and windsurfing equipment, certification by a sanctioned organization, or the passing of a qualification test given by the chief instructor, is required. An Island Certification Card is req for use of any diving equipment and/or service.

Tama Hills Recreation Center (JA1OR8)
Yokota Air Base
APO San Francisco 96328-5000

Comm: 81-0425-77-7009
ATVN: 225-1101
Mil: 224-3421-3422

LOCATION: Off base. 15 miles SE of Yokota AB. NMC: Tokyo, outskirts.

DESCRIPTION OF AREA: A 500-acre retreat west of Tokyo, Tama was originally built by the Japanese Imperial Army in 1938 as a munitions storage area. After extensive repairs and renovations the center was reopened in 1983. The lodge and cabins all have private baths. Hot tubs available year round. It is a quiet, wooded getaway offering a large range of facilities.

SEASON OF OPERATION: Year round.

Tama Hills Rec Area, Cont'd

ELIGIBILITY: Active/Retired/DOD Civilians.

RESERVATIONS: Required up to 3 months in adv. Address: Tama Rec Center, 475 ABW/SSRL, Yokota Air Base, APO San Francisco 96328-5000. Comm: 81-0423-77-7009; ATVN: 224-3421/3422.

CAMP FACILITIES:	NO UNITS	HOOKUPS	FEE
Lodge	19 Rooms		$20.00 daily
Lodge	4 Suites		30.00 daily
Cabins	14 Double and Single		25-35 daily
Camp and Tent Sites	19	Toilets	.50 daily

SUPPORT FACILITIES:			
	Archery/fee	Camp Equip Rntl	Golf (18 holes)
	Grills/fee	Laundry	Picnic Area/fee
	Playground	PX (small)(Th-M)	Rec Equip Rental
	Restaurants	Restrooms	Showers
	Swim Pool (sumr)	Tennis Cts/fee	Trails

ACTIVITIES:	Bicycling	Horseback Riding	Jogging

RESTRICTIONS: Pets allowed.

White Beach Recreation Services (JA13R8)

Okinawa Commander Fleet Activities
FPO Seattle 98770-1100

Comm: 81-631-2264/6
FTS: 09893 8-1111

LOCATION: Off base. On the Pacific Island of Okinawa, S of Japan. On east side of the island on Katsuren Peninsula in Buckner Bay. From Hwy 24, N of Okinawa City, turn E on Hwy 329 to Hwy 8 to White Beach. NMI: Kadena AB, 8 mi W. NMC: Naha, 12 mi S.

DESCRIPTION OF AREA: Beautiful beach, many recreational activities, and Port of Call Club in White Beach. The club is open to all ranks and provides a full-menu dining room, amusement center, ballroom, casual bar, shoppette, post office and package store.

SEASON OF OPERATION: Year round.

ELIGIBILITY: Active/Retired/DOD Civilians.

RESERVATIONS: Required with full payment 72 hrs in adv. Address: White Beach Recreation Services, CFAO Special Services, Box SS, FPO Seattle 98770-1100. Comm: 81-631-2264/2266; FTS: 09893 8-1111.

CAMP FACILITIES:	NO UNITS	HOOKUPS	FEE
Cabins (Smuggler's Cove)	4		$15.00 daily
Camping on beach and in picnic areas; elec in picnic areas.		None	

SUPPORT FACILITIES:			
	Beach	Bowling Alley	Chapel
	Fishing Piers	Grills	Marina
	Picnic Areas	Racquetball	Rec Equip Rental
	Rec Hall	Restrooms	Showers
	Snack Bars	Sports Fields	Swimming Pool

ACTIVITIES:	Boating	Fishing	Swimming

RESTRICTIONS: No pets allowed.

KOREA

Naija Hotel Armed Forces Recreation Center (RKO1R8)

Community, Family & Soldier Support Cmd-Korea
APO San Francisco 96301-0074

Comm: 82-737-5145/8681
ATVN: 293-3133/4/5/6

LOCATION: Off post. Located in downtown Seoul, Korea, at #75 Naija-dong, Chongro-ku. NMI: HQ US Forces Korea (Yongsan Compound), 15 minutes away. Shuttles available 10 times daily.

DESCRIPTION OF AREA: The Naija (pronounced Nay'ja) is in 3 separate buildings. It is near the American Embassy, palaces, cultural centers and museums. Only 20 min to Kimpo International Airport. Full range of mil fac at Yongsan Compound.

SEASON OF OPERATION: Year round.

ELIGIBILITY: Active/Retired/DOD Civilians.

RESERVATIONS: Required 3 wks in adv with one night's deposit. Priority given lower enlisted grades. Address: Naija Hotel, AFRC, CFSSCK, APO San Francisco 96301-0074. Comm: 82-2-737-8681/2/3/4; ATVN: 293-3933/4/5/6.

LODGING: 75 rooms and 4 family suites. All rooms have A/C, central heat, telephones and color TV. Most have shared baths; 7 have priv baths.

FEE:	
Single Room	$22.00 daily
Studio Room	30.00 daily
Double/Twin Room	30.00 daily
Suite, 2 bdrm	55.00 daily
Suite, 3 bdrm	75.00 daily
Cots	5.00 additional

SUPPORT FACILITIES:			
	Barber Shop	Boutique/Men's	Cafeteria
	Cocktail Lounge	Game Room	Laundry
	Money Exchange	Pack-n-Wrap Svc	Package Store
	Post Exchange	Restaurant	Tour & Travel Ctr

ACTIVITIES: Sightseeing

RESTRICTIONS: No pets allowed.

PHILIPPINES

Camp John Hay Armed Forces Recreation Center (RPO2R8)

John Hay Air Station
APO San Francisco 96298-5000

Comm: 63-442-2101
ATVN: 392-1110

LOCATION: On base. In northern Luzon, the largest island of the Republic of the Philippines. From Clark AB or Subic NB go N on Rt-11 (MacArthur Hwy); after approx 70 mi take a R and climb the Zig Zag Road (or Kennon Rd) to John Hay Air Station. The Recreation Site Lodging Office is in Bldg 400 in the center of the base. NMC: Baguio City, 2 mi NW.

Camp John Hay AFRC, Cont'd

DESCRIPTION OF AREA: John Hay Air Station, a beautiful retreat 5,200 feet high in the mountains of northern Luzon, was created by Act of Congress in 1903. Average temperature is 64 degrees. There have been many improvements and additions to facilities in the last few years. Daily bus service from Clark AB. Full range of recreation and support facilities on base.

SEASON OF OPERATION: Year round.

ELIGIBILITY: Active/Retired/DOD Civilians.

RESERVATIONS: Required: up to 90 days in adv for AD and DOD Civ; up to 30 days in adv for Retired. Address: Recreation Services, 6020 Support Squadron/SVH, APO San Francisco 96298-5000. Comm: 63-442-2101; ATVN: 392-1110.

CAMP FACILITIES:	NO UNITS	FEE
Motel-type rooms	14 Non-housekeeping	$10-24 daily*
Cottages/Duplex; Apts	91 Houskeeping	18-40 daily*
Lodge	17 Rooms	10-20 ea pers dly*
Tent Spaces/Tents	500 Spaces (2.5 acres)	Minimal charge

*Prices vary according to number of occupants/beds.

SUPPORT FACILITIES:			
	Car Rental	Chapel	Clubs
	Conference Fac	Gas	Golf
	Laundry	Parks	Picnic Areas
	Playground	Rec Ctr/Game Rm	Rec Equip Rntl
	Restaurants	Skating	Snack Bars
	Swimming Pool	Taxi Service	Tennis Courts
	Theater	Trails	

ACTIVITIES:	Hiking	Jogging	Tours

RESTRICTIONS: No pets allowed.

Grande Island Recreation Area
(RPO1R8)
Subic Bay US Naval Station
FPO San Francisco 96651-1009

Comm: 63-884-9222/9232/9240
Fm RP: 844-9222
ATVN: 882-3011-EX-4-7222

LOCATION: On base. Grande Island is at the mouth of Subic Bay. It is 2 hours by car from Manila or Clark AB and a 30-min shuttleboat ride from Subic Bay Naval Station.

DESCRIPTION OF AREA: This self-contained recreational center is an island which has been developed into a military resort. Once a Spanish fortress, Grande is now a captivating pleasure island. A campground is in planning stages. Free shuttleboats leave Fleet Landing at Subic every 2 hours on the even hours during the week and every hour on the hour weekends and holidays. Water taxis available at minimum cost. Full range of military fac at Subic Bay Naval Sta.

SEASON OF OPERATION: Year round. (Every day, including holidays.)

ELIGIBILITY: Active/Retired/DOD Civilians assigned overseas.

RESERVATIONS: Accepted up to 60 days in adv; up to 1 year in adv for group bookings; walk-ins accepted if there are vacancies. Address: Recreation Services Dept, Box 12, US NAVSTA, FPO San Francisco 96651-1009. Comm: 63-884-9222/9232; ATVN: 882-3011-EX-4-1101.

LODGING:	NO UNITS	FEE
Cottages, 1-4 bdrm	16	$ 14-22 daily*
Fleet Quonset, 8 bed		16.00 daily
Hotel	35 Rooms	10-17 daily*
Grande Lodge	10 Rooms	10-12 daily*
Grande Lodge	Entire facility	102.00 daily

*Prices vary according to number of bedrooms.

SUPPORT FACILITIES:			
	Basketball Cts	Beaches	Boat Rental
	Helicopter Pad	Laundry	Lockers
	Paddle Boats	Pavilions	Picnic Areas
	Playground	Rec Equip Rntl	Restaurant
	Restrooms	Retail Store	Showers
	Ski Boat Rental	Snack Bar	Softball Fields
	Tennis Courts	Theater	TV/Game Room

ACTIVITIES:			
	Bicycling	Boating	Fishing
	Hiking Trails	Horseshoes	Jogging
	Pitch&Putt Golf	Scuba Diving	Sightseeing
	Skin Diving	Snorkeling	Swimming
	Volleyball	Water Skiing	

RESTRICTIONS: No pets allowed.

SPAIN

Rota Travel Camp (SPO5R7)

Rota US Naval Station
FPO New York 09540-1055

Comm: 34-56-620-2780-EX-5051
ATVN: 727-1110-EX-5051

LOCATION: On base. On the Atlantic side of southern Spain. The camp is near horse stables on the NAVSTA. HE: map 61, C/5. NMC: Cadiz, 22 mi S.

DESCRIPTION OF AREA: Situated in a large field near stables. Attractions include: Great beaches on Costa de la Luz, wine harvest (Sep), 3100-year-old Port of Cadiz, and resorts on Costa de Sol. Wide range of military fac on base.

SEASON OF OPERATION: Year round.

ELIGIBILITY: Base access ONLY to military personnel stationed in Spain. No PX or Commissary to retired personnel/third nationals or military personnel without orders to Spain. Also applies to military personnel on leave status. This is a Joint Use Facility with Spanish Forces.

RESERVATIONS: No adv resv. Address: Recreational Services, US Naval Station, Box 14, FPO New York 09540-1055. Comm: 34-56-86-2780-EX-2563/2564; ATVN: 727-1110-EX-2563/2564.

CAMPING FACILITIES:	NO UNITS	HOOKUPS	FEE
Camper Spaces	10 Hardstand	E (110)	Free
Camper Spaces	20	None	Free

SUPPORT FACILITIES:			
	Boat Rental	Camp Equip Rntl	Chapel
	Gas	Golf	Picnic Area
	Quick Stop	Racquet Sports	Restrooms/flush
	Stables		

Rota Travel Camp, Cont'd

ACTIVITIES: Fishing   Horseback Riding Rec Equip Avail

RESTRICTIONS: See "Eligibility" above. The camping facilities are <u>extremely</u> <u>limited</u> and are available only to personnel with access to the base and to Spanish military personnel and their families.

TURKEY

Erdemli Beach Area (TUO3R9)
Incirlik Air Base
APO New York 09289-5000

Comm: 90-711-119062/111285
Fm TU: 90-711-14228
ATVN: 676-1110

LOCATION: Off base. Approx 68 mi SE of Adana, TU, on shore of Mediterranean. NMI: Incirlik AB, 80 mi NW.

DESCRIPTION OF AREA: Campground is located in large, landscaped area shaded by pine trees. The dark sand beach is approx 75-100 yds from the trailers. Full range of military facilities available at Incirlik Air Base.

SEASON OF OPERATION: Year round.

ELIGIBILITY: Active/Retired/DOD Civilians.

RESERVATIONS: Required. Address: Recreation Supply, Incirlik Air Base, APO New York 09289-5000.

CAMPING FACILITIES:	<u>NO UNITS</u>	<u>HOOKUPS</u>	<u>FEE</u>
Campers, 4-person	5	W/S/E	$10.00 daily, 15 wknd & holiday

SUPPORT FACILITIES:	Marina	Sewage Dump Station
ACTIVITIES:	Fishing	Swimming

RESTRICTIONS: Campers must be registered with local Security Forces. No loud music after 2400 hours.

UNITED KINGDOM

Machrihanish Travel Camp (UK 14R7)
Scotland Naval Atomic Weapons Facility
FPO New York 09515-5000

Comm: 44-0586-2341
ATVN: 392-8578

LOCATION: On base. 5 mi W of Campbeltown on southern tip of Kintyre Peninsula on west coast of Scotland. HE: map 8, B/4. NMC: Glasgow, 145 mi E.

DESCRIPTION OF AREA: Coastal area across the North Channel from Northern Ireland. Sightseeing at Mull Island of Kintyre and Inverary Castle (65 mi N).

SEASON OF OPERATION: 1 April-31 October.

ELIGIBILITY: Active/Retired/DOD Civilians.

UNITED KINGDOM
Machrihanish Travel Camp, Cont'd

RESERVATIONS: Required. Address: Recreation Services, NAF, Machrihanish, FPO New York 09515-5000. Comm: 44-0586-2341-EX-291; ATVN: 392-8578-EX-291.

CAMPING FACILITIES:	NO UNITS	HOOKUPS	FEE
Camper Spaces	50 Hardstand	W/E	$5.00 daily
Camper Spaces	50	None	3.00 daily

SUPPORT FACILITIES:	Golf (9 holes)	Restrooms/flush	Showers/hot
ACTIVITIES:	Fishing	Hiking	Swimming

RESTRICTIONS: Pets allowed.

ATTENTION

As we locate new **RV, Camping & Rec Areas** (or learn about cutbacks or closings), we will publish the information in Military Living's all-ranks travel newsletter, the R&R Report. You can keep up-to-date by subscribing now! Please see page 190 for information we obtained as we went to press about a new recreation area. This information was published in the R&R Report but was received too late to be integrated into the text of this edition.

-NOTES-

APPENDIX A
Regional Location Maps

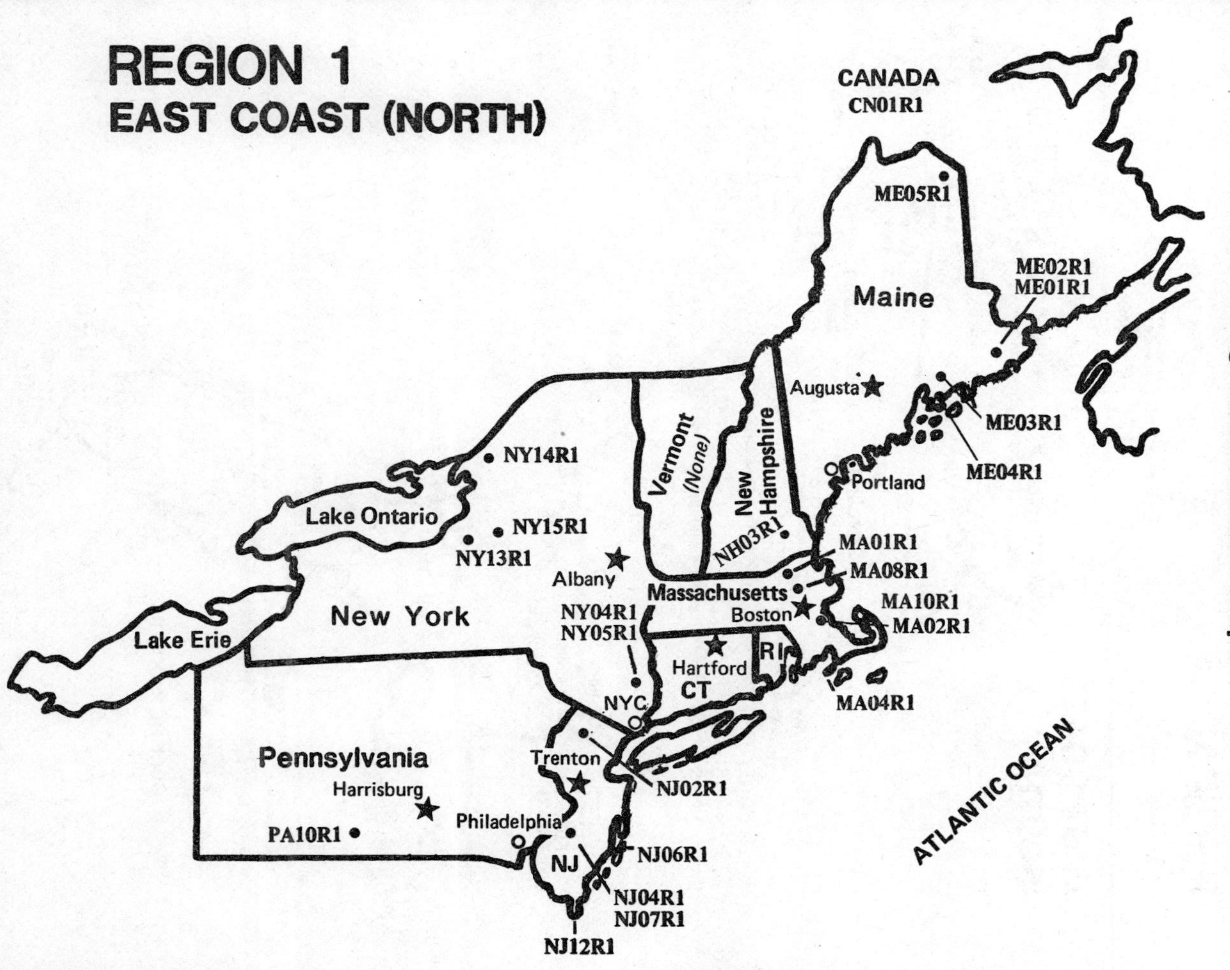

REGION 1

EAST COAST (SOUTH)

REGION 2
CENTRAL (NORTH)

REGION 2
CENTRAL (SOUTH)
Missouri
Kansas City
St. Louis
Jefferson City
MO01R2
Cincinnati
KY03R2
Frankfurt
Louisville
Lexington
Kentucky
KY04R2
KY05R2
Nashville
Knoxville
Tennessee
Fort Smith
TN04R2
TN03R2
Memphis
Arkansas
AR05R2
Huntsville
AL12R2
MS06R2
AL09R2
Birmingham
Mississippi
Tuscaloosa
Alabama
ALO5R2
Shreveport
LA09R2
AL11R2
Jackson
Meridian
Montgomery
Louisiana
AL10R2
AL13R2
LA02R2
LA04R2
MS05R2
Mobile
Baton Rouge
New Orleans
AL07R2
LA03R2
LA08R2
GULF OF MEXICO

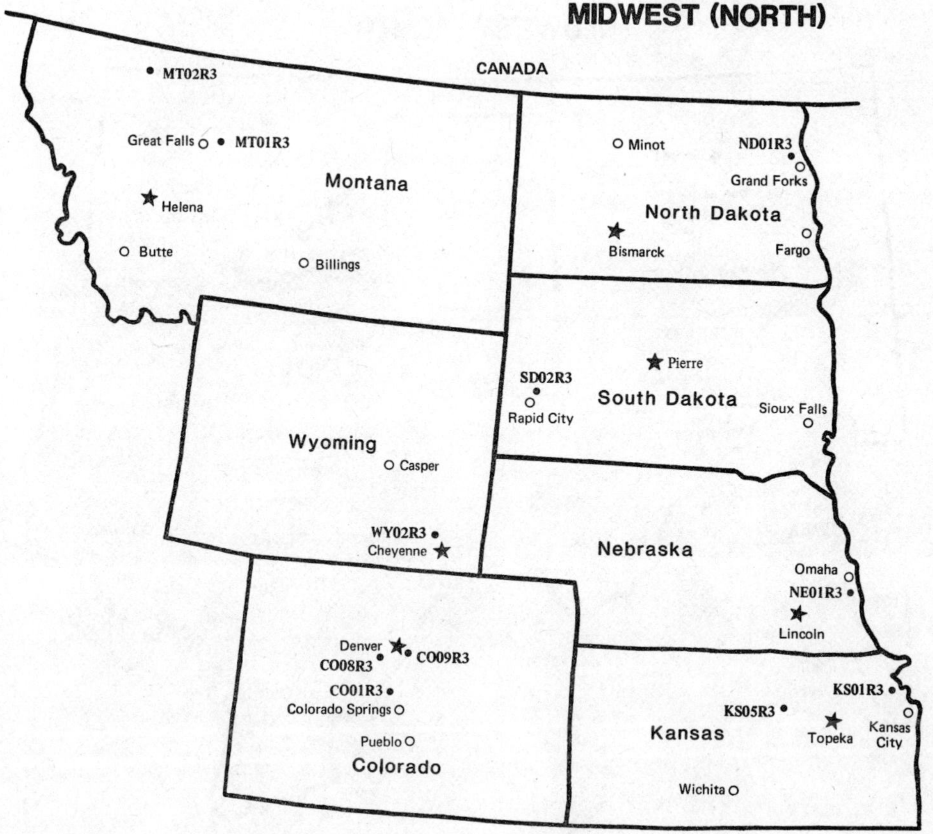

REGION 3
MIDWEST (NORTH)
CANADA
MT02R3
Great Falls
MT01R3
Montana
Helena
Butte
Billings
Minot
ND01R3
Grand Forks
North Dakota
Bismarck
Fargo
SD02R3
Rapid City
Pierre
South Dakota
Sioux Falls
Wyoming
Casper
WY02R3
Cheyenne
Nebraska
Omaha
NE01R3
Lincoln
Denver
CO08R3
CO09R3
CO01R3
Colorado Springs
Pueblo
Colorado
KS01R3
KS05R3
Kansas
Topeka
Kansas City
Wichita

REGION 3
MIDWEST (SOUTH)

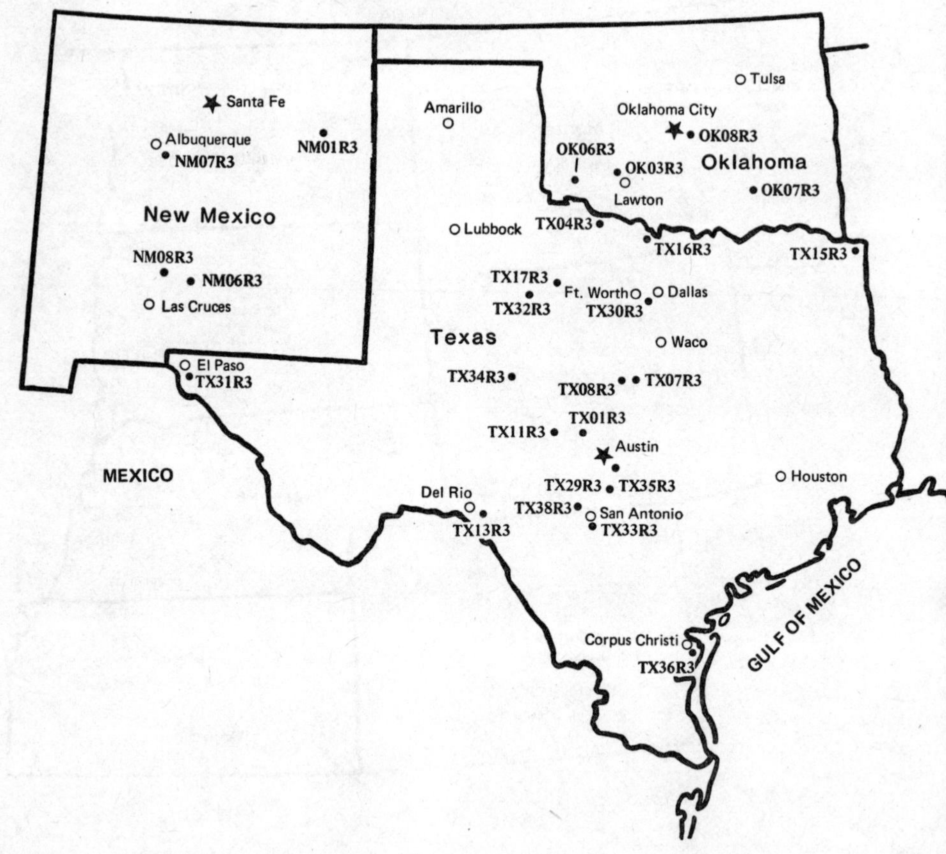

REGION 4
WEST COAST
CANADA
WA12R4
WA07R4
Seattle
Spokane
WA01R4
Olympia
Tacoma
WA13R4
WA14R4
WA03R4
Washington
Portland
Salem
Idaho
Oregon
Eugene
(NONE)
Boise
Idaho Falls
ID03R4
ID02R4
Pocatello
UT03R4
Ogden
UT07R4
UT01R4
CA73R4
UT06R4
Salt Lake City
CA24R4
CA60R4
Reno
Provo
CA68R4
Carson City
Utah
CA66R4
Sacramento
Nevada
CA63R4
Oakland
CA74R4
San Francisco
CA72R4
California
CAO2R4
CAO4R4
Las
NV04R4
Vegas
CA61R4
CAO5R4
AZ11R4
Flagstaff
CA62R4
CA67R4
Arizona
CA70R4
CA69R4
CA11R4
Los Angeles
AZO7R4
AZ15R4
CA76R4
Phoenix
CÂ07R4
CA65R4
CA64R4
San Diego
Yuma
CAO3R4
AZ12R4
CA31R4
Tucson
AZ14R4
AZ10R4
MEXICO
PACIFIC OCEAN

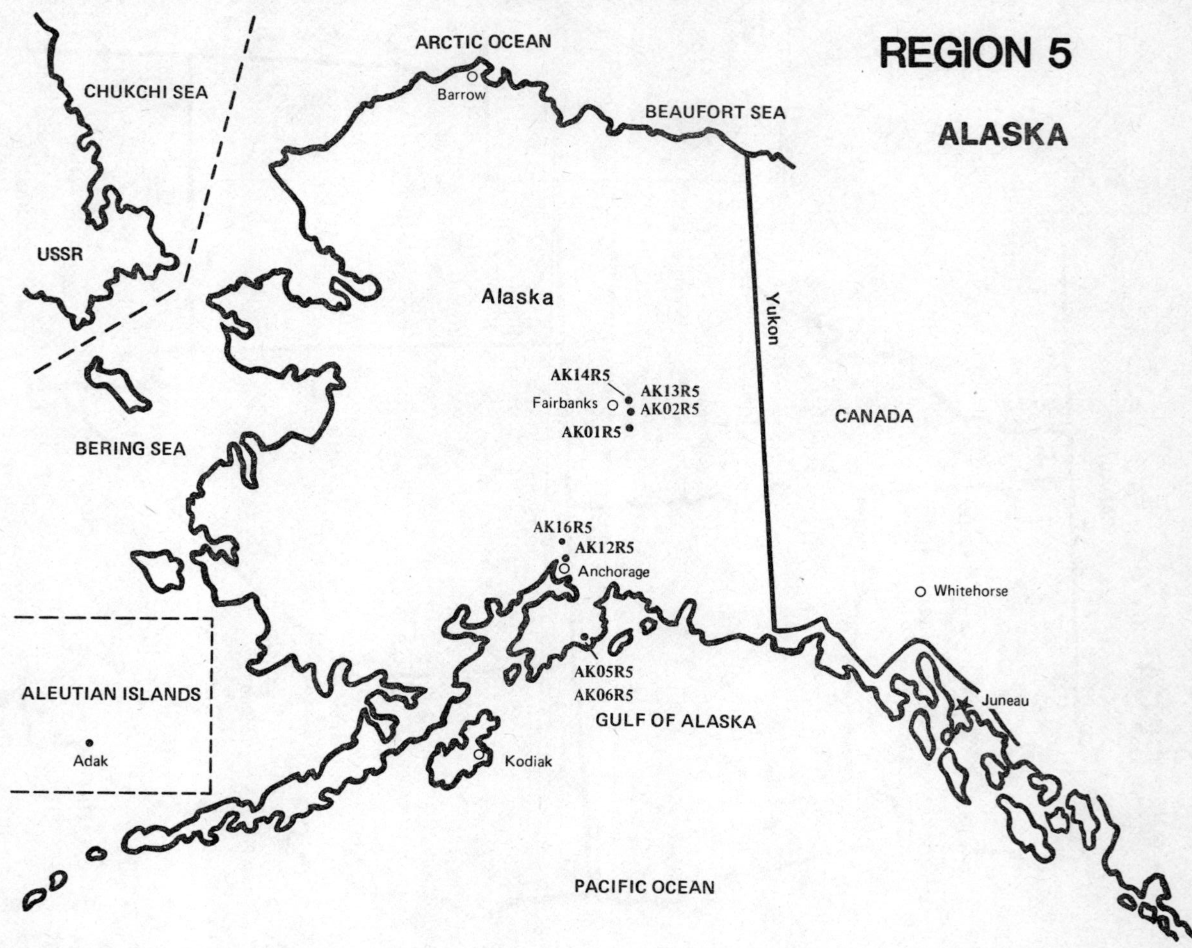

REGION 5
ALASKA
ARCTIC OCEAN
Barrow
CHUKCHI SEA
BEAUFORT SEA
USSR
Alaska
Yukon
CANADA
BERING SEA
Whitehorse
AK14R5
Fairbanks
AK13R5
AK02R5
AK01R5
AK16R5
AK12R5
Anchorage
AK05R5
AK06R5
GULF OF ALASKA
Juneau
Kodiak
ALEUTIAN ISLANDS
Adak
PACIFIC OCEAN

REGION 6

HAWAII

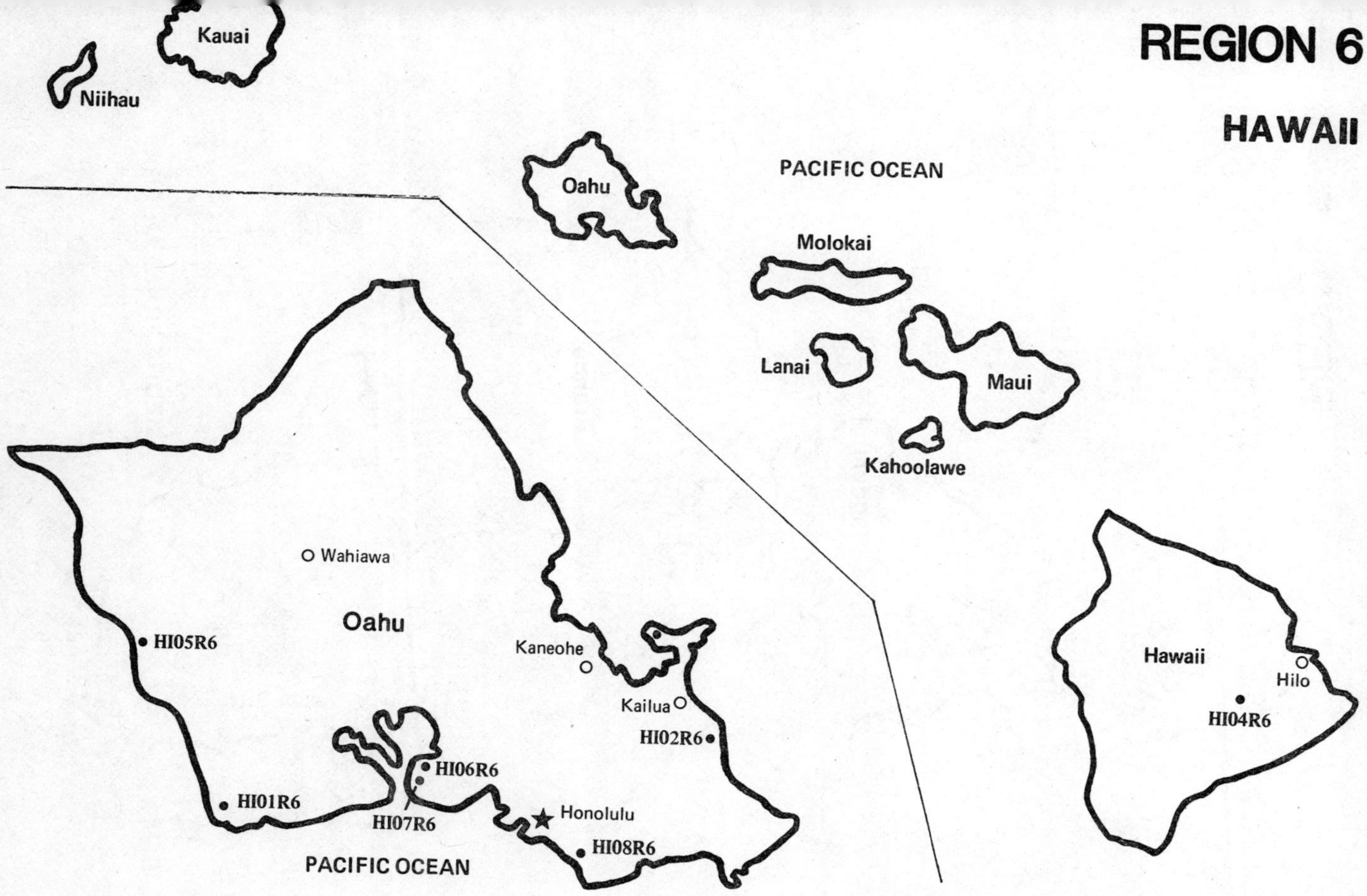

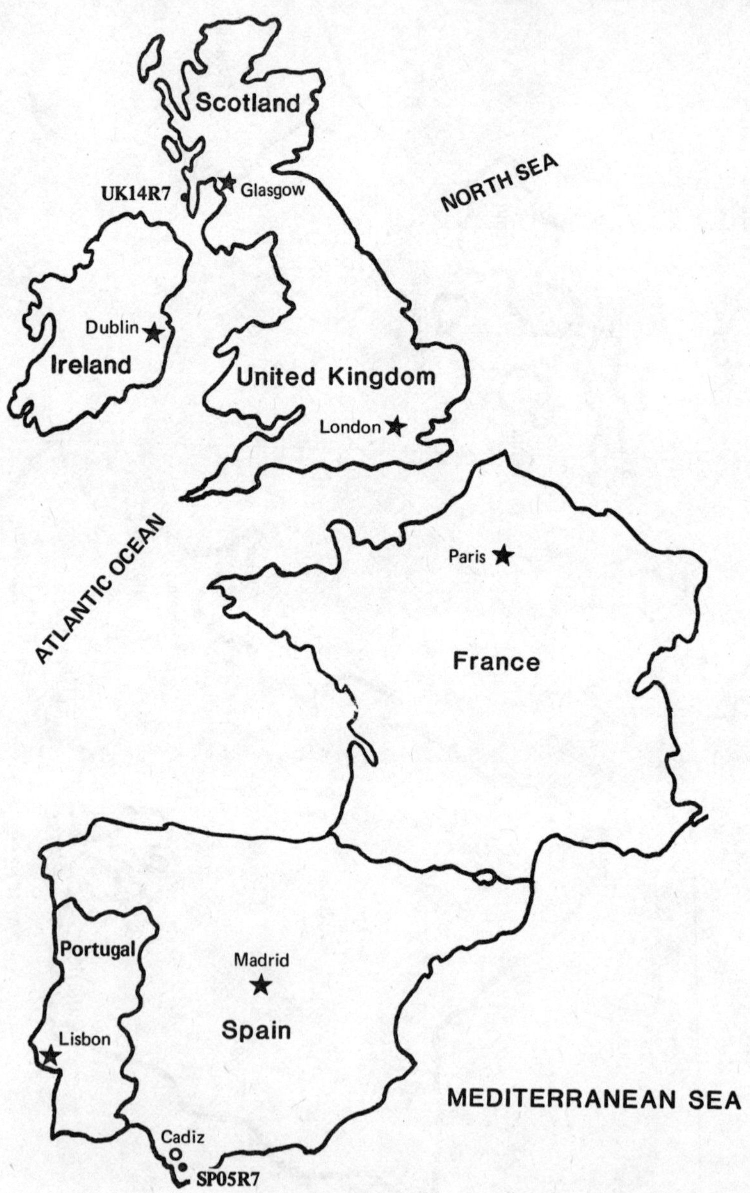

REGION 7
WEST EUROPE
Scotland
Glasgow
UK14R7
NORTH SEA
Dublin
Ireland
United Kingdom
London
ATLANTIC OCEAN
Paris
France
Portugal
Madrid
Lisbon
Spain
Cadiz
SP05R7
MEDITERRANEAN SEA

REGION 7
EAST EUROPE

West Germany
Bonn
GE56R7
GE55R7
GE47R7

GE57R7
GE08R7
GE09R7
Austria
GE07R7
Switzerland
GE10R7
GE58R7
IT09R7
IT08R7
IT15R7
Italy
Florence
Yugoslavia
Belgrade
IT02R7
Corsica
Rome
ADRIATIC SEA
IT03R7
Sardinia
REGION
9
GREECE
GR03R9
TURKEY
TU03R9
Sicily

REGION 8

FAR EAST/PACIFIC

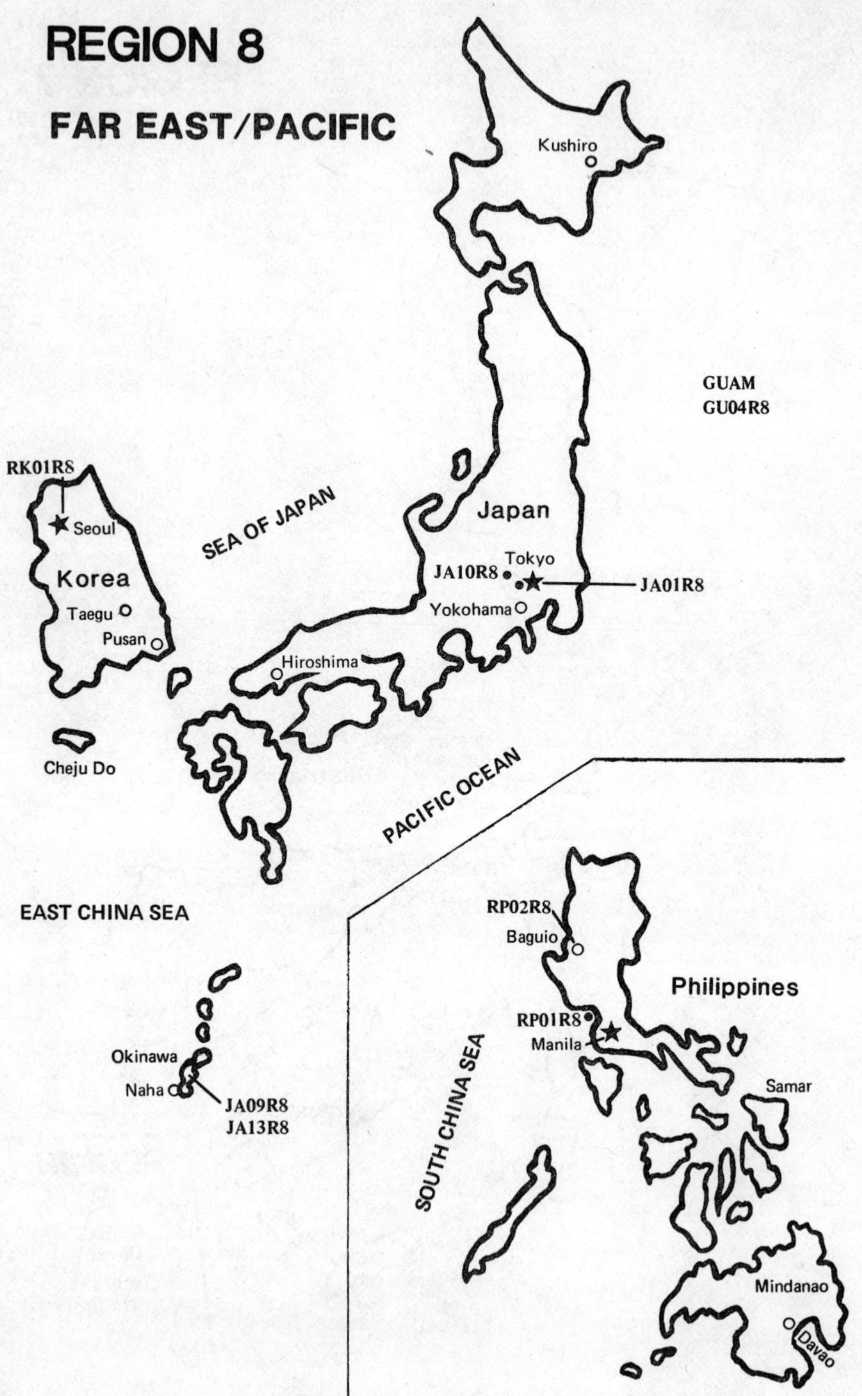

APPENDIX B

CAMPING ON OTHER FEDERAL PROPERTY

Thousands of campsites are available to the public on various types of Federal reserves around the country. These sites are located in national parks, national forests, game and wildlife refuges, Federal water reservoir reserves, Tennessee Valley Authority dam sites, and other federal areas.

Many of these sites are near or on routes to military installations to which you may be traveling. A wealth of information is available from a variety of sources concerning these camp sites and adjacent recreation areas. Again, plan ahead; get this information before you travel or vacation.

If a military installation is not conveniently located along your route, maybe one of the public areas will be. Or, if you cannot get space at a military area, perhaps you can at a nearby public area. You may want to supplement facilities available at military installations with a day's boating, fishing, or swimming at a nearby public recreation area.

Listed below are addresses of federal agencies from which information about camping on federal lands other than military installations can be obtained. Also listed are titles and descriptions of some of the available material.

Superintendent of Documents, US Government Printing Office, Washington, DC 20402. Tel: (202) 783-3238.

GPO prints many items for all the government agencies. You may write for these materials or you may order by telephone using your credit card.

Backpacking, Stock No. 001-000-042475 ($3.50). US Dept of Agr, Forest Service, Program Aid 1239. This 50-page brochure is for backpacking campers who want to make their experience safer and more enjoyable.

National Park Guide 1986-87, Stock No. 024-005-00987-6 ($3.50). This 26-page booklet contains basic information, in chart form, about the facilities and recreational opportunities available to the users of National Park System camping areas.

Lesser Known Areas of the National Park System, Stock No. 024-005-00911-6 ($1.50). Listing, by state, of more than 170 national parks, their accommodations, locations and historical significance.

National Wildlife Refuges, Stock No. 024-010-00680-3 ($1.00). This is a fold-out map showing locations of 300 wildlife refuges. Facilities and best viewing seasons at each refuge, and addresses for more information are listed.

Bureau of Land Management (BLM), Division of Recreation (3700), Washington, DC 20240. Tel: (202) 343-1100.

Camping on Public Lands. Free color map with charts on back indicating facilities and services in areas maintained by the BLM.

US Dept of Agriculture, Forest Service, Washington, DC. Tel: (202) 447-3957.

Information concerning camping sites in National Forests is supplied by regional offices of the Forest Service rather than the Washington, DC, headquarters office. Write to Regional Forester, Forest Service, Dept of Agriculture in one of the following cities: Milwaukee (WI), Atlanta (GA), Denver (CO), Albuquerque (NM), San Francisco (CA), Portland (OR), Ogden (UT), Missoula (MT), or Juneau (AK).

US Army Corps of Engineers, Publications Depot, 2802 52nd Avenue, Hyattsville, MD 20781-1102. Tel: (301) 436-2063.

Lakeside Recreation Series, No. EP 1130-2-411/12/13/14/15/16. This is a set of very nice free pamphlets that are directories of recreational opportunities at Corps projects. They have color maps, facilities charts and written descriptions of each project, divided into six regions of the US: New England, Northeast, Southeast, Midwest, West and Southwest.

Tennessee Valley Authority, Program Support & Information Services, Division of Land & Forest Resources, Forestry Building, Norris, TN 37828. Tel: (615) 494-9800

Recreation on TVA Lakes is a brochure that includes information about camping and other recreation facilities in the TVA region. Pamphlets are also published by some of the TVA states.

Golden Eagle, Golden Age, Golden Access Passports

The Golden Eagle Passport is an annual entrance permit to national parks, monuments, and recreation areas that charge entrance fees and are managed by the Federal government. It admits the permit holder and a carload of accompanying people. It does not cover user fees, such as fees for camping.

The Golden Eagle Passport may be purchased for $10 in person or by mail. Address: National Park Service, Washington, DC 20240. To obtain in person, ask at any area of the National Park System where entrance fees are charged. A Golden Eagle Passport is good for one calendar year.

The Golden Age Passport is a free lifetime entrance permit to those national parks, monuments, and recreation areas that charge entrance fees and are managed by the Federal government. It is available to persons 62 and older. The Passport also provides a 50 percent discount on user fees charged for facilities and services, such as camping, boat launching, and parking. The Golden Age Passport does not cover fees charged by private concessionaires even though they may be located on Federal property.

Those eligible may obtain Golden Age Passports in person at most federally-operated recreation areas where they can be used; therefore, it may not be necessary to obtain the passport in advance of a vacation trip. The Golden Age Passport cannot be obtained by mail.

The Golden Access Passport is a free lifetime-entrance permit, like the Golden Age Passport, for persons who have been medically determined to be blind or permanently disabled. It must be picked up in person at federally-operated recreational areas.

Computer Reservations for Camping Facilities on Federal Property

Computer reservations can be made at over 600 Ticketron walk-in outlets nationwide. Reservations through the computer system may be made up to eight weeks in advance of the anticipated camping date (in-person at Ticketron outlets) or by mail by writing to Ticketron Reservation Office, P.O. Box 2715, San Francisco, CA 94126; or P.O. Box 19992, Washington, DC 20036.

Those writing for reservations will receive a form on which they can make a reservation for a specific date and park. The reservation charge is $1.75 plus the cost of the campsites, which range from $2 to $4 per night. Reservation forms are also available from the parks involved and from National Park Service regional offices and Washington headquarters.

Camp Stamps

Camp Stamps give you a 15 percent discount on camping fees charged at 2000 national-forest campsites in 44 states. They are sold at all Forest Service offices and by participating local merchants.

Not only do they save you money ($8.50 for $10 worth of fees), but you don't have to worry about carrying cash into the woods. The Forest Service saves on administrative expenses so they can spend more on maintaining and improving the facilities. Everyone benefits! For more information contact your local Forest Service office, or write: Camp Stamps, Forest Service-USDA, Dept B, PO Box 2417, Washington, DC 20013.

-NOTES-

APPENDIX C

GENERAL ABBREVIATIONS

This Appendix contains general abbreviations used in this book. Commonly under-
stood abbreviations, e.g., M-F, Monday to Friday, have not been included in
order to save space. Address abbreviations are also not included in most cases
because they have proven to be accurate when used as stated in this book.

AAF- Army Air Field
AB - Air Base
A/C - air conditioning
Acpt - accepted
AD - Active Duty
Add - additional
Adj - adjacent
Adv - advance
AF - Air Force
AFAF - Air Force Auxiliary Field
AFB - Air Force Base
AFR - Air Force Range
AFRC - Armed Forces Recreation Center
AFS - Air Force Station
APO - Army Post Office
Approx - approximately
Apt - apartment(s)
AR - Army
Arpt - airport
ATVN - Automatic Voice Network (Autovon)
Avail - available
Avn - aviation

Bdrm - bedroom
Biwkly - biweekly
Bldg - building
Bltg - billeting
Br - Branch
Btwn - between
BX - Base Exchange

CG - Coast Guard
CGAS - Coast Guard Air Station
Civ - civilian
Cmd - command
Cntr - center
Comm - community
Consol - consolidated
Conv - convenience
Conv S - convenience store
Ct - court
Ctr - center
CTV - cable TV

Dbl - double
Dep - deposit
DH - downhill
Div - Division
Dly - daily
DOD - Department of Defense

DOT - Department of Transportation
DR - dining room
Drv - driv(ing)

E - East
E - electricity
E - telephone extension
Ea - each
Eff - efficiency
Emp - employee
Eq/Equip - equipment
Exc - except
Excel - excellent

Fac - facilities
Fam - family
Fed - Federal
Fm - from
FPO - Fleet Post Office
Ft - fort
FTS - Federal Telephone System
Furn - furniture/furnished

Govt - government
Gp - group

HE: - Hallwag Europe (atlas)
Hq - Headquarters

Info - information
ITT - Information Tour and Travel

JPAO - Joint Public Affairs Office

Kit - kitchen
Km - kilometer
KMC - Kilauea Military Camp

L - left
LI - Location Identifier
Lic - license
Loc - location
LR - living room
Ltd - limited

Max - maximum
MC - Marine Corps
MCAS - Marine Corps Air Station
MCB - Marine Corps Base

Appendix C, Cont'd

MH - mobile home
Mi - miles
Mil - military
Min - minimum
Mo - monthly
MW - microwave oven

N - North
NAB - Naval Amphibious Base
NAEC - Naval Air Engineering Center
NAF - Non-appropriated Fund
NAF - Naval Air Facility
NAS - Naval Air Station
Natl - national
NB - Naval Base
NCU - Naval Communication Unit
NETC - Naval Education & Training Center
NG - National Guard
NMC - nearest major city
NMI - nearest military installation
NS - Naval Station
NSA - Naval Support Activity
NSGA - Naval Security Group Activity
NSWC - Naval Surface Weapon Center
NTC - Naval Training Center
NWC - Naval Weapons Center
NWS - Naval Weapons Station

Occ - occupant(s)
OD/OOD - Officer of the Day
Off - official
Off/S - off-season

Pav - pavilion
PB - private bath
PCS - Permanent Change of Station
Pers - personnel/person
PO - Post Office
Priv - private
Prog - program
PX - Post Exchange

Rec - recreation
Refr - refrigerator
Req - required
Res - Reserve
Resv - reservation
Ret - retired
Rg - range
Riv - river
Rm - room
RM: p - Rand McNally: page
Rntl - rental
RV - recreational vehicle

S - South
S - sewer
Sgl - single
Sl/slp - sleep(s)
Space-A - space-available
Sta - station
Sumr - summer
Svc - service

TAD - temporary attached duty
TBA - to be announced
TDY - temporary duty
Tel - telephone
Tng - training
TV - television
Tvl - travel

USA - United States Army
USAF - United States Air Force
USCG - United States Coast Guard
USMC - United States Marine Corps
USN - United States Navy
Uten - utensils

Veh - vehicle

W - water
W - West
W/ - with
W/D - washer/dryer
W/S/E - water/sewer/electricity
Wk - week
Wkly - weekly
Wknd - weekend

XC - cross country

Enlarged Sample Directory Listing

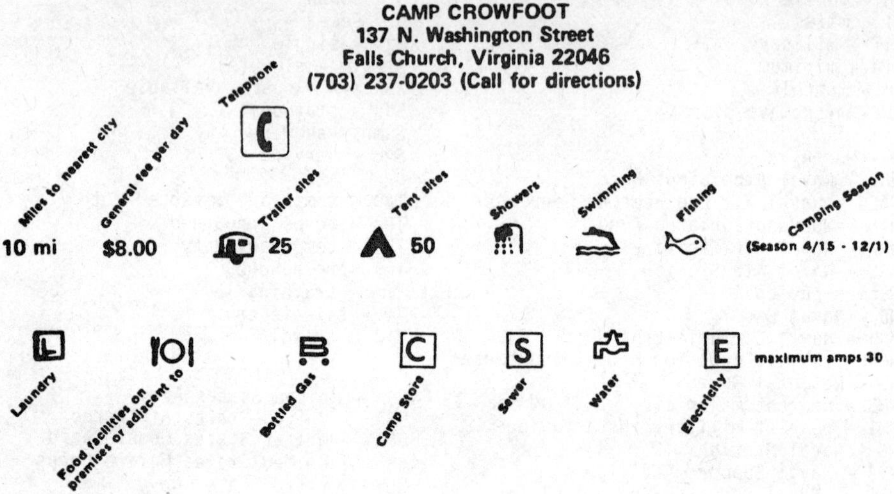

RV/CAMPING, SALES & SERVICE DIRECTORY

Military families especially enjoy using military RV/Camping facilities because they feel "at home" there. Unfortunately, many times, especially during the peak travel seasons, military RV/Camping areas can be fully occupied. Also, there are many areas where there are no military facilities available.

In view of this, we surveyed a number of RV/Camping facilities throughout the USA asking if they were interested in attracting military and their families to their location or business. The ones listed in this directory are expressing a desire to serve you. The next best thing to a military installation where you feel at home is surely a facility which really wants your business.

Some have indicated that they offer military rates, but we suggest you inquire at each location. Please also mention your book, Military Living's **Military RV, Camping & Rec Areas Around the World.**

We hope that each of you have a lot of fun with this book serving as your guide. If you have a favorite camping area which you think should be listed in future editions of our book, please show the book to them and give them our address. Thank you very much.

ALABAMA

Spring Creek Campground
P.O. Box 97
Geneva, Alabama 36340
(205) 684-3891

3 mi $7.50 dly Open all year
🚐 11 ▲ 14 🚿 🏊 🐟
Ⓛ Dump station E up to 50 amps

Ozark Camper Park
Highway 231 N.
Ozark, Alabama 36360
(205) 774-3219

8 mi Ft. Rucker Fee $9.95 dly Open all year
🚐 40 ▲ 5 🚿 🏊
Ⓛ ✕ Ⓒ Ⓢ E 40 (30 amps)

ARIZONA

J and H RV Park
Rt. 11 Box 17-B N. 89
Flagstaff, Arizona 86004
(602) 526-1829

5 mi Fee $10 for 2 Open all year
🚐 55 ▲ 20 🚿 ✕
Ⓢ E 30 amps

Tombstone Hills KOA
Route 80, P.O. Box 99
Tombstone, Arizona 85638
(602) 457-3829

1 mi Fee $12 dly Open all year
🚐 50 ▲ 20 🚿
Ⓛ Ⓒ Ⓢ E 30 & 50 amps

CALIFORNIA

Best Western Cavalier Motor Hotel
& Camperland
710 "E" St., Chula Vista, California 92010
(619) 420-5183

4 blocks Fee $17-24 dly
🚐 17 ▲ 0 🚿 🏊 🐟 ✕
Ⓛ Ⓒ Ⓢ E - yes

Cloverdale KOA
P.O. Box 600, Cloverdale, California 95425
(707) 894-3337

6 mi Fee $14.50/2 (Elec $3, Sewer $1)
Open all year
🚐 98 ▲ 60 🚿 🏊 🐟 ✕
Ⓛ Ⓒ Ⓢ E 15 & 30 amps

CALIFORNIA

Rio Bend R Resort Ranch
1589 Drew Road
El Centro, California 92243-9582
619-352-7061
Fishing, swimming, jacuzzi, walking trails,
putting green, desert golf course, general
store, laundry room, billiards, driving range.

Indianwaters Hideaway
47-202 Jackson, Indio, California 92201
(619) 342-7885

7 blocks Fee $18 dly Open all year
🚐 149 ▲ 0 🚿 🏊
Ⓛ Ⓢ

Edgewater Resort & RV Park
6420 Soda Bay Road
Kelseyville, California 95451
(707) 279-0208

5 mi Fee $14/2 dly Open all year
🚐 50 ▲ 20 🚿 🏊 🐟
✕ Ⓛ Ⓢ E 30 amps

Riverside RV Park
P.O. Box 235
Klamath, California 95548
(707) 482-2523

19 mi Fee $10 dly Season 4/1 to 11/1
92 ▲ 15 🚿 🏊 🐟 Ⓛ ✕
Ⓒ Ⓢ E 30 amps

High Sierra Campsites
P.O. Box 3262, 326 Peninsula Drive
Lake Almanor Peninsula, California 96137
(916) 596-3997/off-season (415) 964-0888

¼ mi Fee $10 up to 4 Season 5/28 to 9/15
🚐 8 ▲ 4 🚿 🏊 🐟 ✕
Dump station E 15 amps/8 sites

Lakeview Terrace Resort
Star Rt. Box 250 MC
Lewiston, California 96052
(916) 778-3803

Fee $13 Open all year
🚐 34 ▲ 0 🚿 🏊 🐟
Ⓛ Ⓢ E 30 amps

Oak Knoll
31718 South Grade Road
Pauma Valley, California 92061
(619) 742-3437

25 mi Fee $12 dly Open all year
🚐 45 ▲ 45 🚿 🏊 Ⓛ
Ⓒ Ⓢ E 15/30 amps

Town & Country Trailer Park
3700 Morse Avenue
Sacramento, California 95821
(916) 487-7454
8 mi Fee $15 dly Open all year
🚐 23 ⛺ 0 L ✕
⌂ S E 30 amps

De Anza Harbor Resort
2727 De Anza Road
San Diego, California 92109
(619) 273-3211
Fee-Wint $21, Sumr $30 Season 5/27 to 9/5
🚐 245 ⛺ 0 🚿 ≋ 🐟 ✕
L 🛒 ⌂ C S E 30 amps

Santa Fe Park
5707 Santa Fe Street
San Diego, California 92109
(619) 272-4051
8 mi Fee-7/1-8/31 $25/2, 9/1-6/30 $18/2
🚐 129 ⛺ 0 🚿 ≋ L ✕
⌂ S E 20 & 30 amps

Eagle Lake R.V. Park
687-125 Palmetto Way
Susanville, California 96130
(916) 825-3133
38 mi Fee $13.50 dly Season 5/15 to 11/15
🚐 63 ⛺ 6 🚿 ≋ 🐟 ✕
L 🛒 ⌂ C S E 30 amps

Victorville KOA
16530 Stoddard Wells Road
Victorville, California 92392
(619) 245-6867
3 mi $15 no hookup, $17 elec, $19 full
🚐 78 ⛺ 25 🚿 ≋ L Open all year
🛒 C S ⌂ E 20 & 30 amps

River Rest Campground
General Delivery, Washington Road
Washington, California 95986
(916) 265-4306
Fee $10-15 dly Open April thru October
🚐 30+ ⛺ 20+ 🚿 ≋ 🐟 ✕
L 🛒 ⌂ C S E 15/20 amps

Parramore's Campground
1675 S. Moon Road
Astor, Florida 32002
(904) 749-2721
Fee $12 dly Open all year
🚐 94 ⛺ 10 🚿 ≋ 🐟
L 🛒 ⌂ C S E 30 amps

Sting Ray Station
Carrabelle, Florida 32322
(904) 697-2638
Fee $7-10 dly Open all year
🚐 49 ⛺ 2 🚿 ≋ 🐟
⌂ C S E 30 amps

Citrus Valley Campground
2500 Highway 27 South
Clermont, Florida 32711
(904) 394-4051
12 mi fr $12.95 RV. $10.75 Tent
🚐 335 ⛺ 62 🚿 ≋ 🐟 L ✕
⌂ C S E 20 & 30 amp Open all year

Oceanus Mobile Village & Campground
152 Crescent Beach Drive
Cocoa Beach, Florida 32931
(305) 783-3871
2 mi Fee $13 dly Open all year
🚐 50 ⛺ 10 🚿 ≋ 🐟 L
✕ 🛒 ⌂ C S E 20-30-50 amp

Ginnie Springs Camp & Dive Resort
Rt. 1, Box 153
High Springs, Florida 32643
(904) 454-2202
8 mi $8 Adult, $4 7-14, Free 6 & under
🚐 49 ⛺ Unlimited 🚿 🛒 Open all year
≋ 🐟 ✕ C ⌂ E 30 amp

Hanna Park and Campground
500 Wonderwood Road
Jacksonville, Florida 32233
(904) 249-4700 — 249-2316
Next door to Mayport Naval Station

East Lake Fish Camp
3680 E. Boggy Creek Road
Kissimmee, Florida 32743
(407) 348-2040
9 mi Fee $7 dly Open all year
🚐 43 ⛺ 40 🚿 🐟 L
✕ 🛒 ⌂ C S E 100 amps

Mill Creek RV Resort
2775 Michigan Avenue
Kissimmee, Florida 32743
1 mi   Fee $16+ tax   Open all year
185   Sumr only   E

Countryside RV Park
Rt. 1, Box 60 (I-75 exit 64)
Lake Panasoffkee, Florida 33538
(904) 793-8103
2.5 mi   Fee $12 dly   Season 1/1 to 12/31
59   0   E 100 amps

Lake Whippoorwill Beach & RV Park
12343 Narcoossee Road
Orlando, Florida 32827
(407) 277-5075
12 mi   Fee $9.95-$18.50   Open all year
154   10   E 30 amps

Turkey Lake Park
3401 S. Hiawassee Road
Orlando, Florida 32811
(407) 299-5594 — 299-5581
7 mi   Fee varies   Open all year
32   P50   E 20 & 30 amps

Wesgate Motel and Campground
1627 S. Highway 19-98-27A
Perry, Florida 32347
(904) 584-5235
Fee $10 dly   Open all year
60   4   E 20-30-50 amps

Canoe Creek Campground
4101 Canoe Creek Road
St. Cloud, Florida 32769
(305) 892-7010
5 mi   Fee $13 (10% dis.)   Open all year
178   178   E 30 amps

Katie's Wekiva River Landing, Inc.
190 Katie's Cove
Sanford, Florida 32771
(407) 322-4470
27 mi   Fee $14 dly   Open all year
55   10   E 50/30

Stage Stop Campground
700 W. Highway 50
Winter Garden, Florida 32787
(407) 656-8000
Fee $12 for 2, $2 ea addl. Open all year
248   248   E 20-30 amps

ILLINOIS

Vandalia KOA Kampground
RR 2, Box 55A
Brownstown, Illinois 62418
(618) 427-5140
5 mi   Fee $9.90-14.50 Season 4/1 to 10/31
58   15 acres   E 30 amps max

Gages Lake Camping, Inc.
18887 W. Gages Lake Road
Gages Lake, Illinois 60030
(312) 223-5541
Fee $18 up family of 4 Season 4/1 to 11/1
150   0
Dump station   E 30 amps

Enchanted Shores-Chicago-Kankee
Rt. 45 & Peotone-Wilmington Road
Peotone, Illinois 60468
(312) 258-6040
40 mi   Fee $14 (10% M. dis.) S-May-Nov.
31   5   E 30 amps

Mr. Lincoln's Campground
3045 Stanton
Springfield, Illinois 62704
(217) 529-8206
2 mi   Fee $10   couple/Tents $5 per person
42   50   E 30/50 amps Season 4/1-12/31

Carriage Lane RV Resort
RR 2
Streator, Illinois 61364
(815) 672-2419
2 mi   Fee $10   Season 4/15 to 10/15
75   Unlimited

Fox Harbor Campground & Marina
RR3, Box 289
Sullivan, Illinois 61951
(217) 728-7312
4 mi   Fee $8 base/2   Season 4/1 to 10/31
148   115   E 20&30 amps

KENTUCKY

Otter Creek Park
Route One
Vine Grove, Kentucky 40175
(502) 942-8686 or 583-3577
5 mi Fort Knox Season March thru Nov.
151 10 E 30 amps

MAINE

Kennebunkport Camping & Tenting Park
RR1, Box 784, Old Cape Road
Kennebunkport, Maine 04046
(207) 967-2732
1 mi Fee $13 family of 5 Open 5/15-10/15
18 33 E 30 max.

MARYLAND

Cherry Hill Campcity, Inc.
9530 Rosehill Avenue
College Park, Maryland 20740
(301) 474-5069
Open all year
E 30, some 50 amps

Double G Ranch & Campground
P.O. Box 25, Mosser Road
McHenry, Maryland 21541
(301) 387-5481
30 mi Fee $10 dly Season 5/15-10/15
128 60 E 20 amps

MASSACHUSETTS

Peters Pond Park
Box 999
Sandwich, Massachusetts 02563
(508) 477-1775
5 mi $12 base fee Season 4/15 to 10/15
450 50 E 30 amps

NEW HAMPSHIRE

Len-Kay Camping Area
Hall Road
Barrington, New Hampshire 03825
(603) 664-9333
8 mi Fee $17.50 dly Season 5/15-9/15
100 25 E 20 amps

NEW HAMPSHIRE

Broken Branch KOA
P.O. Box 6, Rt. 175
Woodstock, New Hampshire 03293
(603) 745-8008
Fee $15 dly Season 5/1-10/15
130 E 30 amps

NEW JERSEY

Maple Lake Campground
P.O. Box 1209
Jackson, New Jersey 08527
(201) 367-0177
4 mi Fee $19.50 dly Season 4/22-10/15
140 140 E 20 & 30 amps

Havenwoods Campground
1316 Stagecoach Road
Palermo, New Jersey 08230
(609) 390-1726
5 mi Fee $15 Tr, 12 Tent Open 4/15-10/31
71 32 E 30 amps max

NEW MEXICO

Logan's Mobile Haven
11072 Hiway 180 West
Silver City, New Mexico 88061
(505) 538-3331
2 mi Fee $8.50+tax Open all year
20 15 E 30 amps

NEW YORK

Mohawk Campground
RD 2, Box 62
Cherry Valley, New York 13320
(607) 264-3241 or 547-2712
2 mi Fee $12+ Season 5/1 to 10/1
40 10 Dump Station E 20 amps

Deer River Campsite, Inc.
HCR-01, Box 101A
Malone, New York 12953
(518) 483-0060
16 mi Fee $10/2 Season 5/1 to 11/30
63 5 E 30 amps

NEW YORK

Blue Ridge Falls Campground
Blue Ridge Road
North Hudson, New York 12855
(518) 532-7863
8 mi $10 Basic tent Season 5/15 to 10/15
41 14 E 15 amps

Lake Placid-Whiteface Mountain KOA
Fox Road, Wilmington, New York 12997
(518) 946-7878
9 mi $15 less 10% w/mil ID Open all year
100 100 Log cabins w/fireplaces
E 30 amps

Birchwood Acres Campground
P.O. Box 482
Woodridge, New York 12789
(914) 434-4743
8 mi Fee $18.50 Season 5/1 to 10/10
126 100 E 30/20 amps

NORTH CAROLINA

Alpine Woods RV Park
Rt. 9, Box 565
Hendersonville, North Carolina 28739
(704) 692-6011
1½ mi Season Open all year
103 6 E 20/30/50 amps

OHIO

Findlay East KOA
Vanlue, Ohio 45890
(419) 387-7738
15 mi 3 hole reg. golf course Open 5/1-9/30
168 0 E 20/30 amps

OKLAHOMA

Jamestown RV Park & Campground
POB 25965/1-40 & S. Rockwell
Oklahoma City, Oklahoma 73125
(405) 787-5992
5 mi Fee $15 Season Open all year
126 25 E 30 amps

OREGON

Sea Ranch RV Park
P.O. Box 214
Cannon Beach, Oregon 97110
(503) 436-1268
2 bls Fee $13 to $4 Season Open all year
41 30 E 20 amps

PENNSYLVANIA

Spring Gulch Resort Campground
475 Lynch Road
New Holland, Pennsylvania 17557
(717) 354-3100
Basic fee $10 Season 3/25 to 11/1
250 50 E 30 amps

Mill Bridge Village & Campresort
Box 86
Strasburg, Pennsylvania 17579
(717) 687-8181/1 (800) 645-2744
8 mi Fee $11 to $22 Season 3/15 to 12/10
120 65 E 30 amps

RHODE ISLAND

Oak Embers
547 Escoheag Hill Road
Escoheag, Rhode Island 02821
(401) 397-4042
15 mi Fee $12-14 Season 2/1 to 12/31
20 30 E 30 amps

TENNESSEE

Bar-W Campground
Rt. 1, Box 38
Gatlinburg, Tennessee 37738
(615) 436-3239
3 mi Fee $12 dly Season 4/1 thru 11/30
22 15 E 30 amps

Shady Oaks Campground
500 Conner Heights Road
Pigeon Forge, Tennessee 37863
(615) 453-3276
½ mi Fee $8 to $12+ tax Open all year
84 40 E 15/30 amps

TEXAS

Breeze Lake
1710 N. Vermillion
Brownsville, Texas 78521
(512) 831-4427
6 mi Fee $10/2 Open all year

187 ▲ 187 🚿 🏊 🎣 L ✕
🚐 🐾 Ⓒ Ⓢ E 50, 30, 20 amps

57 Trailer Park
2550 Main Street
Eagle Pass, Texas 78852
(512) 773-5676
2 mi Fee $6 w/o A/C Open all year
🚐 15 ▲ 1 🚿 L ✕
🐾 Ⓢ E 30 amps

Evening Shadows RV Park
Rt. 3, Box 236
Tool, Texas 75143
(214) 432-3455
1½ mi Fee $9 dly Open all year
🚐 98 ▲ 100 🚿 🏊 🎣 L
✕ 🐾 Ⓢ E 30 amps

Weatherford-Fort Worth KOA
2205 Tin Top Road
Weatherford, Texas 76086
(817) 594-8801
25 mi $12 w, el/$13 w, el, s Open all year
🚐 60 ▲ 20 🚿 🏊 L
🚐 🐾 Ⓒ Ⓢ E 20, 30 50 amps

VIRGINIA

Cherrystone KOA
P.O. Box 545
Cheriton, Virginia 23316
(804) 331-3063
4 mi Fee $12 Open all year
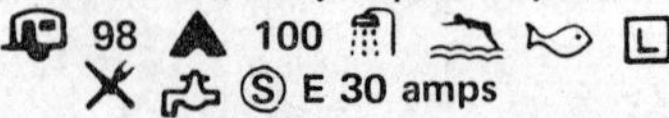
600 ▲ 95 🚿 🏊 🎣 L ✕
🚐 🐾 Ⓒ Ⓢ E 30 amps

Christopher Run Campground
Rt. 1, Box 326
Mineral, Virginia 23117
(703) 894-4744
8 mi Fee $13 dly Season 4/1 to 10/31
🚐 200 ▲ 25 🚿 🏊 🎣 L ✕
🚐 🐾 Ⓒ Ⓢ E 30 amps

VIRGINIA

Southfork Ranch RV Park
P.O. Box 1116, State No. 3
Oak Grove (Colonial Beach), VA 22443
(804) 224-7093
6 mi Fee $12 dly Season 4/1 to 10/31
🚐 100 ▲ 0 🚿 🏊 🎣 L ✕
🚐 🐾 Ⓒ Ⓢ E 30 amps

Bay Haven Farm
1400 Public Landing Road
Virginia Beach, Virginia 23457
(804) 721-6680
12 mi Fee $9 dly Open all year
🚐 ▲ 30 sites 🚿 🎣
🐾 Ⓒ Ⓢ E 30 amps

Best Holiday Trav-L-Park
843 S. Birdneck Road
Virginia Beach, Virginia 23451
(804) 425-0249
1½ mi $14-26 dly Open all year
🚐 700 ▲ 400 🚿 🏊 L ✕
🚐 🐾 Ⓒ Ⓢ E 30-50 amps

Fair Oaks
901 Lightfoot Road
Williamsburg, Virginia 23185
(804) 565-2101
4 mi $9.50-13 Open all year
🚐 400 ▲ 50 🚿 🏊 🎣 L
✕ 🚐 🐾 Ⓒ Ⓢ E 20, 30, 50 amps

WASHINGTON

Aero Park Campground
P.O. Box 1340
Airway Heights, Washington 99001
(509) 244-2744 / (509) 455-8137
6 mi $10 full hook-up Open April thru Oct.
🚐 14 ▲ 10 🚿 2 mi fr Fairchild AFB
🐾 Ⓢ E 110 amps

WEST VIRGINIA

Pine Hill Campground
RD 3, Box 233-AA
Bruceton Mills, West Virginia 26525
(304) 379-4612
20 mi Fee $10 dly Season 4/1 to 11/1
🚐 50 ▲ 100 🚿 🎣
🐾 Ⓢ E 110 amps

WEST VIRGINIA

Harpers Ferry KOA Kampground
Route 3, Box 1300
Harpers Ferry, West Virginia 25425
(304) 535-6895
1 mi $14 w/o elec Season 4/1 to 11/1
200 ▲ 100 E 30 amps

Milleson's Walnut Grove Campground, Inc.
P.O. Box 400
Springfield, West Virginia 26763
(304) 822-5284
3.2 mi Fee $6.50 up Season 4/1 to 12/15
40 ▲ 40 E 50, 30, 20 GFI

WISCONSIN

Holiday Shores Campground & Resort
3900 River Road
Wisconsin Dells, Wisconsin 53965
(608) 254-2717
4 mi $12.50-16.50 Season 5/1 to 10/15
99 ▲ 40 E 20 & 30 amps

Wisconsin Dells KOA
S 235 Stand Rock Road
Wisconsin Dells, Wisconsin 53965
(608) 254-4177
8 bl Base $13.50 Season 4/17 to 10/12
98 ▲ 27 E 30 amps

SERVICE

Dick Shrock RV Center
13660 N. Tamiami Trail
Naples, Florida 33963
(813) 597-8500

The Good Sam Club
P.O. Box 500
Agoura, California 91301
1-800-234-3450
Save on overnight camping, propane gas, RV parts and accessories. Low cost RV & auto insurance plans, free trip routing, etc.

SALES

LazyDays R.V. Center
11028 North Florida Avenue
Tampa, Florida 33612
(In Fla 1-800-282-7800) 1-800-626-7800
"World's Largest HOLIDAY RAMBLER Dealer." Used Travel Trailers-Used Motor Homes.

Cruise America
5959 Blue Lagoon Drive
Miami, Florida 33126
(305) 262-9611

26 great places to check in to in Oklahoma, Kansas and Missouri:

OKLAHOMA:
Checotah/Henryetta KOA . . . . . .(918) 473-6511
Elk City/Clinton KOA . . . .(405) 592-4409
Sallisaw KOA . . . .(918) 775-2792

KANSAS:
Emporia KOA . . . .(316) 342-2236
Fort Scott KOA . . . .(316) 223-3440
                     or 223-5100
Garden City KOA . . . .(316) 276-8741
Lawrence/Kansas City KOA . . . . .(913) 842-3877
Topeka KOA . . . .(913) 289-3419
Wakeeney KOA . . . .(913) 743-5612
Wellington KOA . . . .(316) 326-6114
Wichita KOA . . . .(316) 722-1154

MISSOURI:
North Branson/Musicland KOA . .(417) 334-0848
South Branson KOA . . . .(417) 334-4414
Hayti/Portageville KOA . . . .(314) 359-1580
Jonesburg/Warrenton KOA . . . . .(314) 488-5630
Joplin KOA . . . .(417) 623-2246
Kansas City East/Oak Grove KOA (816) 625-7515
Lebanon KOA . . . .(417) 532-3422
Osage Beach/Lake Ozark KOA . .(314) 348-3445
Rock Port KOA . . . .(816) 744-5485
St. Louis South KOA . . . .(314) 479-4449
St. Louis West KOA . . . .(314) 257-3018
Stanton KOA . . . .(314) 927-5215
Springfield KOA . . . .(417) 831-3645
Sullivan/Meramec KOA . . . .(314) 468-8750
Willow Springs KOA . . . .(417) 469-9098

For more information on each campground's location, facilities, and nearby attractions, please refer to your KOA Directory.

GIANT RV SALE

PRE-OWNED AND MAINTAINED BY US—
1987 (& SOME '86) MOTORHOMES
BY WINNEBAGO, FLEETWOOD & COACHMEN

Cruise America operates and sells the largest company-owned rental fleet in the world. All our fully-equipped motorhomes have documented maintenance histories.

And we back every motorhome with a 12 month/12,000 mile **limited powertrain warranty plan** at no additional charge. Right-smart financing too, with up to 10 year terms.

YOU'LL NEVER BUY FOR LESS. NO GIMMICKS. NO REBATES. NOW'S YOUR CHANCE TO OWN OR UPGRADE AT HUGE SAVINGS.

Call our retail sales center.
**Twenty Sales Centers in
California, Texas, Florida,
Colorado, Illinois, Georgia, Washington,
Oregon, Utah, and New Jersey**

or call us toll free
1-800-327-7778

America's Largest Retailer of New and Used Motorhomes.

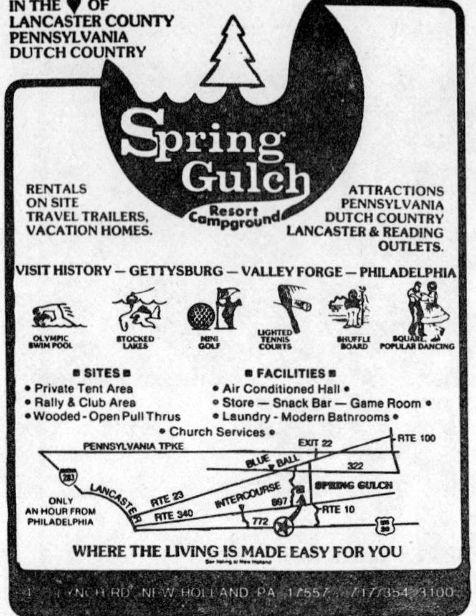

OVER 150 CAMPING SITES

$8.00 Tent Only
10.00 with Water & Electric
11.00 with Electric & Sewer

30 Miles South-West of Louisville off Hwy. 1638, near Fort Knox, Ky. Dixie Highway to Hwy. 1638 in Muldraugh. Follow the park signs.

For More Information, Call

502-583-3577 or 502-942-8686

Situated on 3000 acres of beautiful Kentucky woodland, overlooking the Ohio River, Otter Creek offers:

Fishing, Hiking, Boat Ramp, Public Pool, Frisbee, Golf, Tennis/Basketball, Nature Center, Picnic Areas, Park Store/Restaurant, Laundromat, Playground, Heated Showers

Naturalist Available

*Sorry-**NO PETS** (accredited kennel ¼ mile away)*

Daily & Weekly Rates Available

CHERRY HILL CAMPCITY, INC.

P-90
9530 Rosehill Avenue
College Park, MD 20740

(301) 474-5069

On U.S. Hwy. 1 & I-95 at Exit 25A. Just north of Capital Beltway (I-95/I-495) behind the Holiday Inn.

Enchanted Shores of Killarney

SWIMMING 10 A.M. - 6 P.M.
Daily Swimming Rate $2.50 Adult $1.50 Child
RV CAMPING Route 45-52
Hot Showers · Full Hookups · Rec Hall

Ph. 312-258-6040 Bus.   Peotone, IL. 60468

3 Miles West of Interstate I-57 at Peotone-Wilmington Exit

MOHAWK CAMPGROUND
CHERRY VALLEY, NEW YORK 13320   (607) 264-3241 or 547-2712
WRITE OR CALL FOR BROCHURE

- Hookups and tent sites
- 170 acres of nature trails
- Heated pool
- Fishing — boat rentals
- Fully stocked camp and RV store
- Recreation Hall
- Video games arcade
- Hay rides
- Laundry facility
- Propane filling

"World's Largest HOLIDAY RAMBLER Dealer"

Presenting the finest selection of 1988 Models

PACE ARROW

WINNEBAGO

BOUNDER

ALLEGRO

TIOGA MINI-HOMES

TRAVELCRAFT VANS

14 ACRES · 275 Units
$7,000,000 Inventory

And Over 150 Pre-Owned R.V.'s
Used Travel Trailers · Used Motor Homes

11028 North Florida Avenue
Tampa, Florida 33612

Challenge Us! USE This
Toll Free Customer Hot-Line:

1-800-282-7800
(In Florida)

1-800-626-7800
(Out of Florida)

Membership
in the Good Sam RV Owner's Club
has benefits!

- ★ Save 10% on overnight camping
- ★ Save 10% on propane gas
- ★ Save 10% on RV parts and accessories
- ★ Low cost RV and auto insurance plans
- ★ Free trip routing
- ★ Free mail forwarding service (set quarterly postage charge)
- ★ Emergency Road Service plans for RV's and much, much more!

Special new member price for Military Living readers:
One year for only $12

Use the coupon below, or for fastest service or more information call toll-free 1-800-234-3450.

The Good Sam Club P.O. Box 500 • Agoura, CA 91301

O.K., I'm interested, sign me up for one year at $12

☐ My check or money order is enclosed.
☐ Please charge my ☐ VISA ☐ MasterCard

Card # ____

Signature ____

Name ____

Address ____

City ________________________ State __________ Zip __________

7G-MILI-468

Space-A Travel Newsletter
(Space-A Air . . . Space-A RV & Camping . . . Space-A Temporary Military Lodging)

FREE COPIES FOR PURCHASERS of THIS BOOK

"TRAVEL ON LESS PER DAY.... THE MILITARY WAY"

We'd like to acquaint you with our travel newsletter, Military Living's R&R Report. It gives late breaking info on Space-A air travel, new info on military camping and rec areas, and temporary military lodging plus informative and helpful reader trip reports.

We'll send you two free copies (a $4.00 value) if you will send $1.00 to cover the cost of postage and handling.

To get your copies, send your name and address and $1.00 to:
Military Living R&R (Dept. SA)
Box 2347
Falls Church, VA 22042

CENTRAL ORDER COUPON

MILITARY *Living* ™

MILITARY LIVING PUBLICATIONS
P.O. Box 2347, Falls Church, VA 22042
Telephone. (703) 237-0203.

Publications	Qty.	Publications	Qty/ Yrs.
The One Everyone is Talking About **Military Space-A Air Opportunities Around the World*** **$15.45 ea.**		Assignment Washington A Guide to Washington Area Military Installations $7.45 ea.	
You Can Have Fun With This Book! **Military RV, Camping & Rec Areas Around the World*** **$9.45 ea.**		*The World-Wide Travel Newsletter* **Military Living's R&R Report** 5 yrs. - $42.00 2 yrs. - $20.00 3 yrs. - $27.00 1 yr. - $12.00 (6 issues)	
Our All Time Best Seller! **Temporary Military Lodging Around the World*** **$11.45 ea.**		*Local Washington Area Magazine* **Military Living** 3 yrs. - $16.00 1 yr. - $7.00 (12 issues) 2 yrs. - $12.00	
U.S. Forces Travel Guide U.S.A. & Caribbean Areas* **$9.45 ea.**			
Subtotal: $		Subtotal: $	

*If you are an R&R subscriber, you may deduct $1.00 per book. (No discount on R&R Report itself.)

For 1st Class Mail, add $1.00 per book

Mail Order Prices are for the U.S., APO & FPO addresses. Please consult Publisher for International Mail Price. Sorry, no billing. GREAT FUND RAISERS! Please write for wholesale rates.

Total: $______

VA addresees
add 4½% sales tax $______
(Books only)

Total Amount $______
Enclosed

We're as close as your telephone. . .by using our Telephone Ordering Service. We honor Visa, American Express, Choice or Mastercard. Call us at **(703) 237-0203** and order today! Sorry, no collect calls. Or. . . fill out the info in the mail order coupon below.

Name: __________________________

Street: __________________________

City/State: __________________________

Phone: __________________________
(with area code)

Signature: __________________________

☐ Active Duty
☐ Retired
☐ Widower
☐ 100% Disabled Veteran
☐ Guard
☐ Reservist
☐ Other __________

Rank: ________________ or Rank of Sponsor: ____________________

Branch of Service: ________________________________

Please mail check or money order to: Military Living, P.O. Box 2347, Falls Church, VA 22042.

CENTRAL ORDER COUPON

MILITARY *Living* ™

MILITARY LIVING PUBLICATIONS
P.O. Box 2347, Falls Church, VA 22042
Telephone: (703) 237-0203.

Publications		Qty.	Publications	Qty/Yrs.
The One Everyone is Talking About Military Space-A Air Opportunities Around the World* **$15.45 ea.**			Assignment Washington A Guide to Washington Area Military Installations **$7.45 ea.**	
You Can Have Fun With This Book! Military RV, Camping & Rec Areas Around the World° **$9.45 ea.**			*The World-Wide Travel Newsletter* Military Living's R&R Report 5 yrs. - $42.00 2 yrs. - $20.00 3 yrs. - $27.00 1 yr. - $12.00 (6 issues)	
Our All Time Best Seller! Temporary Military Lodging Around the World° **$11.45 ea.**			*Local Washington Area Magazine* Military Living 3 yrs. - $16.00 1 yr. - $7.00 (12 issues) 2 yrs. - $12.00	
U.S. Forces Travel Guide U.S.A. & Caribbean Areas* **$9.45 ea.**				
Subtotal: $			**Subtotal: $**	

*If you are an R&R subscriber, you may deduct $1.00 per book. (No discount on R&R Report itself.)

For 1st Class Mail, add $1.00 per book

Mail Order Prices are for the U.S., APO & FPO addresses. Please consult Publisher for International Mail Price. Sorry, no billing. GREAT FUND RAISERS! Please write for wholesale rates.

Total: $_______

VA addresees add 4½% sales tax $________
(Books only)

Total Amount $_______
Enclosed

We're as close as your telephone. . .by using our Telephone Ordering Service. We honor Visa, American Express, Choice or Mastercard. Call us at **(703) 237-0203** and order today! Sorry, no collect calls. Or. . . fill out the info in the mail order coupon below.

Name: _______________________________

Street: _______________________________

City/State: _______________________________

Phone: _______________________________
(with area code)

Signature: _______________________________

☐ Active Duty
☐ Retired
☐ Widower
☐ 100% Disabled Veteran
☐ Guard
☐ Reservist
☐ Other _______________

Rank: _______________ or Rank of Sponsor: _______________

Branch of Service: _______________________________

Please mail check or money order to: **Military Living, P.O. Box 2347, Falls Church, VA 22042.**

COMING SOON!!! THE NAVY'S NEWEST REC AREA. Look for a new listing in the next edition of this book. Meanwhile, here is some info to get you going. (Copyrighted material reprinted with permission, Military Living's R & R Report)

"Ocean Getaway," New Navy Rec Center

WE ARE LOOKING FOR GREAT MILITARY TRAVEL DEALS.... and the following gold nugget of info arrived on our desk at press time! Thanks to the Romanes of Bremerton, WA, who let us know what's new in their area! From the KITSAP Ret'd Officer Association Newsletter, Feb. 1988. Editor Cdr. Donald V. Gorman, USN, Ret'd, reported on a visit to a new Navy Rec facility at Pacific Beach, Washington. (Some info and rates have been updated 15 Mar 88 by R&R.)

"Called the **Pacific Northwest Fleet Recreation and Education Support Center,** it is located on the site of the former Pacific Beach Naval Communications Facility which was decommissioned about a year ago and will be for the use of active duty personnel and retired military personnel on a space available basis. When fully operational (probably by 1 May 1988) the Center will offer 24 furnished Capehart cabins and 5 suites (located in the former BOQ and for

adults only). Several cabins and suites are now ready for occupancy. RV pads are on the drawing board and should be completed by June 89. (A CB detachment from Whidbey Island NAS will lay the pads.)

Depending on location and size and rank, rates are as follows: Enlisted, E1-E5, east side $12-26; oceanside $14-28. E6-9, east side $14-30; oceanside $16-32. Officers, east side $16-34; oceanside $18-36. Lodging can be reserved from two nights up to two weeks. When space is available, extensions may be granted. The furnished cabins have kitchen appliances, TV, linens, towels, cooking and eating utensils. Furnished suites have TV, linens, towels and a refrigerator. Maid service is provided every three days. It is a picturesque site, located on a cliff with a sweeping view of the ocean and with trails leading down to broad, sandy beaches. It is located about 13 miles north of Ocean City on Highway 109 and just south of the Quinault Indian Reser-

vation border. The Center will have to make it on its own as no appropriated funds are available to support it. For information on reservations call (206) 526-3579 or write to **Recreation Services, Naval Station Puget Sound, 7500 Sandpoint Way NE, Seattle, WA 98115-5014.** Ocean Getaway is 161 miles from Puget Sound. Active duty may make reservations 90 days in advance. All others to include retired military may request reservations 60 days in advance of the dates desired.

MOVING TO WASHINGTON COUPON

"One Shot" Help

MOVING TO WASHINGTON?
Make one call or send this coupon & help will be on its way. As a military wife, one of my chief goals is to boost military family morale . . . so mail this coupon today & help will be on its way.
Hope to hear from you soon.

Ann Crawford, Publisher
Military Living Magazine

TO: Mrs. Ann Crawford, Publisher, Military Living
P.O. Box 2347, Falls Church, VA 22042
Phone: (703) 237-0203

Our Family Is:
- ☐ Army
- ☐ Navy
- ☐ Air Force
- ☐ Marine
- ☐ Coast Guard
- ☐ P.H.S.
- ☐ NOAA
- ☐ Other
- ☐ Active
- ☐ Retired
- ☐ 100% DAV

Military member's name/rank _______________________

Spouses Name _______________________

Address: _______________________

City/State/Zip: _______________________

Tel: _______________________
Total number in family: ______
Number of children: ______

Area assigned to: _______________________

We expect to arrive: _______________________

We would like info, if possible, on the following:
- ☐ House ☐ Apt. ☐ Condo
- ☐ Renting ☐ Buying
- ☐ Car
- ☐ Furniture
- ☐ Major Appliances

Short Term Housing
- ☐ Military Lodging
- ☐ Hotel/Motel ☐ B & B
- ☐ Short Term Apt.

Other things we need: _______________________

- ☐ Banking/Checking Accounts
- ☐ Employment Opportunities for spouse
- ☐ Real Estate Career Opportunities
- ☐ Legal Services/Settlement Atty.
- ☐ College Opportunities
- ☐ Investment Opportunities
- ☐ Travel in nearby areas
- ☐ Back Issues of Military Living
- ☐ Window Treatments
- ☐ Dentist ☐ Doctor

4/88

Space-A Travel Newsletter
(Space-A Air . . . Space-A RV & Camping . . . Space-A Temporary Military Lodging)

FREE COPIES FOR PURCHASERS of THIS BOOK

"TRAVEL ON LESS PER DAY.... THE MILITARY WAY"

We'd like to acquaint you with our travel newsletter, Military Living's R&R Report. It gives late breaking info on Space-A air travel, new info on military camping and rec areas, and temporary military lodging plus informative and helpful reader trip reports.

We'll send you two free copies (a $4.00 value) if you will send $1.00 to cover the cost of postage and handling.

To get your copies, send your name and address and $1.00 to:
Military Living R&R (Dept. SA)
Box 2347
Falls Church, VA 22042